Citizen Politics in
Post-Industrial Societies

URBAN POLICY CHALLENGES
Terry Nichols Clark, Series Editor

Cities are critical. From the Los Angeles riots of 1992 to the Hong Kong reversion of 1997, cities represent in microcosm the problems and potentials we face at all governmental levels.

Focusing on cities can help clarify our most challenging issues. Most key decisions affecting our lives are made locally. Although national governments collect the majority of funds, most welfare state programs around the world are provided by local governments. Urban leaders play key roles in encouraging economic development, maintaining quality public services, and mandating reasonable taxes.

And they are pressed to do more: provide attractive physical environments, improve amenities such as bike paths, help encourage recycling, assist disadvantaged groups to achieve broader acceptance and access to public facilities, keep streets safe, and fill the gaps in health and social services.

Books in the *Urban Policy Challenges* series will explore the range of urban policy problems and will detail solutions that have been sought and implemented in cities from around the world. They will build on studies of leadership, public management, organizational culture, community power, intergovernmental relations, public finance, citizen responsiveness, and related elements of urban public decision-making.

These approaches to urban challenges will range from case studies to quantitative modeling. The series will include monographs, texts, as well as edited volumes. While some works will target professional and student audiences, many books will elicit attention from thoughtful public leaders and informed citizens as well.

BOOKS IN THE SERIES

Citizen Politics in Post-Industrial Societies

EDITED BY

Terry Nichols Clark
and Michael Rempel

WestviewPress

A Division of HarperCollins*Publishers*

The Political Economy of Global Interdependence

Copyright © 1997 by Westview Press, A Member of the Perseus Books Group

Published in 1998 in the United States of America by Westview Press, 5500 Central Avenue, Boulder, Colorado 80301-2877, and in the United Kingdom by Westview Press, 12 Hid's Copse Road, Cumnor Hill, Oxford OX2 9JJ

Library of Congress Cataloging-in-Publication Data
Capital controls in emerging economies / edited by Christine P. Ries
And Richard J. Sweeney.
    p. cm. — (The political economy of global interdependence :
174)
   Includes bibliographical references (p.)
   ISBN 0-8133-6697-6
   1. Capital movements. 2. Monetary policy. 3. Capital market.
4. Corporations—Finance. I. Hekman, Christine Ries, 1947– .
II. Sweeney, Richard J. (Richard James), 1944– . III. Series.
HG3891.C357 1997
332.'041—dc21   97-18280
                                                 CIP

10   9   8   7   6   5   4   3   2   1

Contents

Part 1—Introduction

Part 2—Cultural Shifts and Politics:
Is Materialism Rising, Declining, or Both?
Implications for Political Activism

Part 3—The New Middle Class Politics:
What Is Special About the Politics of Professionals
and Other Middle Class Persons?

Part 4—New Issues, Ideologies, and Cleavages:
What Mobilizes Citizens?

     Political Candidates and Campaigns in Illinois, 1956-1992 161
     G. Allen Mayer

9   Contemporary Ideological Cleavages in the United States 195
     Michael Rempel

10   The Social Origins of Feminism and Political Activism:
     Findings from Fourteen Countries 209
     Paul Butts

     Bibliography 245
     About the Book 261

Tables and Figures

Tables

Figures

About the Editors and Contributors

Steven Brint is Professor of Sociology at the University of California, Riverside. He is the author of *In an Age of Experts: The Changing Role of Professionals in Politics and Public Life*. His most recent book is *Schools and Societies*.

Clem Brooks is Assistant Professor of Sociology at Indiana University. In addition to his research with Jeff Manza, he is starting work on a project examining the role of values and social problems in explaining political change in the U.S. since the 1960s. He is also working on several projects that analyze data from a new national survey of voters conducted after the 1996 elections. Using the survey's experimental design, these projects examine the role of competing ideologies in policy reasoning.

Paul Butts received an M.A. in Sociology from the University of Chicago and was a graduate student there when he completed his chapter. He is now working in Paris.

Terry Nichols Clark is Professor of Sociology at the University of Chicago. He has published some 25 books, including *City Money* and *Urban Innovation*, and is editor of *Research in Urban Policy* (JAI Press, seven volumes to date). He is Coordinator of the Fiscal Austerity and Urban Innovation Project, a survey of all U.S. cities with populations over 25,000, and parallel surveys in 38 other countries. He has taught at Columbia, Harvard, Yale, the Sorbonne, and UCLA.

Eileen M. Crimmins is Professor of Gerontology at the University of Southern California. She is co-author with Richard Easterlin of *The Fertility Revolution: A Supply-Demand Analysis* (1985).

William L. Cunningham is a Ph.D. candidate in Sociology at Yale University. He is currently working to complete his dissertation on the political representa-

xii About the Editors and Contributors

tion of the U.S. - Canadian Free Trade Agreement. He also manages the Information and Technology Services Education Program at Yale University.

Richard A. Easterlin is Professor of Economics at the University of Southern California. He is co-author with Eileen Crimmins of *The Fertility Revolution: A Supply-Demand Analysis* (1985).

Ronald Inglehart is Professor of Political Science and Program Director of the Center for Political Studies at the University of Michigan. He also chairs the Steering Committee for the World Values Survey, and he is a co-investigator of the Euro-Barometer surveys. His recent books include *Modernization and Postmodernization: Cultural, Economic and Political Change in 43 Societies, Value Change in Global Perspective* (co-authored with Paul Abramson), and *Culture Shift in Advanced Industrial Society.*

Rebecca S. K. Li is a Ph.D. candidate in Sociology at the University of California, Riverside. She is currently working on her dissertation, which compares three rebellions and one revolution in China between 1644 and 1911. Her goal is to examine the conjunctures of structural factors that cause varying degrees of societal disintegration in each event. Her other research interests are emotions and interaction rituals.

Jeff Manza is Assistant Professor of Sociology at Pennsylvania State University. With Clem Brooks, he is writing a book on the social bases of voter alignments since the 1950s, and working on a study of policy experts and the New Deal.

G. Allen Mayer received a B.A. in Political Science from the University of Chicago in 1993. Since then, he has managed several Democratic political campaigns, and served as a legislative aide to an Illinois state representative. He is currently completing graduate study at the University of Illinois College of Law.

Michael Rempel is a Ph.D. candidate in Sociology at the University of Chicago. His research interests include class politics, political culture, and contemporary social theory. He is currently writing a dissertation that develops a social systems theory of postmodernity.

Naoyuki Umemori is Assistant Professor of Political Science and Economics at Waseda University in Japan. He received his Ph.D. in Political Science from the University of Chicago.

Preface

This is one of three volumes about post-industrial politics. The conceptual origin of all three was "The New Political Culture" (Clark and Inglehart 1989, 1990). It contrasted class politics with the New Political Culture (NPC), and formulated 22 propositions about where and when class politics or the New Political Culture are more important. This volume generally uses the term "post-industrial politics" rather than "New Political Culture," but they strongly overlap. The revised NPC paper is the introduction to Clark and Hoffmann-Martinot (1997), a companion volume to this which builds on international data for municipalities. This volume differs in using primarily citizen survey data. The introduction to this volume also stresses the media more, and adds other specifics, such as distinguishing types of social liberalism. Michael Rempel, senior co-author of this volume's introduction, helped give it a distinctive twist. The third volume is Clark (1994), which tests propositions about the New Political Culture with American urban data and analyzes policies like growth control and new management techniques as implementing this political culture. The New Political Culture propositions have been adapted to several contexts, such as Western Europe, Australia, and Japan (Clark and Hoffmann-Martinot 1997), and in more detail, Switzerland (Geser 1994); post-communist Eastern Europe (the NPC paper was translated into Polish and Hungarian, and recast for Eastern Europe in Clark 1993; see also Surazska 1995); Spain (Rojo 1990); and Latin America (Landa 1995, 1996). The propositions also helped spark an ongoing exchange about whether "social class is dying" or yielding to post-industrial politics (Clark and Lipset 1991; Clark, Lipset, and Rempel 1993; Hout et al. 1995).

The propositions suggest several processes. Some concern individual citizens (e.g. more highly educated persons should be more socially liberal), while others concern social/political system characteristics (e.g., the more ideologically coherent are political parties, the less likely is the emergence of New Political Culture). The propositions are sufficiently complex that several subprojects were pursed to address them, with overlapping teams and different types of data. While some ideas have been presented to professional meetings and in journal articles, these three volumes report the main results. Each volume pursues those propositions most appropriate to test with a particular type of data or national context. Similarly, individual chapters in this volume differ somewhat in substantive focus, data, and method. For instance, surveys for tens of thousands of citizens in many countries and over time are analyzed to document changes in values (by Inglehart; Easterlin and Crimmins; Brint, Cunningham, and Li). By contrast, Mayer focuses on a dozen or so key political campaigns, documenting shifts in programs and packaging appeals to citizens. Umemori focuses on why Japan is different from the West, and uses it as a special case to show the importance of religion, nationalism, and consumerism—which also shift some post-industrial processes described in the West.

The three volumes are team efforts. Some initial propositions were sparked by discussions of post-industrial developments in conferences of the Fiscal Austerity and Urban Innovation (FAUI) Project. As we compared interpretations, we might hear that "bureaucrats are more important in Oslo," "Japan has few new social movements," etc. Dozens of such observed differences challenged us to build an analytical framework to interpret them. Our goal throughout has been to explain cases and exceptions by articulating a general theory, which we understand as a set of propositions and assumptions about conditions where the propositions hold. For example, rather than just stating that class politics is important in France, and post-industrial politics more important in the U.S., we formulate more abstract propositions, such as more education for citizens, and weak political parties, should promote post-industrial politics. These propositions should in turn capture key processes to explain differences between France and the U.S., but also differences elsewhere.

Much past research is on one or a few nation-states. Results often differ from one country to the next. This is inherent in "small N" studies: nations are scarce animals, and distinct in part for idiosyncratic reasons. What then? Some suggest in-depth case studies of one or two nations (e.g., Skocpol 1979), or comparing a few nations using procedures like "Boolean analysis" (e.g., Ragin 1987). While each such approach can add insight, we find it useful to conduct case studies of nations or cities identified as theoretically distinct and thus interesting to build on for generalizing. We simultaneously try to join case studies with comparative work. The comparative work locates the cases and indicates the generality or distinctiveness of each case. For comparative work, we find it methodologically compelling to increase the N and then undertake conceptually informed comparisons via testing propositions. Put differently, can we build a science better using a handful of scarce dinosaurs, or with thousands of fruit flies? Our approach builds on the methodological innovations in cross-national comparative research of persons like Stein Rokkan in the 1960s. Alas, there has not been substantial methodological progress since. Our assessment is shared by others, for example, in recent reviews by Erwin Scheuch and Henry Teune (in Oyen 1990) and Kaase and Newton (1995).

General methodological discussions repeatedly stress the value of a large number of cases to permit unraveling causal processes. A large N can reduce idiosyncrasies to "noise," which we have sought to achieve by analyzing either (1) citizens in different countries to assess the importance of individual characteristics like education or age, or (2) local governments to analyze local system characteristics, like income inequalities or party strength. We have correspondingly spent over a decade assembling and analyzing data for more than 60,000 citizens and 7,000 cities around the world, reported in these three volumes.

We often build on the FAUI Project. Initiated in 1983, the FAUI project has become the most extensive study of local government in the world. It includes over 550 persons in 35 countries. Participants meet in conferences, via the Internet, and analyze a core of comparable data. Participants have collected and shared data concerning citizens, local public officials, and socio-economic characteristics of localities, regions, and nations. Many items have been included specifically to map post-industrial politics. Most of these data can now be made available to researchers via the Internet. Contact: tnc@cicero.spc.uchicago.edu.

Persons who kindly assisted with this volume are listed at the beginning of each chapter. The Computer Resource Center of Chicago artfully produced camera-ready text and graphics. We gratefully acknowledge financial and institutional support from the Center for the Study of Urban Inequality, University of Chicago, through funds made available by the Ford, MacArthur, and Rockefeller Foundations; from Burton Ditkowsky; and from Urban Innovation Analysis.

Terry Nichols Clark

Citizen Politics in
Post-Industrial Societies

1

Overview of the Book

Michael Rempel
and
Terry Nichols Clark

This volume explores new developments profoundly transforming politics as we know it. Our Introduction (chapter 2) presents a general framework interpreting core components of *post-industrial politics*. Subsequent contributions expand on this framework. Most provide comprehensive reports of political trends, with extensive evidence from citizen surveys. The contributors use diverse methods to illuminate recurring themes: the rise of social issues, fragmentation of classic left-right binaries, and the importance of education, age, religion, and country of origin for politics. Some contributors provide intriguing contrasts, not all of which are yet resolved in this dynamically changing field.

Our volume's convergence on the politics of *post-industrial society* builds on past work such as Daniel Bell (1973) and Ronald Inglehart (1990). Our framework is unique in incorporating political trends that grew more pronounced over the last two decades. For example, this period saw little growth in real incomes of most citizens in Western Europe and the United States. Yet, differing from past recessionary periods, the political views of many middle class persons and left parties around the world became more fiscally conservative. During the same period, social conservatism mounted on some issues (like treatment of criminals and immigrants), but social liberalism increased on other issues (like women's roles). As another example, party politics changed. Green/ecology-oriented and anti-immigrant nationalist parties emerged in Europe as vital political forces. This occurred while traditional social democratic parties declined or reshaped their platforms to adapt to the diminishing import of class-based industrial politics.

This volume seeks to provide a clear assessment of such profoundly important changes, without taking a strong ideological stand. Our cross-national focus is especially important. It permits us to identify patterns that both do and do *not* transcend national boundaries. Isolated studies of single nations can be misleading in drawing attention away from cross-national socio-economic and political influences. Emphasizing socio-economic and political variables can transcend "national character" interpretations, while provoking policy-sensitive thinking about modes of intervention.

Part One.
Introduction: Post-Industrial Politics:
A Framework for Interpreting Citizen Politics Since the 1960s

Our Introduction suggests that shifts in technology toward a *post-industrial society* encourage fundamental political changes, including: (1) increased influence of the mass media, (2) less influence of traditional statuses like social class or religion, (3) the decline of "left-right" ideological polarization, (4) the rise of single-issue politics, (5) more influence of public political discussion, (6) institutionalization of new social movements (e.g., concerning feminism, civil rights, or environmentalism), and (7) a divergence between the political orientations of citizens and of many parties and pressure groups; (8) these changes are especially manifest among young, well-educated, and non-religious citizens, and in societies where such citizens are more numerous. These components combine to generate *post-industrial politics*. To illustrate their impact, we analyze numerous results concerning four specific post-1960s trends in: (1) social liberalism, (2) economic liberalism, (3) issue priorities, and (4) political activism. Apparent contradictions surface in the evidence on each trend. We find some liberal and some conservative trends. We seek to resolve the contradictions by formulating specific propositions that point to mediating effects of the eight political changes just listed. The result is a theory of post-industrial politics in the form of general propositions and specifications about where they apply. For instance, one general proposition is that *education encourages social liberalism*. But effects vary by country. We thus specify conditions that do and do not lead education to encourage social liberalism, thereby clarifying results detailed in later chapters.

The subsequent chapters report original analyses of citizen surveys. National surveys of citizens in the United States, many countries in Western and Eastern Europe, Australia, and Japan are mined for new patterns. Many patterns emerge. Some fit clearly into the Introduction's framework. Others do not, which sparks discussion by the contributors as to why. In particular, we include contributions to two ongoing debates. The first debate concerns whether or not materialism is rising. Easterlin and Crimmins challenge Inglehart's *postmaterialist* interpretation, with each author reassessing and integrating the other's results. Second is the debate over "are social classes dying?" Clark, Lipset, and Rempel (1993) suggested that social classes are declining in political importance in many societies. This interpretation was challenged by, among others, Hout, Brooks, and Manza (1993, 1995), who suggested that social class has *not* declined in its impact on political behavior. Their results, they suggested, undermined the entire post-industrial politics interpretation. Brooks and Manza have moved beyond this earlier position. In the present volume, they present a deeper and more subtle approach to class politics, showing instances of its persistence but also how its expression has changed in current, post-industrial societies. They carefully map the forces driving the contrasting trajectories of professionals to the Democrats, and managers to the Republicans over the past several decades. This analysis permits a careful testing and partial reconciliation of competing interpretations about class and post-industrial politics.

Part Two.
Cultural Shifts and Politics: Is Materialism Rising, Declining, or Both? Implications for Political Activism?

The first two chapters in this part document trends in cultural values as background for understanding recent *political* developments. Ronald Inglehart extends his past work showing that value priorities of Western publics are shifting from *materialism* to *postmaterialism*: from an emphasis on physical and economic well-being to the quality of life, self-expression, and more democracy. Using quite recent data, Inglehart demonstrates that virtually all industrialized societies show a clear twentieth-century trend toward postmaterialism. Short-term economic fluctuations do generate blips: economic downturns elicit more emphasis on material needs. But over the long haul, because successively younger generations exhibit more postmaterialism than their elders, the predominant shift throughout the industrialized world is toward postmaterialism.

Richard Easterlin and Eileen Crimmins present apparently discrepant findings. They report that from the early 1970s through the late 1980s, *private materialism* increased greatly among United States youth. Reviewing annual surveys, they find that goals relating to family life increased somewhat, public interest concerns diminished modestly, and the goal of personal self-fulfillment declined sharply. Also, jobs offering money and status became more preferred, relative to those providing opportunities for self-fulfillment or public service; and there was a corresponding retreat from political involvement. Commenting on these findings, Inglehart notes that they concern values in just one country, during a decade and a half when there was frequent economic stagnation, and that data are only for quite young persons (high school seniors and college freshpersons). Inglehart suggests that Easterlin and Crimmins may therefore miss the "big picture" of burgeoning postmaterialism since World War II. Easterlin and Crimmins reply to Inglehart, pointing out areas of persistent disagreement and rapprochement. Our Introduction proposes a reconciliation of the two findings. Inglehart's survey items, we suggest, capture a shift towards postmaterialism in *public* values, concerning what society and government should promote, often via public policies: for example, more civil liberties, ecological values, and democratic participation. By contrast, Easterlin and Crimmins's items focus on a shift toward materialism in *private values,* concerning what people would like to obtain individually—in a context that broader public policies make possible.

Naoyuki Umemori makes some important general points using original materials from Japan. Consistent with Inglehart, he documents rising postmaterialism in Japan after World War II. As Inglehart theorizes, this trend stems largely from the increased postmaterialism of successively younger generations, not from generations changing as they age. Yet, sharply disconfirming Western interpretations, Umemori reports that political *activism*, notably in socially liberal new social movements, is *not* rising. To the contrary, Japanese youth show growing political apathy, coupled with expanding concerns to enjoy a rich and satisfying life of private consumption. These rising consumer orientations match the Easterlin and Crimmins evidence of growing materialism in the United States. To interpret the political patterns, Umemori also discusses Japanese religion and nationalism as important factors often ignored in Western studies. His contribution clarifies these contradictory but critical tensions found in many post-industrial societies.

Part Three.
The New Middle Class Politics: What Is Special About the Politics of Professionals, and Other Middle Class Persons?

The previous three chapters focus on *generational politics*, providing extensive evidence of trends among younger persons. The next two assess the impact of social class background, a concern of social scientists for decades. Indeed, many contrast the class focus of politics in industrial societies with the weaker class content of post-industrial politics. The chapters included here focus on *the new middle class politics,* which is analytically critical, since the middle classes illustrate core tendencies of post-industrial politics in general.

Steven Brint, William Cunningham, and Rebecca Li provide a comprehensive examination of the politics of middle class *professionals* across five industrialized societies. They identify four broad characterizations of professionals in past writings: (1) a conservative business-oriented class, (2) a moderate "balance wheel" between forces of left and right, (3) a left-of-center "new class," whose interests primarily concern social rather than economic issues, and (4) a class that combines economic conservatism and social liberalism. Brint et al. show that the fourth characterization provides the most accurate portrait. Yet, they also reveal that professionals are highly divided in their views. Economic liberalism is more common among professionals in "social and cultural" occupations, and less common among lower-income and younger professionals. Social liberalism is greater among younger, better educated, and less religious professionals. Brint et al. also report tremendous variation in the politics of professionals across the five countries in their study. Professionals in countries like the United States and Australia, with a business-oriented political culture, tend to be conservative in outlook, while professionals in countries like Italy and Germany, with a more welfare-oriented political culture, tend to be more social democratic.

Jeff Manza and Clem Brooks focus on the United States, but explore specifics of three types of middle class politics: among managers, the self-employed, and professionals. All three groupings hold pivotal middle class locations, as compared for instance with blue-collar workers. American professionals were often politically conservative in the 1950s, but changed over the next two decades. Why? Manza and Brooks consider competing theories, and conclude that professionals' liberalism on social issues led them increasingly to identify with the Democratic party. By contrast, the more conservative social views of managers and the self-employed, coupled with the broadly conservative economic views that all three middle classes share, led the latter two classes to identify more with the Republican party. The Manza and Brooks portrait of all three middle classes as comparatively conservative regarding an activist government on *economic* issues confirms a key conclusion of Brint et al.: that even the more liberal professionals do not challenge the dominant ideology of advanced industrial societies. To this assessment, however, Brint et al. add that the historical ethic of "social responsibility," particularly salient in professional ideologies from 1870 to 1920, could plausibly lead professionals toward more forceful opposition if social protest should rise in the future.

Part Four.
New Issues, Ideologies, and Cleavages: What Mobilizes Citizens?

The final three contributions document new issues, cleavages, and political styles emerging with post-industrial politics. Allen Mayer provides a lively and engaging case study of political campaigns since the early 1970s. He advances *new fiscal populism* as the political culture of the future. It joins social liberalism with economic conservatism, a combination that Brint et al. and Manza and Brooks apply especially to professionals. New fiscal populism also contains other elements that he clarifies and documents with campaign flyers, speeches, and other data. New fiscal populists oppose patronage, support clean government, and make extensive use of electronic media in campaigns—rather than personal contacts by local party activists. New fiscal populist candidates downplay their *ideology*, or ties to established parties, portraying themselves as non-ideological "outsiders," stepping in to make government more "efficient." Mayer provides evidence that changing citizen demographics—greater affluence and education, and a larger suburban population—will increasingly oblige successful Democrats to embrace new fiscal populist themes.

Mayer shows both ideological change and more subtle changes that left-right ideological distinctions cannot capture. Michael Rempel, by contrast, focuses on the *ideological* constituents of post-industrial politics. Rempel considers five sets of ideological divisions: (1) a single, class-based left-right cleavage, (2) separate cleavages on economic and social issues, (3) separate cleavages on welfare-oriented *redistributive* economic programs and on *non-redistributive* or "middle class" spending programs, (4) separate cleavages on new social movement and "law and order" social concerns, and (5) a single-issue politics perspective, which rejects any general cleavages. Rempel finds the least support for the first and fifth positions, but some support for the other three. However, he qualifies the trend away from left-right divisions. He finds that well-educated and politically active citizens remain consistently on the left or the right across different issues, much more than the general population. Thus many activist citizens still unite multiple issues under a classic left-right framework.

In the final contribution, Paul Butts explores some central issues raised by post-1960s new social movements: political activism and feminism. Butts analyzes surveys from citizens in fourteen countries. This rich data set permits him to show how many would-be interpretations are remarkably nation-specific. Assessing political activism, he finds high educational attainment and low religiosity are its most consistent cross-national predictors. One notably ambiguous finding is that younger respondents are *more* likely to be politically *active*, but *less* likely to indicate an *interest* in political issues. This joins with Umemori's findings of rising political apathy among Japanese youth. Perhaps education, the media, and new social movements encourage younger persons to become politically active when concerned about an issue; but compared most obviously to the 1960s generation, young persons today show fewer political concerns. Turning to feminism, Butts creates five distinct measures of feminist views, permitting a more subtle analysis than past studies. Female sex, low religiosity, high educational attainment, and youth are the strongest predictors of feminist views, although results vary across the five feminism measures. Another interesting finding is that controlling for social background, pro-feminist respondents are more politically active. Butts concludes that this bodes well for the future spread of feminism.

The book does not directly explore political leaders, government institutions, parties, and their decision-making processes. Although central components of post-industrial politics, they are difficult to capture using citizen survey data, the main foundation of this volume. Our companion volume pursues these other components (Clark and Hoffmann-Martinot 1997).

Part 1

Introduction

2

Post-Industrial Politics: A Framework for Interpreting Citizen Politics Since the 1960s

Michael Rempel
and
Terry Nichols Clark

Politics in advanced industrial societies has changed dramatically in the past few decades. Many forces driving these changes emerged after World War II, but their main political effects did not surface until the 1960s. Until then political discussion had focused largely on economic issues, such as unemployment, labor relations, and economic growth. But in the 1960s, a young and dedicated corps of activists rallied around new protest issues, such as free speech and the Vietnam War in America, or "green" issues in Europe. New groups and political parties subsequently developed on issues like environmental protection and immigration policy. "New social movements" took shape concerning the environment, women's rights, and other "new left" causes. Citizens grew more concerned with non-economic issues like crime and the threat of nuclear war. Some of these patterns persisted into the 1990s, while others shifted.

This volume seeks to clarify and interpret these and related developments. Our main focus is on *citizen* politics. Two companion volumes focus on parallel changes among elected leaders and organized groups, one for the United States (Clark 1994) and one international (Clark and Hoffmann-Martinot, 1997).

AUTHORS' NOTE: We thank Steven Brint and Mark Gromala for many helpful comments. Brian David Jacobs and Helge Larsen were provocative discussants of this and related papers at the July 1994 World Congress of Sociology in Bielefeld, Germany. Dennis Merritt and Leszek Porebski provided invaluable assistance in preparing tables. William Cunningham, G. Allen Mayer, and Lucy Stanfield helped with the ISSP, GSS, and related data analyses. Andres Villarreal helped with research on the media.

Franklin, Mackie, and Valen (1992) provide a complementary treatment of political parties. Dalton and Kuechler (1990) consider "new social movements."

A Summary of Post-1960s Political Trends

The social, economic, and political changes of recent decades render obsolete many previous theories and everyday understandings. Consider some political trends in the advanced industrial societies of Western Europe, North America, Australia, and Japan:

- Despite widespread generalization about trends in "social liberalism"— "leftism" in European parlance—liberalism is up since the 1960s on some social issues (like the environment, and civil rights for women and minorities) but down on others (like crime and drug use). These conflicting trends are most evident among the young.
- Despite widespread generalization about trends in "economic liberalism," liberalism has declined on abstract questions about taxation and government intervention, while often rising on questions about spending for specific programs (e.g., crime-fighting and health care). Even for a citizen who, in principle, may oppose taxes and government intervention, an interest in the social benefit of a particular program may generate support for spending more money on it. These trade-offs have grown more subtle than many past observers appreciated.
- Among *all* citizens, the correlation between social and economic liberalism is weak. However, among citizens who are highly educated, politically informed, or politically active, the correlation rises. In contrast to the view that citizens do not maintain consistent ideological positions, this result suggests that an important subset of citizens *does* continue to consider issues in general "left-right" terms. They put social and economic issues together under one ideological framework.
- It is widely said that the political activism of the 1960s raised the public's consciousness of *social* issues, like the environment, women's rights, and peace. Political activism on those issues has indeed risen. However, the inactive majority seems now to care *less* about those issues than in the 1960s. In "most important problem" surveys since the early 1970s, only a negligible fraction of respondents mention any *social* issues as "most important," whereas at least a plurality—and on some surveys a majority—mention *economic* issues like unemployment, inflation, and governmental budget deficits. This apparent rise of popular *economic* concerns probably results from the recessionary and generally unstable economic conditions in most advanced industrial societies since the early 1970s.
- Two characteristics strongly correlated with citizen political activity—high education and low religiosity—are becoming more widespread (albeit more in Europe than in the United States). These two trends should increase political activ-

ism. Accordingly, there is some evidence of increased activism (in the Butts chapter), but other evidence shows increased political *apathy* and the replacement of political with *consumer* concerns (in the chapter by Umemori and Rempel).

To explain these seeming discrepancies—in some cases, outright contradictions —between different findings, we point in this introductory chapter to mediating effects of eight general political changes. We unite these under the term *post-industrial politics*, as they derive largely from the transition to a technologically advanced *post-industrial society*.

The Eight Components of Post-Industrial Politics

We are undergoing a profound shift not just in political "trends" but in their cumulative meaning and interpretation. This marks a shift in political culture. Culture is a society's body of commonly held meanings and ideas—shared values, beliefs, and worldviews—and its members' ways of demonstrating, debating, and transmitting those meanings. Political culture is the body of shared political meanings and ideas, and the underlying "rules of the game" for the conduct of politics, among citizens, parties, pressure groups, government institutions, or the media.

Here are the eight components of post-industrial politics:

1. *Mass media gain in political influence.* This occurs via news outlets such as, in the United States, the major free television networks and the cable networks, CNN and CSPAN. "Soft" news media also emerge, but their influence is less direct; they include television "newsmagazines" and the burgeoning computer Internet. G. Allen Mayer identifies *political advertising*, aired via electronic media, as an increasingly widespread and effective means for electoral candidates to sway citizen opinion. (See Mayer, this volume; Sabato 1981.)

2. *Political orientations grow relatively less determined by pre-industrial or industrial social cleavages (e.g., social class, region, or religion) but more determined by multiple "new" cleavages (e.g., education, gender, or contemporary race/ethnic divisions).* The earlier cleavages, social class in particular, undeniably persist as influential social forces. Class affects access to both wealth and political power, whether one defines classes only as blue- or white-collar or using multiple, more specific class distinctions (cf. Hout, Brooks, and Manza 1993; Verba, Schlozman, Brady, and Nie 1993; Wright 1985). But the political *expression* of class interests has declined, at least relative to other cleavages. This results in part from the growing influence of "middle class" subgroups, whose most salient issues do not always concern economics or *class interests* per se. For instance, Manza and Brooks (this volume) report that since the early 1970s, professionals in the United States have demonstrated growing support for the Democratic party, largely due to their liberal views on *social* issues of civil rights, gender equality, and abortion.

Another development which may importantly affect social cleavages is the spread of national (and increasingly international) electronic media; these media disseminate political information *across* class and other subgroup lines. The heightened access of citizens to a non-class-specific political discussion (or "discourse" to use the term of recent cultural analysts) may make political views more "sociotropic"—more responsive to the public interests of the collective, as opposed to the private interests of locality, subgroup, or self. Ronald Inglehart suggests this development: "The electorates of advanced industrial societies do not seem to be voting their pocketbooks, but instead seem primarily motivated by 'sociotropic' concerns: rather than asking, 'What have you done for me lately?' they ask 'What have you done for the *nation* lately?'" (1990: 1295; *italics in original*). At the same time, the media and other social developments may lead subgroup divisions besides traditional ones, such as class or religion, to become more prominent. We explore this below. (See Manza and Brooks, this volume; Clark and Lipset 1991; Clark, Lipset, and Rempel 1993; Franklin, Mackie, and Valen 1993; Inglehart 1987.)

3. *Polarization between classic "left" and "right" ideologies declines.* It is still commonplace to speak of a political "left" and "right." However, in this volume, Mayer and Rempel each examine why political views become increasingly distinct within at least *two* left-right cleavages—one on economic and the other on social issues. Mayer theorizes that the prevalent trend is toward "new fiscal populism," combining social liberalism and economic conservatism. Meanwhile, Brint, Cunningham, and Li, as well as Rempel, suggest that on economic issues the left is becoming more defined by support for moderate, "middle-income," non-redistributive programs than by support for classic rich to poor redistributive programs.

Further, Mayer posits that in a certain sense *all* ideological cleavages are weakening. He observes that for considerable numbers of United States citizens, an overriding concern with the *efficiency* of program delivery has replaced *ideology* as the basis of their personal political outlooks. Current Vice-President Al Gore illustrates this emphasis in frequent mentions of his plan to "re-invent" government by streamlining services in numerous government agencies. (See Brint, Cunningham, and Li, this volume; Mayer, this volume; Rempel, this volume; Clark and Ferguson 1983; Heath et al. 1991 for British evidence.)

4. *Single-issue politics rises in salience.* From consumer advocates to civil rights defenders to anti-smoking activists, political groups more often address single issues. Both the numbers of single-issue groups and concerns they address have expanded tremendously in recent decades (Berger 1981). Also, individual citizens are now more likely to evaluate issues piecemeal, without reference to organizing ideologies. However, as Rempel confirms for the United States, ideological consistency rises among better-educated, informed, and politically active citizens. (See Rempel, this volume; Clark and Lipset 1991.)

5. *Public political discussion gains in influence.* Those who can *slant* public

discussion their way (e.g., via the media) can better spread their views to others, thus helping their favored causes. *On a given issue, a given side's impact on public discussion rises as that side exhibits greater (1) citizen passion, (2) organized activism, or (3) possession of competitive resources, such as money, staff, political contacts, or access to the media.* This should hold especially in a post-industrial context, where activists have relatively greater opportunities to use their resources to gain access to the media and to other technologies for disseminating its views (component #1). Also, as left-right ideological polarization weakens and citizens grow more apt to evaluate issues piecemeal (components #3 and #4), citizens are more often swayed by discussion from one side of a single issue than by an overarching ideology.

Much survey research stresses the political impact of citizens' background characteristics, such as income, education, and age. This leads to findings like citizens with social background characteristics *a*, *b*, *c* are more likely to hold political views *x*, *y*, *z*. For example, many studies report advanced education to be the background characteristic most strongly associated with liberal views on many social issues. Since education is rising in nearly all industrialized societies (Table 2.2, below), this logic suggests that socially liberal views should also be rising. Yet as we show below, liberalism is *declining* on many social issues. To explain this, component #5 points to the issue-specific influences of *public political discussion.* Liberalism on a particular issue may decline if prominent discourse slants towards the conservative side. The slant may be due in part to the disproportionate passion, activism, or resources of conservatives. Therefore, in addition to citizen background characteristics, we stress here the rising importance of the content of public political discussion. (See especially Mayer, this volume.)

6. *New social movements become institutionalized.* These movements address not workplace but quality of life issues (e.g., women's rights, gay rights, and the environment). The "left-libertarian" and "green" parties in Western Europe formed largely out of new social movement concerns (Franklin, Mackie, and Valen 1992; Kitschelt 1990). Their institutionalization into parties and pressure groups generally leads the new movements to become less radical in their demands and tactics; but this change can help them achieve a more stable, enduring presence on the political map. (See Dalton and Kuechler (eds.) 1990; Offe 1987.)

7. *Citizens' political orientations diverge from those of many political parties and pressure groups.* This happens in two ways. First, citizens' ties to classic left and right ideologies loosen, while most long-standing, established parties in industrialized countries resist abandoning *their* historical roots in a class-based left-right continuum (Lipset and Rokkan 1967). This leads many citizens to turn to candidates who seem weakly tied to parties and pressure groups; citizens may perceive such candidates more as responsive to popular views and hence have more ability to defy "business as usual." In the 1992 United States presidential election, the widespread belief that H. Ross Perot stood apart from established parties and pressure groups—correct or not—helped him take 19 percent of the

vote, the second-largest share ever taken by a candidate from either of the country's two major parties (New York Times 1992). Still, candidates seeking to demonstrate independence need not abandon party ties altogether; Mayer observes that many candidates keep nominal party ties but distance themselves from party influence and ideology. This lets them embrace the less "ideologically consistent" views more popular among citizens. To adapt to this new electoral climate, established parties may eventually modify their long-standing positions. In this regard, Franklin et al. (1992) observe that during the 1970s and 1980s, leftist parties throughout the industrialized world backed away from strong pro-socialist positions. (See Mayer, this volume; Franklin, Mackie, and Valen 1993; Lipset 1991.)

Second, "new social movements," and "new left" and "new right" parties also diverge substantially from the concerns of most citizens. These movements and parties stress *social* issues; but to a steady plurality—and often a majority—of citizens, the economy remains paramount, while other issues come later. (This is a hotly debated point among theorists, but James Carville, a lead staffer in Bill Clinton's 1992 presidential campaign captured it in what became the campaign's guiding slogan, "It's the economy, stupid.") This continued salience of the economy among citizens partly explains the continuing success of more established political parties, even in continental European countries where alternative "new left" and "new right" parties have arisen. (See Franklin, Mackie, and Valen 1992; Kitschelt 1990.)

8. *The foregoing components most influence the political orientations of young, well-educated, and non-religious citizens.* Such citizens have weaker ties to traditional family and social institutions. This renders them more open to new cultural and political influences—arising, for instance, from national (and international) versus local media. Young persons are especially responsive to the new because of their recent socialization; older persons tend to support the political cultures dominant during their own youth. (See Brint, Cunningham, and Li, this volume; Inglehart, this volume.)

Mapping Political Change

Figure 2.1 summarizes our theoretical perspective. It maps connections among four types of changes: (1) the technological and social structural transition to a post-industrial society, (2) changing cultural values, (3) the rise of post-industrial politics, and (4) trends among ordinary citizens in their social liberalism, economic liberalism, issue priorities, and political activism. The transition to a post-industrial society drives many other changes. This transition includes progress in informational and other *technologies* and change in the *social structure*— both in the social organization of the workplace and of the larger society.

Figure 2.1 shows changing *values* as an intervening cause of political change, mediating the connection between post-industrial and political developments.

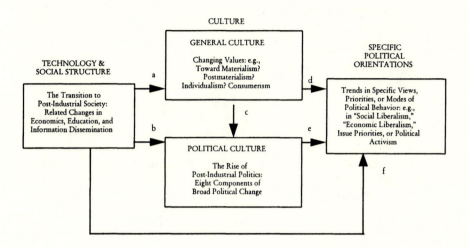

FIGURE 2.1 Mapping Political Change: Structural, Cultural, and Political Cultural Changes Which Interact to Drive Forward Changes in Specific Political Orientations

We do not suggest that *all* current values derive from post-industrial technological and structural influences but only that such influences are a prime cause of *recent* value *changes*. Since each country *enters* the post-industrial transition from a distinct cultural and political past, major cross-national differences in values should persist even as the post-industrial transition proceeds. This is a key conclusion of Brint, Cunningham, and Li (this volume). In five countries, they find that a person's country of origin remains a stronger determinant of political views than certain cross-nationally changing socioeconomic variables (e.g., income, occupation, education, etc.).

The next section examines the technological and structural origins of post-industrial politics (arrow b, Figure 2.1). We then look at how changing values intervene between technological and structural change and change in political culture (arrows a and c, Figure 2.1). The final section examines specific political orientations, such as social liberalism and economic liberalism (arrows d, e, and f, Figure 2.1).

The Technological and Structural Origins of Post-Industrial Politics

The transition to a post-industrial society has both technological and social structural dimensions. First, whereas the main workplace technologies in *industrial* society involve heavy manufacturing, the main technologies in *post-industrial* society are advanced scientific and technical knowledge, and information-handling tools like computers and telecommunication networks. Second, as technologies grow more sophisticated, more jobs in workplace social structures require mental rather than manual labor; this means that possessing an advanced education or technical training becomes more important (Bell 1973; Reich 1991).

Advanced technologies create more than new industries and jobs; consumer advertising, new forms of entertainment, and other subtle forms of information reach citizens with increasing speed and efficacy during their leisure hours, not just in the workplace. Indeed, post-industrial society implies fundamental changes in the *mode of information*—the way that informational signs and symbols reach people, at work, home, or leisure, and correspondingly influence their social and cultural perceptions. Numerous forms of electronic communication—television, telecommunications, and computers—increasingly pervade social life, displacing person-to-person and printed communications (Poster 1990). This change produces a more fragmented, rapidly changing, "schizophrenic" culture that can constantly shake even people's personal identities (e.g., Gergen 1991).

As technologies affecting most areas of life expand and grow more complex, public issues do too. This makes it more challenging for "generalists" (both political leaders and ordinary citizens) to understand details of multiple issues—from acid rain to social welfare programs to the effects of deindustrialization. At the same time, "specialists" emerge on many such issues. Some specialists build on their technical expertise to spearhead new social or political movements. Also, many citizens develop a detailed interest in a few select issues but withdraw from broader, general commitments—which established political parties continue to represent.

Figure 2.2 links specific post-industrial changes to the eight components of post-industrial politics. We identify post-industrial changes in three areas of life: (1) the economy, (2) education, and (3) the dissemination of information.

The Economy

Industrialized countries enjoyed considerable economic growth from 1945 to the early 1970s (Summers and Heston 1988)—especially in high-technology *service* industries, like finance, accounting, and computer-related industries (Bell 1973). The higher-level "knowledge workers" in these industries earn more and have more on-the-job autonomy than their manual-laboring counterparts in heavy industry. This rise of well-paid knowledge workers brings profound changes in

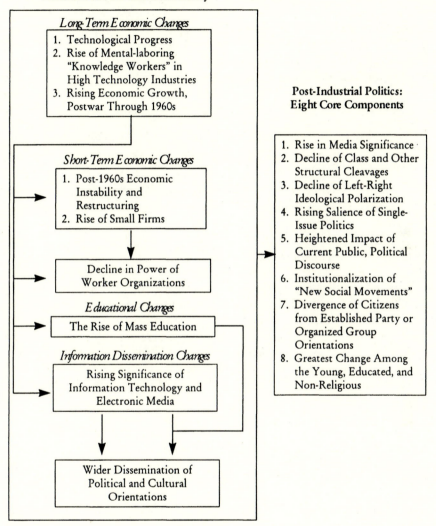

The Technological and Social Structural
Transition to Post-Industrial Society

Long-Term Economic Changes

1. Technological Progress
2. Rise of Mental-laboring "Knowledge Workers" in High Technology Industries
3. Rising Economic Growth, Postwar Through 1960s

Short-Term Economic Changes

1. Post-1960s Economic Instability and Restructuring
2. Rise of Small Firms

Decline in Power of Worker Organizations

Educational Changes

The Rise of Mass Education

Information Dissemination Changes

Rising Significance of Information Technology and Electronic Media

Wider Dissemination of Political and Cultural Orientations

Post-Industrial Politics: Eight Core Components

1. Rise in Media Significance
2. Decline of Class and Other Structural Cleavages
3. Decline of Left-Right Ideological Polarization
4. Rising Salience of Single-Issue Politics
5. Heightened Impact of Current Public, Political Discourse
6. Institutionalization of "New Social Movements"
7. Divergence of Citizens from Established Party or Organized Group Orientations
8. Greatest Change Among the Young, Educated, and Non-Religious

FIGURE 2.2 Schematic of the Technological and Structural Origins of *Post-Industrial Politics*

Note: This figure is an expansion of the two boxes connected by arrow b in Figure 2.1.

the income structures of industrialized countries. From the late 1940s to the early 1970s, the percentage of total income received by the most affluent tenth of the population (i.e., the top decile) declined in seven of nine industrialized countries (Roberti 1978).[1] By contrast, in eight of those countries, the "upper-middle-income" sector (seventh through ninth deciles) *gained* in relative income. Many skilled "knowledge workers" were in this upper-middle-income bracket, earning less than the wealthiest decile, but rising to challenge it in income and social power. This same study shows that since the 1940s, the bottom three deciles have *declined* in relative income, indicating that despite the rise of a new "middle class," a large part of the population still does not enjoy economic success.

Consider the political ramifications of these developments.

I. The rise of high technology industries and of highly skilled, well-paid "knowledge workers" reduces bipolar conflict between management and workers; this weakens classic left-right polarization.

In much of the twentieth century, the manual laboring class was conceived as the major force driving classic leftist politics. Therefore, as knowledge workers acquire some of the political influence of manual laborers, that should weaken leftist politics. In particular, there should be less support for redistributive economic programs, from which knowledge workers themselves would see little direct benefit. Brint, Cunningham, and Li (this volume) support this proposition in reporting that blue-collar workers are the most liberal subgroup on *redistributive* spending, whereas middle-income professionals are the most liberal subgroup on "middle-class" spending (e.g., for the arts, environment, and education).

Mayer (this volume) deepens our understanding of changing popular opinion. He notes that increasingly, political statements in the United States stress improving "efficiency" rather than expanding or cutting spending. This indicates an "ideologically neutral" or "pragmatic" outlook. New York City Mayor Rudolph Giuliani embraced this outlook in a 1994 interview. Asked if his spending cuts reflected a fiscally conservative "ideology," Giuliani replied that he had no such ideology but wished only to raise governmental efficiency as a "practical" response to growing budgetary constraints.[2] Giuliani, a Republican, again showed his pragmatism in endorsing New York's Democratic Governor Mario Cuomo for reelection in 1994, explaining that his decision was based on his practical fear that policies advocated by the Republican candidate, George Pataki, would jeopardize New York City's fiscal stability. While we do not suggest that such political "pragmatism" is ideologically neutral, we stress its increased visibility among growing numbers of citizens and political officeholders.

II. As the economic and political power of labor unions and leftist political parties declines, so do class politics and classic left-right polarization.

Debate on these issues continues. Some suggest that by the early 1970s, union radicalism and power waxed rather than waned (Bowles and Gintis 1987; Brown 1990; Hardiman 1990). Bruce Western (1995) confirms that across eighteen advanced industrialized countries, unionization levels remained roughly constant from 1950 to 1970, and then *rose* following the strike waves of the late 1960s. Only subsequently, in the aftermath of the 1970s oil shocks, did unions finally go into decline in most countries; and even so, Western finds that this decline did not extend to *all* advanced industrialized countries until the early 1990s.

The decline of union power that began in the early 1970s is linked to growing economic instability, mass unemployment, and related "post-Fordist" restructuring processes, affecting both labor markets directly and the role of the state as an intermediary in labor disputes (Aglietta 1987). Central to economic restructuring is the growing prevalence of small firms (Brown 1990; Hardiman 1990). The rise of small firms first grew salient in the early 1970s (Birch 1979), just as unions began to decline. Small firms are more apt to hire part-time or temporary workers, given those firms' sensitivity to short-term economic fluctuations (Baron 1984; Beck, Horan, and Tolbert 1978). Small firms are also less likely than larger firms to invest in worker training, high wages, and benefits. Yet small-firm workers less often protest over inferior employment conditions, since their temporary, unstable, and decentralized form of employment makes it difficult for them to organize into effective unions. The rise of small firms can also undermine the political and economic power of large-firm workers. Since many small-firm workers can shift to superior large-firm jobs if given the chance, this gives large-firm employers more leverage in dealing with *their* more-often-unionized employees. In the United States, harder bargaining with unions, and reduced wages and benefits, grew more common in the 1980s, as large firm employers often made explicit arguments that they had to respond to competition by smaller firms, domestically and internationally. Workers in automobile, steel, and other industries often accepted "give-backs," inconceivable a decade or so earlier. In the 1990s these issues sparked major strikes in Western Europe.

Some researchers stress other aspects of small firms in the post-industrial transition: lower wages and less satisfactory jobs. Harrison and Bluestone (1988) and Harrison (1994) suggest that post-industrial *service* growth (e.g., in small firms) has been more in menial, unsatisfying jobs than in high technology industries, as Bell (1973) maintains. However, on this point, recent research by Esping-Andersen (1994) indicates that the specific post-industrial sectors that grow the most vary greatly by country. In general, from analyzing changes in jobs and income in the United States, Germany, and Sweden from the 1960s to 1980, Esping-Andersen reports that post-industrial service growth more often produces a job *upgrading* and declining job polarization. This suggests that any deleterious effects on

TABLE 2.1   Popular Support for the Republican Party Has Risen, 1972-1993

Party Identification	1972-76	1977-82	1983-87	1988-93
Strong Democrat	17.0%	16.7%	18.1%	14.6%
Not Strong Democrat	25.8%	25.9%	22.2%	21.4%
Independent, Near Democrat	13.0%	13.1%	12.1%	10.3%
Independent	11.9%	13.6%	11.3%	12.4%
Independent, Near Republican	7.6%	8.5%	9.6%	9.7%
Not Strong Republican	14.8%	14.2%	16.2%	19.6%
Strong Republican	7.3%	7.4%	9.6%	11.2%
Other Party	2.7%	.6%	1.0%	.8%
	100%	100%	100%	100%

Source: General Social Survey (GSS), 1973-1993.

workers remain more subtle than some maintain. Yes, the nature of post-industrial *service* labor represents a decided upgrading from the past. Still, labor in
advanced industrial societies remains more temporary or part-time and more in
small firms than in the past; such conditions pose new barriers to the ability of
service *and* traditional manufacturing workers to promote economic and political interests concerning employment stability, health care and other job benefits, and social welfare protections for the unemployed.

Evidence: Western (1995) reports that economic restructuring is a significant
determinant of the decline of unions but is careful to point out country-specific
differences. For instance, before the 1990s, union density did *not* decline in Belgium, Denmark, Finland, and Sweden; he attributes this to high initial density
and national, collective bargaining procedures—involving institutionalized representation by business, labor, and the state—that were firmly in place. This
made unions in those countries less vulnerable to the 1970s economic stagnation. Western finds that by the early 1990s, what finally brought union decline
even in those countries was abandonment of national collective bargaining and
declining popularity of leftist, social democratic parties which, while in power,
had supported unions. Also, two countries initially *low* in union density elected
anti-union leaders, Margaret Thatcher and Ronald Reagan, which weakened
unions.

Indeed, parties with strong leftist positions have declined in most industrialized countries over the past two decades (Franklin et al. 1992; Lipset 1991; Western 1995). For instance, Table 2.1 shows, from 1972 to 1993, slowly but steadily
declining citizen identification in the United States with the traditionally pro-
union Democratic party and rising identification with the conservative Republican party. Manza and Brooks (this volume) analyze the party identification
trends for three specific social classes: (1) professionals, (2) managers, and (3) the

self-employed. They report that since 1952, professionals have become more Democratic, while managers and the self-employed have become more Republican. They find that the largely conservative economic views held by all three of those classes (although by the self-employed most especially) have influenced them in a pro-Republican direction. It is therefore professionals' liberalism on social issues that has made the difference in that class's becoming more Democratic on net. A shift of "middle class" subgroups like professionals towards leftist political parties may thus importantly contribute to the shift in the ideologies of those parties away from strident, old left positions and towards platforms that emphasize social issues and spending on "middle class" programs, like education, health care, or the arts (see Brint et al., this volume; Rempel, this volume).

Of course, it is difficult to assess the causal direction between the decline of unions and strong left parties, but both betoken the decline of class politics. This is especially evident in countries like the United States, where both union and leftist party power declined throughout the 1970s to 1990s. Class appeals often declined and ideologically moderate or "pragmatic" policies were adopted, even by political parties and groups traditionally sympathetic to unions. The magnitude of the change was made clear when a new Democratic president in the United States actively opposed major unions on a key issue where they took a visible and firm position. The case in point was the 1993 public debate over the North American Free Trade Agreement (NAFTA). Despite vigorous opposition from unions and others on the left, President Clinton garnered support for NAFTA from a coalition of political moderates, economists, and business leaders. It finally passed.

Education

Educational expansion is integral to the post-industrial transition. This holds whether the expansion is driven by students seeking more general education or for other reasons, including demands from business for a more literate, technically able, and disciplined work force (Apple 1979; Bowles and Gintis 1976; Tyack 1974). Some question whether an advanced education actually imparts useful work skills at all, and not just symbolic credentials (Collins 1979). In any case education has expanded dramatically during the twentieth century, in parallel with economic developments, as Table 2.2 shows. This supports our general stress on formal education as central to the rise of a high-technology, information-based society.

Yet how education works is more complex than earlier work suggested. Many studies find a positive correlation between advanced education and liberal views on social issues like women's equality, political liberties, and the environment (Brint and Kelley 1983; Flanagan 1982a; Smith 1982). In this volume, both Brint et al. and Butts find this association for numerous industrialized countries. But

TABLE 2.2   Secondary School Enrollment Ratios, 1950-1990 (secondary school enrollment by school age population for given country)

Year	Can.	USA	Arg.	Belg.	Czech.	Den.	Fin.
1950	31	77	22	—	—	59	—
1955	38	84	29	—	28	64	—
1960	49	86	30	—	36	66	—
1965	52	96	38	75	39	65	57
1970	65	—	45	81	31	78	102
1975	91	92	55	84	62	80	89
1980	92	90	59[a]	88	89	105	97
1985	103	99	70	96	84	105	102
1987	104	98	74	103	82	107	106
1989	105	90	71	102	87	109	112
1990	104	—	—	102	83	108	117

Year	Fran.	W. Ger.	Hung.	Ire.	Italy	Neth.	Nor.
1950	—	—	15	20	17	—	—
1955	—	54	20	25	24	50	—
1960	46	55	26	31	35	60	62
1965	56	60	36	45	47	59	70
1970	74	36	63	74	61	75	84
1975	82	71	63	88	70	89	88
1980	85	94	70	93	73	93	94
1985	93	99	72	96[b]	75	104	97
1987	92	101	70	98	75	103	93
1989	97	107	76	99	78	97	98
1990	99	107	81	101	75	96	101

Year	Pol.	Spain	Swe.	UK	Aus.	Isr.	Jap.
1950	30	12	46	51	46	25	71
1955	35	16	54	58	56	—	77
1960	48	20	54	68	61	—	79
1965	58	31	85	68	72	48	85
1970	62	56	86	73	82	57	86
1975	72	73	78	83	73	66	91
1980	77	87	86	83	71	72	93
1985	78	98	83	85	79	76	96
1987	80	105	91	82	81	83	95
1989	81	108	91	83	82	83	96
1990	83	—	90	86	81	85	—

[a]Data for 1981
[b]Data for 1984
Source: UNESCO Statistical Yearbook, 1963-1993.

there are exceptions. To explain the disparate results, we propose two propositions, building on Weil (1985) and Muha and Jackman (1984):

> *IIIA. A national education system fosters support for a country's ascendant ideas—*
> *ideas consistent with the country's founding or ascendant political, cultural, and*
> *religious principles.*

> *IIIB. In a country with a political system based on democratic principles (especially*
> *on individual rights), educational expansion fosters liberalism on issues like those*
> *addressed by new social movements—provided that other cultural influences do not*
> *exert strong contrary effects.*

These propositions challenge the so-called enlightenment thesis (see Davis
and Robinson 1991), which holds that an advanced education consistently fosters tolerant or "enlightened" attitudes characteristic of the liberal sides of social issues. We suggest instead that education—especially state-administered
public education—has more of a *homogenizing* than an enlightening effect. Cur-
ricula in most countries' public education systems are broadly similar across
regions, and hence should generate similar views, usually those consistent with
the countries' founding or "ascendant" principles (Weil 1985; Muha and Jackman
1984). In political systems constitutionally founded on principles of democratic
government and individual rights, those principles are stressed in public education; this should foster socially liberal views on civil-rights issues and other
concerns of new social movements.

Butts's results support propositions IIIA and IIIB. In predominantly Catholic
Ireland, Italy, Spain, and Belgium, Butts finds weaker linkages than elsewhere
between educational attainment and liberalism on sexual freedom issues. In
those countries, a restrictive Catholic-inspired sexual morality may reinforce
conservative *religious* principles, partly offsetting the liberalizing effects of democratic *political* trends.

Information Technology

Information technology has advanced for decades, but in the 1960s the pace of
change accelerated dramatically. Television coverage in the 1960s of the Vietnam War and civil rights protests in the U.S. and student protests in Europe and
Japan magnified the socio-political effects of these events. Table 2.3 shows the
enormous growth of television viewership in America, most especially of world
events and national elections. Joining television are the burgeoning computer
networks, including the Internet and commercial on-line services, that offer
immediate access to information on an endless variety of political topics. And
these are still in their infancy.

TABLE 2.3   Citizen Reliance on Television, Versus Other Media Sources, for Obtaining Political Information

A. Where U.S. Citizens Obtain Most of Their World News

Date	TV Only	Newspapers Only	TV and Newspapers	Newspapers and Others, But Not TV	TV and Others, But Not Newspapers	Media Other Than TV or Newspapers
1959	19	21	26	10	6	17
1959	19	21	26	10	6	17
1961	18	19	27	11	7	15
1963	23	21	24	8	8	13
1964	23	20	28	8	6	12
1967	25	18	30	7	8	10
1968	29	19	25	6	5	13
1971	31	21	22	5	7	13
1972	33	19	26	5	5	12
1974	36	19	23	4	6	12
1976	36	21	23	4	5	11
1978	34	19	27	3	6	11
1980	39	21	20	3	5	12
1982	41	21	20	3	5	10
1984	46	22	15	2	3	11
1986	50	22	13	1	2	10
1988	44	22	18	2	3	10
1990	44	19	22	2	3	10
1991	54	11	23	1	4	6
1992	44	20	21	2	4	9

Source: Mayer (1993); Originally Published by Roper Organization Surveys for Television's Information Office; Question: "I'd like to ask you where you usually get most of your news about what's going on in the world today—from the newspapers, or radio, or television, or magazines, or talking to people or where?" [multiple responses permitted].

B. Where U.S. Citizens Obtain Most of Their Campaign Information

Date	Newspapers	Radio	Television	Magazines	More Than One of These	None	N
1952	23	28	32	5	3	6	1,672
1956	24	11	49	5	3	8	1,742
1960	23	5	60	4	3	5	1,813
1964	24	4	58	7	4	3	1,448
1968	21	4	62	5	2	5	1,332

Source: Mayer (1993); Originally Published by the Survey Research Center/Center for Political Studies, University of Michigan, American National Election Studies; Question: "We're interested in this interview in finding out whether people paid much attention to the election campaign this year [four questions preceded the one for which we show results]. . . . Of all these ways of following the campaign, which one would you say you got the most information from—newspapers, radio, television, or magazines?"

(*continues*)

TABLE 2.3   *(continued)*

C. What Sources Best Inform U.S. Citizens of Presidential and Vice-Presidential Candidates (dates since the early 1970s)

Date	Newspapers	Television	Radio	People	Magazines	Other
1972	26	66	6	5	5	2
1976	20	75	4	3	5	1
1984	19	75	4	3	3	2
1988	20	70	4	3	3	2
1992	18	74	6	7	2	1

Source: Mayer (1993); Originally Published by Roper Organization Surveys for Television's Information Office; Question: "And what about candidates in the national election—for President and Vice-President?" [the question follows three, whose initial introduction is: During the last election campaign, from what source did you become best acquainted with the candidates running in local elections . . . from the newspapers, or radio, or television, or magazines, or talking to people or where?"]

How large are media effects? Assessment is complex. The first serious media research, on radio in the 1940s and 1950s, found far more limited effects than many expected. Ever since, empirical social scientists tend to dismiss the "media hype" surrounding effects reported by journalists, advertisers, or critical theorists. Yet extrapolating from past research is misleading when media changes in recent years are so large. Unfortunately, the major changes we identify remain understudied to date. Consider, however, some effects that are likely, building on limited past research.

Neuman (1993) reports that on certain issues—such as wars or domestic crises like the AIDS epidemic—the media have a critical *attention-generating* effect. By contrast, media effects on more abiding issues, like poverty, crime, and pollution, seem less pronounced, although Neuman still finds significant media effects on public attention to certain long-term but fluctuating problems, like unemployment and inflation.

Brody (1991) likewise uncovers media effects on citizen attention to issues. When in 1972, at the beginning of Richard Nixon's second presidential term, the media greatly increased its coverage of domestic versus foreign policy issues, Brody found that domestic, macroeconomic indicators began to exert a heightened impact over citizen evaluations of government and presidential performance. Coverage was measured via the size of newspaper headlines, locating a story on the front pages of a newspaper (or early in a TV broadcast) and the volume of coverage. Page and Shapiro (1992) add that media effects on citizen attention rise especially on issues distant from most citizens' personal experi-

ences, for example, unemployment, criminal victimization, foreign policy decisions. Employed citizens, for example, report more concern over unemployment when the media covers it more extensively.

The media not only affect citizen *attention*; some research indicates that media
reports affect the *direction* of citizens' views on specific issues. Bartels (1993) finds
that during American presidential campaigns, media reports have small but
significant effects on citizens' views on both issues and candidates. Bartels notes
that these effects increase on new issues and new and unfamiliar candidates.
Also, using regression analysis techniques, Page and Shapiro (1992) find that on
certain issues, nearly half of the variance in popular opinion change between
two test times results from TV news coverage (adjusted R2 = .41). Page and
Shapiro distinguish many TV news effects and, in their regression model, estimate impacts of each separately. They find that *news commentary* (e.g., from a
commentator) has the greatest impact, as one "probably pro" commentary on a
policy generates over four percentage points of positive opinion change. They
also find that stories on expert opinion or scientific research strongly influence
popular opinion; if a TV news story indicates that experts favor a policy, public
support rises on average by three percentage points. A persistent point in these
and most serious studies is the caution that even when measured media effects
are relatively small over *short* periods, over longer periods—harder to study
rigorously—the media may play a substantial role in the gradual construction of
a citizen's political views.

While the media sometimes influence citizens directly, indirectly they often
reflect or *mediate* the influence of political officeholders or other opinion leaders.
Political leaders and organized activists, recognizing this potential, may consciously adjust statements and activities to generate more favorable and extensive media coverage. Blumenthal (1981) explores this in more depth, evoking
Democratic party pollster Pat Cadell's concept of "the permanent campaign"; it
stresses that modern American presidents must constantly "sell" their personal
image and policies through deliberate use of the mass media. Special press conferences, on-site visits to the "Heartland," and adjustments of grooming and
mannerisms exemplify tactics which Cadell advocated for modern leaders to
improve personal and policy ratings. Indeed, many elected officials regularly
report that their entire workweek is structured to heighten media impact (e.g.,
Miller 1989).

Page and Shapiro (1992) find that *popular* presidents are especially effective at
using the media to advance their policy views. They report that American presidents with an approval rating over 50percent change public opinion by .58 percentage points per "probably pro" speech, while presidents with lower approval
ratings change public opinion by only .05 percentage points per speech. Through
repeated, media-covered speeches over several months, Page and Shapiro find
that popular presidents can generate a 5-10 percentage point shift in public opinion on an issue. They add that it is when presidents are unpopular that *direct*

media effects—especially of news commentaries—become most influential.

Several authors emphasize the connection between the rise of the electronic media and of single-issue politics, that is, components #1 and #4 of post-industrial politics. Iyengar (1991) points out that the media cover issues *episodically*—as major events happen—rather than *thematically*—or in connection with overarching, continuing themes. Episodic coverage encourages citizens to see events and issues one-by-one, rather than in broad, ideological schemas. Gitlin (1980) illustrates this media effect through his history of newspaper and TV coverage of the New Left organization Students for a Democratic Society (SDS) in the 1960s. SDS was the leading radical student group in the U.S. in the 1960s. It was a multi-issue organization with a broad ideological vision at its founding. But media stories on SDS emphasized specific events with a single-issue focus. This undermined the concern of many activists to publicize a more general program for social change. Over time, Gitlin suggests that the media affected SDS's internal organization; by stressing the antiwar issue, the media caused an influx of second-generation SDS members with a more specific, militant antiwar agenda than the comprehensive agenda of the organization's founders. Gitlin's stress of the media impact on the rise of single-issue politics cautions us against attributing these developments *exclusively* to non-media "natural" changes in citizens' ideological proclivities.

Mayer elaborates on media effects in this volume. He shows that over the past two decades, successful candidates for offices like governor and United States senator have increasingly used electronic media in their campaigns. Broadcast advertising, though much more expensive than traditional personal-contact methods, allows a candidate to reach millions of voters instantly. Mayer concludes that the electronic media, and paid consultants sophisticated in using them, have largely supplanted traditional political organizing. Information and statistical technologies have encouraged the increasing use of sophisticated polling and other methods to identify and reach potentially supportive voters (Blumenthal 1981). These undermine traditional organizing methods, as candidates can direct carefully crafted messages to select constituencies, illustrating the power of "niche marketing."

Concerning television, Mayer adds a vital caveat: While television holds a growing influence over *major* contests, candidates for *local* offices can still depend heavily on clientelistic, personal ties. Most such candidates have neither the money to buy television time nor the prominence to gain free exposure through coverage by news outlets. For instance, from just the 1980s to early 1990s, Mayor Richard M. Daley of Chicago transformed his main campaign efforts from the personal/clientelist approach he learned from his father to a far more media-based approach. But Chicago is a large city whose politics are regularly televised; smaller locations have less coverage. This suggests a schism between major- and minor-office campaign methods. We generalize:

IV. Candidates for major political offices, to the extent that they do not depend on party or clientelistic ties for media access, increasingly use the media (especially television), while bypassing personal-contact methods.

Modern media technology does not automatically replace clientelistic ties. Even major office-seekers must gain *access* to the media somehow. Japan, even in national politics, is closer to Chicago's past in that established political parties control most funding for major campaigns, and make extensive use of clientelistic personal contacts. This limits the ability of candidates there for major, or minor, offices to use the media to bypass traditional contacts.

Beyond new campaign tools, the new electronic media have broader cultural and political effects:

V. The rise of centralized electronic media fosters national articulation of political issues; this reduces the political influence of social background characteristics like class, ethnicity, and religion.

Like nationwide public education, a nationwide media apparatus fosters homogeneity in priorities and modes of political understanding. This may undercut the influence of subgroup-based outlooks (e.g., arising from class, race, ethnicity, or locality). Television audiences especially tend to favor national over local networks; by contrast, for radio and newspapers, local outlets are often favored. The growing computer-network industry increasingly serves a national—and sometimes global—audience. These general patterns seem to vary by type of user, with younger, more sophisticated, and critical persons acquiring information from a wider range of media, and combining ideas more selectively through personal evaluations and informal discussions. Many interpretative writers have commented on these developments, but we lack serious research on them.

Still, proposition V is implicitly supported by Smith's (1985) finding that subgroup variations have declined in American citizens' choices of the country's "most important problem." Franklin et al. (1993) similarly find that, in much of the industrialized world, social background statuses like class, religion, and age have fallen as predictors of citizen voting.

Figure 2.3 provides further support. It shows a consistent decline from 1972 to 1993 in the impact of social background characteristics (e.g., age, income, educational attainment, race) on the political attitudes of United States citizens. Neither the figure nor the evidence reported on just above identifies a *media* effect per se; but the results are consistent with Proposition V.

Still, the media are rapidly changing. The nationalizing trend of proposition V may have held in the 1950s to 1990s, but could weaken. Why? Some media forecasters predict the rise of more highly personalized, niche-like developments—with cable TV channels replacing the major national networks, more computer-retrievable information, lower broadcasting costs, greater use of closed-circuit TV, and similar developments making access to the media far easier for smaller and local groups. But this is mainly a future prospect, to alert us against projecting linear patterns.

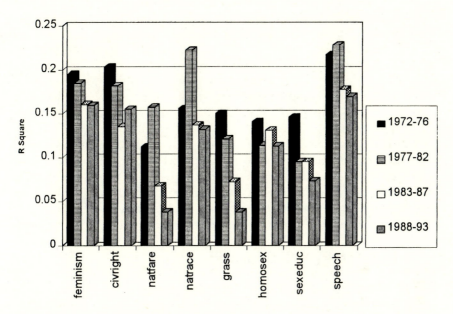

FIGURE 2.3 Declining Impact of Social Background Characteristics on United States Citizens' Political Views, 1972-1993

Note: The figure shows the Adjusted R square statistics from regressions performed separately for eight political questions during the four sub-periods spanning 1972 to 1993. The Adjusted R square indicates the percentage of variation in citizen responses to eight political attitudes explained by nine social background characteristics: age, education, marital status, occupational prestige, race (African American or other), region (Northeast, South, Pacific Coast, or other), religion (Catholic or other), and sex. Although we traced changes in the R square in a much larger battery of political questions, we exclude questions for which the initial R square, in the 1972-76 period, was less than 0.1. For all eight political questions that we do include, the R square declines from the first sub-period (1972-76) to the last (1988-93). This means that these nine social background characteristics, taken together, have declined since 1972 as predictors of liberal versus conservative responses to each of the eight items. The text of each item is in the appendix. (For "natfare" and "natrace," see the appendix for chapter 9.)

Changing Values

Advanced industrialization changes values. Values are desired goals, or conceptions of what is good for the individual or society. We focus on changes in values broadly related to politics, asking (1) what values (if any) are changing, and (2) what are the political ramifications of these changes?

The Nature of Change in Values

Since the 1970s, Inglehart's *postmaterialism* thesis has driven much of the debate on changing values. Inglehart asserts that values are growing less *materialistic* (concerned with money) and more *postmaterialistic* (concerned with nonmaterial goals like democracy, love, or intellectual satisfaction). Why? For Inglehart, technological progress and economic growth (especially 1945 to 1970) satisfied material needs enough for at least the young and the more affluent to turn towards postmaterial concerns. Inglehart (this volume) concludes that postmaterialism has continued to rise in most industrialized countries from the 1970s to the 1990s.

Inglehart's results have become so widely discussed that we feel obliged to consider some specifics. Do they contradict other studies? They clearly show value changes of *some* kind, but one can reinterpret the results. Scott Flanagan (1982a, 1982b) questions whether the items literally index *postmaterialism*. He notes that Inglehart, in his four-question postmaterialism index, classifies "maintaining order in the nation" as materialist, although that value lacks any clear economic content; similarly, Inglehart defines other values as materialist on his twelve-question index which reflect more of a social-order or control orientation than economic concerns. Flanagan suggests that the items do not comprise a single materialist versus postmaterialist dimension but *two* dimensions: (1) *materialism* versus *nonmaterialism*, and (2) *libertarianism* versus *authoritarianism*. The first contrasts materialist economic values, like "fighting rising prices," with all others. The second contrasts, among the *nonmaterialist* values, concerns for individual rights, self-actualization and achievement (*libertarian* values) versus concerns for domestic order, national defense, or other forms of social control (*authoritarian* values). Thus reclassified, Flanagan suggests that only libertarian values are rising, and that they have gained only against authoritarian but not against materialist values. He also notes that while Inglehart emphasizes affluence as driving value change, others find that education and youth are the background characteristics most associated with libertarianism.

Flanagan, while thus concluding that materialist values as measured by Inglehart's value items are not declining, notes that this instrument taps only into *public*, not into *private* values. He calls *public* those values that represent broad social goals that may or may not pertain to individual, personal aspirations. He then hypothesizes that *private* materialist values, unlike the public ones measured by Inglehart, are *declining*—this is because, as private values grow more oriented toward individualism, or toward libertarian self-actualization, money declines as a private concern. Money remains an important *public* concern because citizens continue to value the favorable material conditions that better enable them to achieve their ultimate, nonmaterialistic, private ends.

However, Flanagan's argument involves a subtle sleight of hand. Noting that Inglehart's index includes only *public* values, Flanagan nonetheless posits—but offers no evidence—that *private* libertarianism is rising; from *that*, he then reaches the consequently tenuous conclusion that private materialism must be declining.

By contrast, Richard Easterlin and Eileen Crimmins (this volume), using national survey data for the United States, find that private materialism has *risen* since the 1960s among the young—the age group that should best reflect Flanagan's alleged *decline* in private materialism.

Easterlin and Crimmins study trends from the late 1960s among American high school seniors and college freshpersons on four private values: (1) materialism, (2) family life, (3) personal self-fulfillment, and (4) personal dedication to the public interest. They find that private materialism has risen sharply, family life slightly, and both personal self-fulfillment and serving the public interest have either declined slightly or hardly changed, depending on the specific question.

In a related study, Crimmins, Easterlin, and Saito (1991) find that the "goods aspirations" of American high school seniors rose dramatically from 1976 to 1986. There were increases of 10 percentage points or more in the proportions of high school seniors aspiring to own "at least two cars," "clothes in the latest style," "major labor-saving appliances (washer, drier, dishwasher, etc.)," "a high-quality stereo," and "a vacation house." There were smaller increases in the percentages professing five out of seven other goods aspirations, with small declines appearing on only two—both concerning the aesthetic surroundings of one's house (e.g., yard, garden, and lawn), as opposed to purchasable commodities (1991: 123). This supports the view that a *consumer culture* has grown, promoting demand for consumer luxuries and money to buy them (see Horkheimer and Adorno 1991 [1944]; Turner 1988).

Crimmins, Easterlin, and Saito conclude that goods aspirations have risen *at the expense of aspirations for what cannot be bought*—for the individualistic, "libertarian" pursuit of self-actualization:

> some analysts have argued that there is an ongoing trend away from material aspirations, toward higher, nonmaterialistic ends along a Maslowian hierarchy of needs (Inglehart, 1981; Yankelovich 1981; Maslow 1954). If so, it is not apparent in today's American youth. They have displayed a clear turning away from intellectual/philosophical concerns of the type one might associate with Maslow's "self-actualization" (1991: 130).

Contrary to Flanagan and Inglehart, this more critical analysis suggests that rising "individualism" does not involve "libertarian"-like individuality in personal philosophy, or self-actualization; it may simply mean individuality about which consumer niche to join, or which commodity to buy next. Still, as Inglehart emphasizes in this volume, Easterlin and Crimmins's measures differ from Inglehart's, many of which focus more on public, political values. So the two sets of results are not strictly contradictory. We next seek to incorporate them into more *political* analyses.

Political Ramifications

One should explicitly distinguish the political ramifications of changes in public versus private values. First, *public* libertarian values, such as free speech, democratic participation, and environmental beautification, overlap with and entail support for liberalism on new social movement issues—especially environmental protection, and equal rights for women and for racial, ethnic, and sexual minorities. Second, rising consumerism in *private* values may undermine the cultural and political influence of class and status distinctions. Why? Since consumer imagery can cut across the barriers posed by traditional distinctions and define new subgroups (such as subcultures within schools), it can either generate a new common culture, or a multiplicity of new niche cultures, that supersede traditional distinctions (see Turner 1988). Unfortunately, we have little systematic research that explores specific connections between "consumerism" and politics.[3]

Trends in Specific Political Orientations: Evidence of Post-Industrial Politics at Work

This section considers trends in four types of citizen political orientations: (1) social liberalism, (2) economic liberalism, (3) issue priorities, and (4) political activism.

Social Liberalism

All political issues are social in affecting several persons. But political analysts often define *social* issues to contrast with economic ones. Social issues thus include (1) personal, political, or civil rights; (2) the environment and related "quality of life" issues; and (3) the waging or avoidance of war. The socially liberal (or leftist) sides support civil rights, environmental protection, and nonmilitaristic policies.

Many studies report increases in social liberalism in industrialized societies from World War II to the present (Clark and Ferguson 1983; Flanagan 1982a, 1987; Smith 1982). Two major explanations are the expansion of public educa-

TABLE 2.4   Social Liberalism Trends in the United States

YEAR	FEM-INISM	CIV-RIGHT	ABANY	SEX-EDUC	SPEECH	HOMO-SEX	CAP-PUN	GRASS	WIR-TAP
72	2.39	2.25	—	—	2.20	—	—	—	—
73	—	—	—	—	2.27	1.37	—	1.37	—
74	2.38	2.62	—	2.64	2.22	1.40	1.67	—	1.66
75	2.33	2.53	—	2.59	—	—	1.71	1.43	1.66
76	—	2.22	—	—	2.20	1.47	1.63	1.58	—
77	2.29	2.27	1.75	2.57	2.19	1.43	1.56	—	1.62
78	2.39	—	1.67	—	—	—	1.59	1.61	1.60
80	—	2.31	1.82	—	2.23	1.41	1.57	1.51	—
82	2.51	2.47	1.77	2.69	2.18	1.38	1.55	—	1.65
83	2.51	—	1.69	2.72	—	—	1.46	1.42	1.61
84	—	2.43	1.77	—	2.29	1.41	1.50	1.47	—
85	2.51	2.45	1.74	2.68	2.23	1.38	1.41	—	1.53
86	2.51	—	—	2.68	—	—	1.50	1.37	1.54
87	—	2.47	1.79	—	2.28	1.33	1.62	1.34	—
88	2.56	2.53	1.72	2.74	2.32	1.36	1.48	1.36	1.57
89	2.56	2.53	1.81	2.75	2.38	1.42	1.43	1.34	1.45
90	2.63	2.52	1.87	2.80	2.39	1.37	1.41	1.34	1.53
91	2.62	2.59	1.85	2.76	2.41	1.41	1.48	1.37	1.49
93	2.67	2.65	1.91	2.70	2.43	1.56	1.53	1.47	1.52
Change	+.28	+.40	+.16	+.06	+.23	+.19	−.14	+.10	−.14

Source: General Social Survey (GSS), 1972-1993; from left to right, the nine issues are: FEMINISM (index of 4 questions on women's rights), CIVRIGHT (index of 4 questions on civil rights towards African-Americans), ABANY (question on whether abortion should be legal under any circumstances), SEXEDUC (question on allowing sex education in schools), SPEECH (index of 2 questions on the free speech rights of persons with radical views), HOMOSEX (question on tolerance of homosexuality), CAPPUN (question on the death penalty), and WIRTAP (question on whether the police use of wiretapping should be allowed). Dashes indicate that the question(s) not asked in the year in question, or that there was an insufficient number of responses to obtain a valid statistic. See appendix A for more complete question wordings.

tion and the decline of religiosity. In this volume, Butts and Brint et al. confirm that persons with advanced education and low religiosity hold more socially liberal views. Nevertheless, countervailing factors must be at work, for while liberalism is still rising on some social issues, it is only unchanged or declining on many others, especially among the young. Such contradictory findings have seldom been seriously confronted. How can we interpret them? We begin with the United States, formulate some explanatory propositions, and then test them with cross-national data.

James Davis (1992) conducted an extensive analysis of 42 United States General Social Survey (GSS) questions from 1972 to 1989, mostly on "social" issues. (The GSS is the main survey repeating identical items near-annually for national samples of American citizens over many years.) Davis found that liberalism rose on free speech, race, and sex and gender; changed little on religion; and declined on crime.

With Table 2.4, we update Davis's analysis through 1993 on nine issues chosen to contrast socially liberal and conservative sides: civil rights for women, civil rights for African Americans, civil rights for homosexuals, sex education in the schools, abortion, free speech, legalization of marijuana, the death penalty, and the use of wiretapping. (See appendix 2.A for question wording.)

Liberalism rose from 1972 to 1993 on seven of the nine issues, declining only on the death penalty and wiretapping. In addition, from an analysis we conducted focusing just on young persons, aged 18-25, liberalism for them rose significantly on just three (women's rights, African-Americans' rights, and abortion), was constant on two (sex education and homosexuals' rights), and declined on four. (And only small surges of liberalism in the last two years generated a net rise on women's rights and a net non-change on sex education.) We thus find differences from earlier studies that stressed a consistent liberalizing trend. The young in 1993 are *not* more socially liberal overall than their immediate generational predecessors.

Another important finding is that, in all age groups, liberalism is rising on some social issues but declining on others. Philip Converse (1992) proposed the germ of an idea (in a four-page commentary on Davis 1992) that we develop here. He suggests that the crime and religious issue domains are "conservative-resonating," while the race, sex/gender, and free-speech issue domains are "liberal-resonating." He then proposes that the direction of *resonance* crucially affects the direction of change in public opinion.

It seems that items in the liberal domains show end point changes that tend toward liberalism, whereas responses to more conservative issues are tending toward conservatism. If this is true, then the preponderance of liberal issues (tested by Davis) has to matter, and if it were redressed, it is not clear that the observed faint liberal trend overall would survive. It might even be reversed (1992: 310).

This hypothesis is provocative but demands elaboration. First, concerning the concept of "resonance": What exactly does it mean for an issue to "resonate" with the liberal or conservative side? Second, Converse does not say *why* we should expect an association between the direction of an issue's resonance and the direction of change in public opinion. Third, it remains unclear what the criteria are that identify political issues respectively as liberal- or conservative-resonating.

Component #5 of post-industrial politics extends Converse's hypothesis. First, it suggests a definition of *resonance*: We understand an issue to "resonate" with a particular side if that side exhibits greater (1) citizen passion, (2) organized activism, or (3) possession of competitive resources. Second, component #5 indicates why it is useful to know with which side an issue resonates; in a post-industrial political context, where public discussion can have more influence on citizen opinion, the side with more control over that discussion is more likely to spread its views.

Finally, what criteria define an issue as liberal- or conservative-resonating? Propositions VI and VII address this.

VI. The more that organizations growing out of "new social movements" take up a social issue, the more likely the issue is "liberal-resonating."

VII. The more that a social issue concerns rights or opportunities of persons labeled by conservatives as socially "deviant," especially criminals and accused criminals, the more likely the issue is "conservative-resonating."

Proposition VI follows from component #5 and #6 of post-industrial politics, which noted that single-issue politics have been spreading (#5), and that new social movements have become institutionalized (#6). Several new social movements have reinforced one another's efforts at popularizing their issues through national lobbying and other political activities, like mass demonstrations. The rapid emergence of many important "NSMs" (new social movements) in the late 1960s and early 1970s led them to borrow significant elements from each other's speeches and tactics. Surely leaders watched each other's largest and most successful demonstrations, which in these years comprised highly televised marches on Washington by many thousand followers. A common style spread—in language, lobbying tactics, and organizational structure. Since then, even such a "moderate" interest group as the one which represents the elderly named itself "the Grey Panthers"—adapted from one of the most militant 1960s organizations—the Black Panthers.[4]

Proposition VII derives from the manifest dominance of the conservative side, in the United States especially, over public discussions of "law and order" issues, such as crime, drugs, and rights of the criminally accused. Conservative "law and order" themes grew more dominant in the late 1980s, championed by Republican Presidents Ronald Reagan and George Bush through anti-drug and anti-crime speeches and campaign advertisements. In contrast to the issues raised by liberal NSMs, law and order issues are less often addressed by visible and activist *groups*. Nevertheless, the growing passion of conservative *citizens*—perhaps amplified by certain conservative political leaders—has clearly attracted the attention of other political leaders and the media. The power of anti-crime issues in the U.S. in the 1980s and 1990s even led some liberal elected officials to embrace many conservative "law and order" demands. For instance, Bill Clinton, during his presidential campaign in 1992, made a special symbolic visit to his home state of Arkansas—of which he was then governor—to witness the execution of a man found guilty of murder but deemed mentally incompetent. Then in 1994, President Clinton signed, and most Democratic U.S. senators and representatives voted for, a crime bill opposed by most experts but which included many provisions long advocated by anti-crime conservatives—expanded use of the death penalty, lifetime prison terms for repeat offenders, and mandatory minimum sentences for certain minor offenses.

GSS survey results indicate that public opinion generally changed in a manner consistent with propositions VI and VII. United States citizens moved clearly toward liberalism on civil rights for women and African-Americans, two important new social movement issues. Further, consistent with Proposition VII, liberalism declined significantly on law and order issues—for the entire population on the death penalty and on wiretapping, and for young persons on those issues and also on legalizing marijuana.

Having developed propositions VI and VII with evidence from the United States, we tested them with cross-national results from two International Social Survey Project (ISSP) studies in 1985 and 1990. While spanning just five years, these data still revealed several significant changes in liberalism. Brint et al. (this volume) analyze many ISSP political questions. We focus here on items chosen to test propositions VI and VII. Unfortunately, few ISSP questions concern new social movement issues. The closest items were three on the legality or moral acceptability of the kinds of demonstrative protest tactics that new social movements often used to garner support for their issues, especially early on in the 1960s: *protest*, *strike*, and *obey*. (Table 6.1 of Brint et al. reports question wording.) Rationale: If new social movement mobilization tactics have gained in legitimacy, then NSM substantive themes may have gained in popularity, as proposition VI contends. Table 2.5A confirms significant increases in liberalism (.01 level) on all three protest activity questions in all four countries where asked: Australia, the former West Germany, Great Britain, and the United States. For proposition VII, we analyzed four items tapping conservative-resonating concerns: *tapcrim*, *mailcrim*, *holdcrim*, and *mistake*. Results did not support our expected rise in social conservatism, but differing from the protest activity questions, there was also not a clear rise in liberalism; changes were few, and possibly confounded by question wording (see Table 2.5B).[5]

Additionally, if we look closely at components of Inglehart's twelve-item "postmaterialism" index, one item is "the fight against crime." Support for it should rise, per Proposition VII. Indeed, from 1973 to 1988, the proportion of citizens in nine European countries identifying "the fight against crime" as their #1 or #2 priority rose from 22 to 27 percent; only one other item on the twelve-item index rose this much (1990: 98; N = 10,564 in 1973, N = 11,595 for 1988). Besides supporting proposition VII, this result suggests that Flanagan's hypothesized rise in public "libertarian" values (and Inglehart's "postmaterialist" val-

TABLE 2.5 Trends in Liberalism on Social Issues, 1985-1990

	Australia		West Germany		Great Britain		United States		Italy	
	all ages	*18-24*	*all ages*	*18-24*	*all ages*	*18-24*	*all ages*	*18-24*	*all ages*	*18-24*
A. "New Social Movement" Issues										
PROTEST	+		+	+	+		+	+		
STRIKE	+		+	+	+		+			
OBEY	+	+	+	+	+	+	+	+		
B. "Law and Order" Issues										
TAPCRIM										
MAILCRIM	–	–	–							
HOLDCRIM	+									
MISTAKE			+	–					–	

Source: International Social Survey Project (ISSP) "Role of Government" Surveys, 1985 and 1990; a "+" signifies a statistically significant change on t-tests (.01 significance standard) towards the liberal response between 1985 and 1990; a "–" signifies a statistically significant change towards the conservative response; a blank space signifies no statistically significant change.

ues) should be qualified by adding that some conservative *authoritarian* values have recently spread as much as, if not more than, libertarian values in Europe as well as in the U.S.

If social liberalism is *not* consistently rising across multiple issues, as our evidence reveals, why do so many analysts suggest that it is? Perhaps because the most discussed social issues—the environment, civil rights for women and ethnic minorities, abortion, and peace—all resonate more with liberal concerns. Four contributors to this volume—Butts, Brint et al., Mayer, and Rempel— reflect social science tradition in addressing more new social movement-related issues than issues related to conservative social deviance concerns. Yet a focus on liberal-resonating items overemphasizes liberal trends. Therefore, analysts should be more cautious about making broad claims concerning trends in "social liberalism." More attention is needed on the differing dynamics of these distinct types of social issues.

Economic Liberalism

Economic liberalism, or leftism, entails support for government regulation of the economy and for a large state to administer macro-economic, social-welfare, and other programs. Many studies report declines in economic liberalism in industrialized societies (Flora 1986; Franklin et al. 1992; Lipset 1991; Wilensky 1981; Kaase and Newton, 1995). In this volume, Mayer confirms that demographic changes—specifically rising per-capita wealth and a shift of population to less economically depressed suburbs—encourage economic conservatism. More broadly, by the late 1980s, leftist party platforms across many industrialized countries, from Australia to Scandinavia to Great Britain, ceased to include strident pro-socialist agendas and shifted to support the mere maintenance—or in some countries even scaling back—of existing welfare state programs (Franklin et al. 1992; Lipset 1991; Klingemann et al. 1994).

For an overview, we analyzed changes from 1985 to 1990 in ISSP surveys of fourteen economic policy questions, all offering clear liberal/conservative contrasts (Table 2.6). The questions fell into four types: (1) income equalization between rich and poor, (2) government actions to help the economy, (3) government ownership of key industries, and (4) government "responsibilities" to provide select economic goods, like jobs, health care, or support for the aged.[6]

Against our expectations, the first three types of question items showed no conservative trend in any country except Italy. On nearly half of the 140 tests (70 for the entire population and 70 just for citizens aged 18-24), change was statistically insignificant from 1985 to 1990. Also, except in Italy, about half of the significant changes were in liberal and half in conservative directions.

Questions of the fourth type—about the "government's responsibility" to provide various economic goods—*did* show a marked conservative trend (Table 2.6). Conservatism rose significantly on all six such questions in Australia, on five in West Germany, and on four in both Great Britain and Italy. No such questions showed a liberal trend in these countries. On the other hand, in the United States, three of the six questions showed liberal changes, and there were no conservative changes. This exception is remarkable, since the United States previously led other nations towards economic conservatism with its 1970s citizen tax revolt (Clark and Ferguson 1983).

On the whole, ISSP economic policy questions did not uncover a strong conservative trend, but views on a separate battery of questions on spending for specific government programs—the environment, education, and health care, etc.—shifted decidedly in a *liberal*, pro-spending direction (bottom of Table 2.6). While results in Australia were mixed, the other four countries clearly moved toward liberalism. In West Germany, the ratio of significant increases to decreases on the eight spending questions was six to one; in Great Britain, five to two; in Italy, five to one; and in the United States, four to one.

There were still important differences between the trends on different individual spending questions. For both the entire population and young persons, results in every ISSP country showed increased support for environmental spending, but also—except in Australia—support for less military spending. As the following proposition suggests, these differences may stem from different kinds

TABLE 2.6   Trends in Liberalism on Economic Issues, 1985-1990

	Australia		West Germany		Great Britain		United States		Italy	
	all ages	18-24	all ages	18-24	all ages	18-24	all ages	18-24	all ages	18-24
(1) Income equality										
TAXRICH					+	+				
REDUCE			−				+			
(2) Government actions to help the economy										
PRICES	−				−				−	−
CREATJOB	−		+		−				−	
LESSREG	+		+		+	+	+			
(3) Government ownership of industries										
ELECTRIC	+		−	−	+	+			−	−
STEEL	−		−						−	
BANKING	+	+					+		−	
+/− Ratio for (1)-(3)	3/3	0/1	2/3	0/1	3/2	3/0	3/0	0/0	0/5	0/2
(4) Government responsibilities to provide economic goods										
GOVHEAL	−						+			
GOVJOBS	−		−	−	−	−	+		−	−
GOVPRICE	−	−	−		−	−			−	−
GOVAGED	−	−	−	−	−					
GOVIND	−		−		−	−	+		−	
GOVUNEMP	−		−		−	−			−	−
+/− Ratio	0/6	0/3	0/5	0/2	0/5	0/4	3/0		0/4	0/3
(5) Fiscal liberalism on specific spending programs										
NATENVIR	+	+	+	+	+	+	+	+	+	+
NATAGED	−		+		+		+		+	+
NATARMY	+	−	−	−	−	−	−	−	−	−
NATARTS	+	+	+	+	+	+		+	+	
NATHEAL			+	+			+		+	+
NATORDER	−		+		+		+			
NATUNEMP	−	−			−	−				
NATEDUC			+	+	+		+		+	
+/− Ratio	3/3	2/2	6/1	4/1	5/2	2/2	4/1	2/1	6/1	3/1

Source: International Social Survey Project (ISSP) "Role of Government" Surveys, 1985 and 1990; a "+" signifies a statistically significant change on t-tests (.01 significance standard) towards the liberal response between 1985 and 1990; a "−" signifies a statistically significant change towards the conservative response; a blank space signifies no statistically significant change.

of citizen views on the *social* concerns (e.g., environmental protection, education, or pacifism) which underlie the various spending programs. In general, the evidence indicates that on new social movement issues like the environment, or "postmaterialist" issues like spending for the arts, support for spending is most likely to be on the rise. This pattern is consistent with Inglehart's theory (this volume) and with the analysis of social issues presented above.

VIII. Citizens' views on spending tend to be program-specific, because those views are often influenced by (a) non-economic social priorities and (b) public political discussion.

Regarding (a), citizens who support a program's social purpose, like advancing the fight against crime, may favor spending more money on it, while remaining economically conservative on more general questions, like taxes. On (b), when political leaders, organized groups, or the media address a specific program (e.g., on crime, drugs, or education), they tend to focus on why that one program needs either more or less government attention. Then, at other times, political forces or the media may publicize more general positions, such as fiscal retrenchment as a broad policy goal. This manner of public discussion can foster the detachment of views on specific programs from views on more general or *ideological* standpoints. Also, on why citizens have apparently become more *liberal* on more specific spending programs, that may result from public discussions that emphasize the social *needs* which specific programs meet. The media especially tend to thrive in unearthing *unmet* needs—which thus require more ameliorative spending. Hence the growing political influence of public discussion (component #5 of post-industrial politics) may contribute to the post-1960s trend of citizens more often perceiving that specific programs are underfunded. Still, the media can *negatively* affect support for specific spending programs. For instance, a content analysis showed that media coverage of Social Security from 1980 to 1993 was more frequently negative than positive, and that public support for Social Security declined in periods of greater media coverage (Jacobs, Watts, and Shapiro 1995).

Issue Priorities

This section considers how citizens prioritize issues on a widely used survey item: "What is the most important problem facing this country today?" Propositions VI and VII suggest that liberals focus more on social issues linked to new social movements, while conservatives focus more on issues of social deviance, like crime and drugs. This section asks how salient either of these two types of *social* issues is compared to *economic* issues.

One clear hypothesis is that since the 1960s, citizens place greater emphasis on social issues (Clark, Lipset, and Rempel 1993; Dalton, Flanagan, and Beck

1984; Inglehart 1990). However, "most important problem" trends tell a different story for the United States and selected European countries. Figure 2.4 shows the percentages of respondents to United States Gallup surveys from 1965 to 1994 who mentioned (1) *economic*, (2) *liberal-resonating social*, and (3) *conservative-resonating social* issues.[7] Since the mid-1970s, respondents have mentioned *economic* problems more often than all other types, with just two exceptions. The first was a period of relative national prosperity in the late 1980s, when economic problems briefly dipped under 20 percent; but they surged over 50 percent from November 1991 through September 1993. The second exception was 1994, the last year surveyed, when emphasis on economic issues again declined, but crime rose.[8]

Both liberal- and conservative-resonating social issues have moved in the opposite direction from economic issues since the 1960s. From the mid- to late 1960s, "Vietnam" and "race relations" were often mentioned. But since then, liberal-resonating issues have received negligible mentions except for a mild surge of "fear of war" mentions in the early 1980s, when concern peaked in the threat of a nuclear catastrophe. However, this was for just a single issue, not the gamut of "new social movement" concerns.

Conservative-resonating social deviance issues rose in salience over the 1960s to 25 percent in 1968, continued high in the early 1970s, but fell thereafter. Two recent exceptions are, first, a brief spurt of drugs and drug abuse mentions in 1989 and 1990, prompted by the invasion of Panama by the United States and General Manuel Noriega's arrest for drug smuggling; and second, a sharp rise in 1994 of concern about crime, most likely encouraged by a focus on crime by leaders of both United States political parties.

We computed similar "most important problem" trends for Canada, Great Britain, and France in the 1970s and 1980s (Figure 2.5).[9] Again, mentions of economic problems exceed all others. Also, in Britain and France, more citizens mentioned conservative- than liberal-resonating social issues. Except for one blip in each country, liberal-resonating social issues never received more than 10 percent of mentions. Such blips suggest that issues surge more with short-term political debates than as a result of longer-term social and economic trends. A useful point of these figures is that they include important blips, suggesting the role of the media and related specific events.

Results from three final "most important problem" surveys appear in Table 2.7—for 1984, 1986, and 1988 in France, the former West Germany, England or United Kingdom, Italy, and Spain. Each survey had slightly different question wordings and response options—weakening comparability. Still, the same basic pattern recurs as in the other evidence; economic problems surpassed all others. In 1984 only, "nuclear weapons" surged, at the height of the "nuclear freeze" movement. By contrast, in 1986 and 1988, conservative-resonating social-deviance concerns—especially crime—ranked higher than any new social movement issues in all countries.

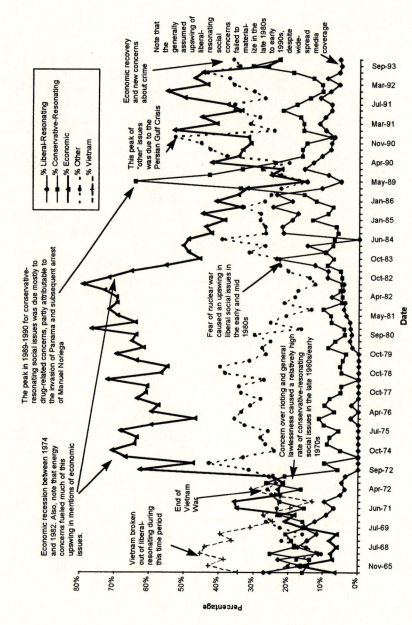

FIGURE 2.4 "Most Important Problem" Trends in the United States, 1965-1994.
Source: Gallup Poll.

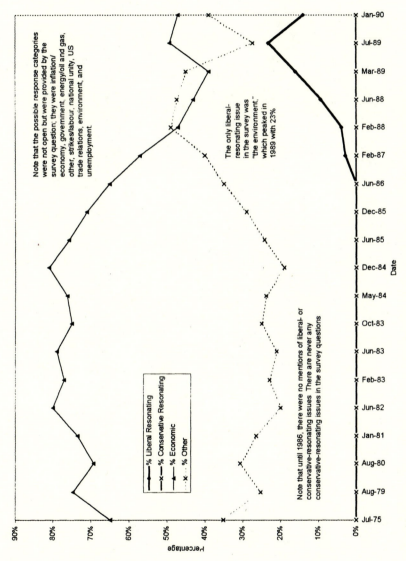

Note that the possible response categories were not open but were provided by the survey question: they were inflation/economy, government, energy/oil and gas, other, strikes/labour, national unity, US trade relations, environment, and unemployment.

The only liberal-resonating issue in the survey was "the environment," which peaked in 1989 with 23%

Note that until 1986, there were no mentions of liberal- or conservative-resonating issues. There are never any conservative-resonating issues in the survey questions

Percentage

Date

— % Liberal Resonating
×— % Conservative Resonating
▲— % Economic
× · · % Other

FIGURE 2.5A Cross-National "Most Important Problem Trends": Canada, 1975–1980

Source: International Survey Index.

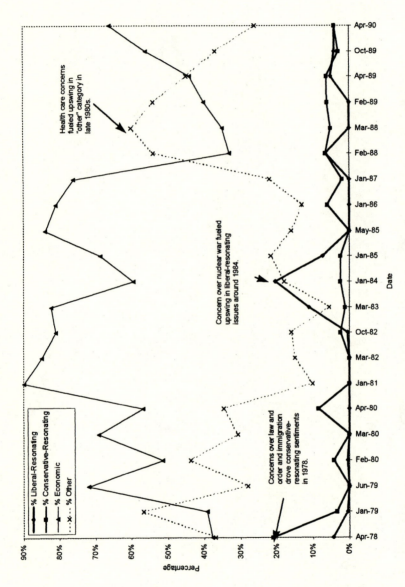

FIGURE 2.5B Cross-National "Most Important Problem Trends": Great Britain, 1978-1990
Source: International Survey Index.

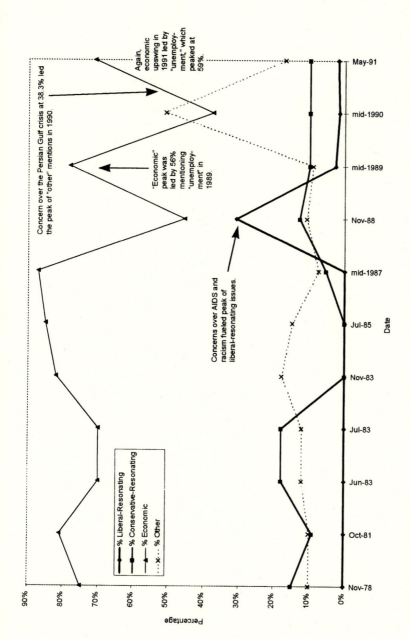

FIGURE 2.5C Cross-National "Most Important Problem Trends": France, 1978-1991
Source: International Survey Index.

TABLE 2.7   The Most Important Problem Facing Citizens in Eight Industrialized Countries in 1984

	France			Germany			U.K.[1]			Italy			Spain		
	1984	*1986*	*1988*	*1984*	*1986*	*1988*	*1984*	*1986*	*1988*	*1984*	*1986*	*1988*	*1984*	*1986*	*1988*
ECONOMIC (%)	**44**	**37**	**72**	**50**	**27**	**30**	**32**	**31**	**40**	**34**	**36**	**52**	**41**	**36**	**61**
Inflation	.12	.13	—	.07	.08	—	.06	.11	—	.11	.14	—	.08	.13	—
Unemployment	.25	.24	.72	.39	.19	.30	.22	.20	.40	.18	.22	.52	.29	.23	.61
Government Deficits	.07	—	—	.04	—	—	.04	—	—	.05	—	—	.04	—	—
SOCIAL: LIBERAL (%)	**23**	**8**	—	**21**	**21**	—	**29**	**9**	—	**27**	**14**	—	**28**	**9**	—
Threat of War	.15	—	—	.10	—	—	.14	—	—	.16	—	—	.17	—	—
Nuclear Weapons	.08	—	—	.11	—	—	.15	—	—	.11	—	—	.11	—	—
Environment	—	.08	—	—	.21	—	—	.09	—	—	.14	—	—	.09	—
SOCIAL: CONSERV. (%)	**9**	**22**	**21**	**7**	**16**	**26**	**13**	**22**	**38**	**16**	**20**	**20**	**12**	**18**	**33**
Crime	.09	.22	.09	.07	.16	.10	.13	.22	.15	.16	.20	.08	.12	.18	.25
Immigrants	—	—	.03	—	—	.08	—	—	.05	—	—	.01	—	—	.01
Wild Youth	—	—	.06	—	—	.05	—	—	.10	—	—	.05	—	—	.04
Loss of Religion	—	—	.03	—	—	.03	—	—	.08	—	—	.06	—	—	.03
OTHER															
Inequality and Injustice	.09	—	—	.09	—	—	.08	—	—	.08	—	—	.11	—	—
Reduce Regional Differences	—	.07	—	—	.08	—	—	.06	—	—	.12	—	—	.13	—
Energy Crisis	.05	.01	—	.03	.05	—	.05	.02	—	.05	.01	—	.04	.01	—
Help Third World	—	.07	—	—	.05	—	—	.09	—	—	.05	—	—	.07	—
Weak Defense	.02	.06	—	.01	.04	—	.04	.09	—	.02	.05	—	.02	.03	—
New Industries	—	.06	—	—	.06	—	—	.06	—	—	.05	—	—	.04	—
Help Consumers	—	.04	—	—	.03	—	—	.04	—	—	.02	—	—	.02	—
Bad Political Leadership	.08	—	—	.05	—	—	.07	—	—	.07	—	—	.01	.06	—

(continues)

TABLE 2.7   (*continued*)

	France			Germany			U.K[1]			Italy			Spain		
	1984	1986	1988	1984	1986	1988	1984	1986	1988	1984	1986	1988	1984	1986	1988
Stressful Living	—	—	.05	—	—	.42	—	—	.20	—	—	.28	—	—	.05
Other/North Americans	.01	.01	.02	.04	.05	.02	.01	.02	.02	.01	n/a	n/a	n/a	n/a	n/a
TOTALS (%)	101	101	100	100	100	100	99	100	100	100	100	100	99	99	100

[1]1984 Survey is of England; 1986 and 1988 surveys are of the United Kingdom.
Source: Elizabeth Hastings and Philip Hastings (1985), *Index to International Public Opinion*, Westport, CT: Greenwood Press; Question in 1984: "In your opinion, what is the most important issue for you and your nation today?"; Question in 1986: "Here are a certain number of problems which have been debated in the European Parliament. Looking at this list, can you tell me which are the three that appear to you to be the most important at the present time?"; Question in 1988: "In your opinion, which of the following problems is the most important one?" Original percentages for 1984 and 1986 exceeded 100% due to multiple responses but were recalculated to be proportional to 100%.

We codify these findings in more general propositions.

IXA. Citizens prioritize economic issues more (1) in periods of slow economic growth, (2) economic instability, and (3) when there are few problems stemming from international war or domestic turbulence.

IXB. Industrialized economies grew little from the early 1970s to 1990s, and experienced substantial restructuring. It is thus consistent with Proposition IXA for more citizens to prioritize economic issues from the early 1970s to early 1990s.

By contrast with the continuous growth of the 1950s and 1960s, from the oil shock in 1973 to the early 1990s, economic growth rates declined in the United States and other industrialized countries. From the early 1970s to late 1980s, annual growth in real GDP per capita dropped and unemployment rates rose in virtually every advanced industrialized country. (See OECD [1987] for cross-national rates of growth in GDP per capita from 1960-1985; see OECD [1981] and OECD [1986] for internationally standardized unemployment rates, respectively from 1965-1969 and from 1970-1985.)

X. Since the early 1970s, with brief exceptions, only a small minority of citizens have cited "liberal-resonating" new social movement issues as "most important."

Does this result contradict the projected political impact on citizens of the post-1960s institutionalization of new social movements (component #6 of post-industrial politics)? Perhaps not. Citizens *may* prioritize new social movement issues more since the 1960s, but not to the point that they become the *one most important* problem. Also, there are *many* new social movement issues—ecology, women's roles, sexual preferences, etc. While leaders of each movement may see theirs as "most important," even followers who support or participate actively in several such movements might not perceive just one which they are inclined to list when asked to name the most important problem facing the "country," "nation," or "government."

Finally, in line with what our results suggest, it is also possible that overall citizen interest in new social movement issues really *has* declined since the 1960s; still, those issues may have become more salient in society as a whole for two related reasons. First, citizens in select demographic subgroups may focus more on new social movement themes than in the past. In this regard, Brooks and Manza (1995) find that in the United States, their liberal views on social issues have exerted an increasing influence on the voting choices of "professionals" since the early 1970s. Second, driven by political activism among professionals, new social movement issues may have become more prominent in organized political *institutions*. On this point, component #7 of post-industrial politics may pertain. It suggests that prominent orientations within established institutions, such as pressure groups or parties, may decreasingly correspond with the most prominent orientations exhibited by the average citizen. Perhaps new social movement issues have become *less* salient for many *citizens* since the 1960s; but because new groups and political parties have arisen, the *institutional* presence of those issues, and hence their influence over political leaders and public policies, has persisted and grown. We indicate this with Proposition XI.

> *XI. Since the 1960s, the institutionalization of new social movements has led "liberal-resonating" new social movement issues to become more salient in organized political institutions, but not among ordinary citizens.*

In toto, results reported in this section lead one to be cautious in assessing the salience of new social movement issues.

Political Activism

Have citizens grown more politically active since the 1960s? The evidence is ambiguous.

Butts (this volume) suggests that activism is rising. Across fourteen industrialized countries, he finds that education predicts a respondent's propensity toward political activism more powerfully than any other social background characteristic. We complemented Butts's research by analyzing *changes* in activism in the same countries he studied between 1981-1982 and 1990-1991. Table 2.8 shows countries where participation in five forms of activism rose or declined by more than 5 percent. In nearly all countries, participation rose in signing petitions; and in most, participation rose in joining boycotts and attending lawful demonstrations. Of the 30 cases of change, 29 were toward more activity.

Nonetheless, Naoyuki Umemori (this volume) contends that in Japan, political *apathy*, not activism, is rising—especially among young persons. He cites numerous Japanese surveys from the 1970s and 1980s. Umemori's interpretation includes some factors specific to Japan, but he also suggests that growing consumerism—common to all post-industrial countries—brings on depoliticization and political apathy. Crimmins, Easterlin, and Saito (1991) uncover a broadly similar pattern among American youth. Neil Howe and Bill Strauss also emphasize this outcome in their best-seller, *13th Generation*, on the youngest, or "13th," American generation. They write that this generation's first rule is:

> Wear your politics lightly. Sure 13ers will tell a pollster they're pro or con on taxes or abortion or any other issue. But most do so without deep conviction or ideological passion. . . . To follow every political story in the news is fine, if you get paid for it—but a waste of time if you don't (1993: 166).

How can we reconcile these seemingly contradictory interpretations of political activism trends? More people are politically active, but their activism is often less "committed." Evidence: Butts (this volume) reports that in most countries, younger persons are *more* likely than older persons to be politically active, but *less* likely to be interested in politics or to discuss political matters with friends and coworkers.

Two of our components of post-industrial politics clarify this apparent contradiction. First, decline of classic left-right ideological polarization (component #3) creates more space for activism on many new issues. Yet, without encompassing ideologies joining issues together, *some* citizens perceive an endless, confusing barrage of information and rhetoric, leading them to become increasingly indifferent to it all.

Second, in many countries, there is a widening divergence between the concerns of ordinary citizens and of key political institutions (component #7). A popular perception that established institutions have grown less responsive to citizens drives some to pursue new, system-challenging forms of activism. Indeed, Hoffman-Martinot (forthcoming) confirms that in many European countries, growing numbers of citizens see established political parties as non-responsive and, for that reason, become proactively involved in new, non-party organizations (concerned with ecology, women's support groups, neighborhood associations, and more). At the same time, rising perceptions of institutional non-responsiveness may lead other citizens to grow apathetic; they may vote less and not join or support political parties or organizations at all; lower turn-

TABLE 2.8   Change in Political Activism, 1981-1982 to 1990-1991

Country	Signing a Petition	Attending Joining a Boycott	Joining a Lawful Demonstration	Unofficial Strikes	Occupying Buildings or Factories
+ = rise of > 5%; + + = rise of > 10%; – = declined of > 5%; – – = decline of > 10%					
Belgium	+ +	+	+ +		
Canada	+ +	–	+		
Denmark	+			+	
Great Britain	+ +	+			
France	+		+		
Ireland	+				
Italy	+ +	+	+ +	+	+
Japan	+ +				
Netherlands	+ +		+ +		
Norway	+	+		+ +	
Spain					
Sweden	+ +	+	+		
United States	+				
West Germany	+ +		+		

Source: World Values Survey, 1981-82 and 1990-91; Question: "I'm going to read out some different forms of political activity that people can take and I'd like to tell me for each one whether you have actually done any of these things, whether you might do it or would never, under any circumstances, do it." All percentage comparisons are for the first choice, indicating that the respondent had done the form of activism in question.

out in elections is a worldwide phenomenon. A slightly cynical, cosmopolitan apathy may thus coincide with bursts of activism on specific issues. A strong version of this pattern is found in Eastern Europe (Swianiewicz and Clark 1995). Why? Because until very recently, institutional leadership in the Communist Party was so powerful, and Marxism so encompassing an ideology, that what followed seemed incoherent by comparison.

Conclusion

Changes toward a *post-industrial society* have driven many recent political developments. We identify eight components of *post-industrial politics*. These capture key ideological and institutional trends since the 1960s. Papers in this volume map some of the most fundamental changes in citizens' political orientations—in social liberalism, economic liberalism, issue priorities, and political activism. This introduction integrates and synthesizes key themes from subsequent chapters, and adds a more general interpretation of post-industrial politics to illuminate specific dynamics of change in citizen preferences.

To interpret cross-national differences, however, patterns that predate the 1960s demand consideration along with post-1960s trends. We find a residue of cultural values from each country's prior cultural and political history. These values help shape reactions to post-industrial developments since the 1960s. While general trends in education, income, and occupation are common to much of North America and Western Europe, specifics still vary from country to country, and even more as one looks further around the world (as the Brint et al. paper shows systematically).

Our conceptual framework (in Figure 2.1) depicts broad processes of social, cultural, and political development. But these take on life through individual participants (like presidents or political activists), whose specific actions greatly influence the speed and direction of change, as well as opposition to certain changes. Leaders take some cues from citizens. But citizen responses also shift as new issues are stressed by leaders and by media coverage. How issues are publicly framed shifts their interpretation by citizens. For example, public discussion in the United States focused on health care more than any other issue in 1994, even though citizens did not mention it enough to appear in Gallup's "most important problem" surveys of preceding years.

Researchers occasionally look back at the social movements of the 1960s as initial expressions of the single-issue politics that we now observe. But many 1960s activists in the 1960s did not limit themselves to single issues like civil rights or the Vietnam war. Many sought a more totalizing *ideological* shift away from the materialistic, apolitical, anti-democratic society that they perceived to be developing, in part due to changes associated with the post-industrial transition (see Gitlin 1980, 1987). Reminiscing on the 1960s, *Nation* contributor Daniel Singer avowed, "The striking novelty of the rebel sixties was the rejection of the so-called consumer society, the repudiation of the ruling religion of growth. Growth for whom? for what purpose? for whose profit?" (1993: 730). Perhaps it is more *since* the 1960s, and the subsequent institutionalization of some of its issues into separate movements and political organizations, that politics has become more single-issue-oriented, fragmented, and incrementalist. In line with this development, many citizens have abandoned "traditional" political parties and leaders who have not adapted their style or programs. Today, the most popular leaders are often those who focus on specialized issues that appeal to small but specific sets of citizens—for example, abortion, women's issues, the environment, or peace. Many citizens do not perceive these issues to dovetail with each other, as if part of a coherent program. This makes politics harder for citizens to join in, harder for leaders to lead, and harder for interpreters to analyze. This book offers a road map to the new world emerging around us.

Appendix A:
Wording for General Social Survey (GSS) Questions

1. FEMINISM: Civil Rights for Women: The following four GSS questions were used to construct the index, FEMINISM, for views on women's rights issues:
   a) FEHOME: "Do you agree or disagree with this statement? Women should take care of running their homes and leave running the country up to men."
   b) FEWORK: "Do you approve or disapprove of a married woman earning money in business or industry if she has a husband capable of supporting her?"
   c) FEPRES: "If your party nominated a woman for president, would you vote for her if she were qualified for the job?"
   d) FEPOL: "Tell me if you agree or disagree with this statement: Most men are better suited emotionally for politics than are most women."

2. CIVRIGHT: Civil Rights for African Americans: The following four GSS questions were used to construct the index, CIVRIGHT, for views on African-American civil rights issues:
   a) RACMAR: "Do you think there should be laws against marriages between (Negroes/Blacks) and whites?"
   b) RACSEG: "Here are some opinions other people have expressed in connection with (Negroes/Black)—White relations. Which statement comes the closest to how you yourself feel. . . . White people have a right to keep (Negroes/Blacks) out of their neighborhoods if they want to, and (Negroes/Blacks) should respect that right."
   c) RACSCHOL: "Do you think white students and (Negro/Black) students should go to the same schools or to separate schools?"
   d) RACPRES: "If your party nominated a (Negro/Black) for president, would you vote for him if he were qualified for the job?"

3. SPEECH: Free Speech: The following two GSS questions were used to construct the index, SPEECH, for views on free speech issues:
   a) SPKATH: "There are always some people whose ideas are considered bad or dangerous by other people. For instance, somebody who is against all churches and religion. . . . If such a person wanted to make a speech in your (city/town/community)against churches and religion, should he be allowed to speak, or not?"
   b) SPKCOM: "Now I should like to ask you some questions about a man who admits he is a Communist. . . . this admitted Communist wanted to make a speech in your community. Should he be allowed to speak, or not?"

4. ABANY: Abortion: "Please tell me whether or not *you* think it should be possible for a pregnant woman to obtain a *legal* abortion if . . . The woman wants it for any reason."

5. HOMOSEX: Civil Rights for Homosexuals: "What about sexual relations between two *adults* of the same sex—do you think it is always wrong, almost always wrong, wrong only sometimes, or not wrong at all?"

6. SEXEDUC: Sex Education in Schools: "Would you be for or against sex education in the public schools?"

7. GRASS: Legalization of Marijuana: "Do you think the use of marijuana should be made legal or not?"

8. CAPPUN: Capital Punishment: "Do you favor or oppose the death penalty for persons convicted of murder?"

9. WIRTAP: Wiretapping: "Everything considered, would you say that, in general, you approve or disapprove of wiretapping?"

Notes

1. This study included Canada, Finland, Italy, Japan, the Netherlands, Norway, Sweden, the United Kingdom, and the United States.

2. From an early 1994 interview on Public Television by Charlie Rose, observed by Michael Rempel.

3. One bit of evidence comes from an ethnographic study of a Chicago junior high school in the 1990s (Mona Abo-Zena, 1993). Its student body was racially mixed, including whites, blacks, Mexicans, and Asian-Americans. These ethnic lines often seem deterministic in their effects on Chicago politics, residential location decisions, and quasi-political voluntary associations. But they were *not* in this school. Students labeled its main cliques by different clothing styles, such as the "Benetton" crowd. This marks a shift from divisions by sports, grades, or ethnicity, identified in past work on youth cultures (e.g., Coleman 1961).

4. At least in the United States, the African-American civil rights movement was arguably the source of most NSMs, even though its constituents were more economically underprivileged than activists of later NSMs, such as the women's or ecology movements. Tactics developed in the civil rights movement—"peaceful demonstrations," sit-ins, etc.—spread around the world in the subsequent decade. In the late 1960s, McAdam (1988) confirms in *Freedom Summer* that there was specific borrowing of tactics from African-American and union groups; 1960s student activists spread these tactics nationally via informal networks, conferences, and newsletters.

5. Since the United States was among the ISSP countries, it is noteworthy that the clear conservative trend on GSS "law and order" issues did not emerge in even the United States ISSP results. The key may be that the ISSP items included a clear political liberties dimension; three of the four ISSP items asked if citizens believe that the police should be allowed to tap the phone, open the mail, or detain a known criminal "without a court order." The latter phrase may suggest to respondents that a conservative answer signifies substantial disregard for basic political liberties. See Table 6.1 of Brint, Cunningham, and Li for full question wording.

6. We considered "liberal" those responses that, for each of the four types of questions, respectively supported more income equality, government action, government ownership, and government responsibility.

7. "Economic," "liberal-resonating" and "conservative-resonating" problems include:

(1) economic: economy in general, high cost of living/inflation, federal budget deficit/ failure to balance the budget, excessive government spending, trade deficit, unemployment, taxes, savings and loan crisis, recession, cost of borrowing/high interest rates, and the energy crisis (of those, the most commonly mentioned were the economy in general, unemployment, cost of living/inflation, and the budget deficit/failure to balance the budget); (2) liberal-resonating (see proposition #2 in the subsection on social liberalism for the liberal-resonating concept): the threat of [nuclear] war, environment/pollution/ ecology, AIDS, racism/race relations, civil rights/race relations; (3) conservative-resonating (see proposition #3 in the subsection on social liberalism for the concept: crime/ looting/violence/lawlessness, drugs/drug abuse, ethics/morals, moral/religious decline, lack of national unity, immigration/illegal aliens, spread of world communism, youth protests/college demonstrations. Although it may not immediately be apparent why ethics/morals and moral/religious decline appear as "conservative-resonating," our working assumption is that persons mentioning such problems were concerned about the "bad morals" thought to be reflected in persons *deviating* from "traditional," law-abiding, nuclear family-based, heterosexual, and/or religious lifestyles. The figure also includes a separate trend line for the Vietnam War, which citizens highly prioritized during the 1960s and early 1970s. Many citizens mentioning the war probably reacted from a "liberal-resonating" orientation toward the growing peace movement; but as this assumption may not apply to all citizens mentioning the war, we chose not to subsume the war under the "liberal-resonating" category.

8. In an earlier analysis of most important problems from 1935 and 1984, Smith (1985) generalized that economic problems rise in salience during recessions and decline during wars and domestic social unrest. Thus from the late 1950s to the early 1970s—when the economy was strong, the Vietnam War growing more intense, and domestic protests rising—economic problems were seldom mentioned.

9. In synthesizing survey results outside the United States, we maintained the same coding of issues into "liberal-resonating" and "conservative-resonating" categories. Outside the United States, responses on some surveys were lumped by the survey organizations into fewer, broader categories permitting less reclassification. Such lumping may have had the unintended effect of raising the apparent salience of economic issues, and, just in Canada, of decreasing the salience of conservative-resonating social issues.

## Part 2

Cultural Shifts and Politics:

Is Materialism Rising, Declining, or Both?
Implications for Political Activism

3

The Trend Toward
Postmaterialist Values
Continues

Ronald Inglehart

Introduction

In 1970 I hypothesized that the value priorities of Western publics were shifting from Materialist values toward Postmaterialist values—from giving top priority to physical sustenance and safety, toward heavier emphasis on belonging, self-expression and the quality of life (Inglehart, 1971). The predicted intergenerational value shift could not be demonstrated until many years had passed; and whether or not it was occurring has been hotly disputed (Boeltken and Jagodzinski, 1985; Van Deth and Thomassen, 1989; Trump, 1991; Clarke and Dutt, 1991). Only in recent years has a sufficiently long time series become available to test the prediction reliably. This chapter examines cross-national survey data over a 24-year period. The results show a clear and statistically significant trend toward Postmaterialist values in almost all of the societies for which we now have detailed time series measurements over this period. These values also show short-term fluctuations linked with changing rates of inflation and unemployment, as the value change thesis implies; but the long-term trend seems to result mainly from intergenerational replacement.

AUTHOR'S NOTE: This chapter draws on material from my forthcoming book, *Modernization and Postmodernization: Cultural, Economic and Political Change in 43 Societies*. Princeton: Princeton University Press, 1997. A more detailed presentation of the theory and evidence concerning intergenerational value change is presented in that book.

The Rise of Postmaterialist Values

Research on the Materialist/Postmaterialist value change has been guided by two key hypotheses (Inglehart, 1977):

1. A Scarcity Hypothesis. An individual's priorities reflect the socioeconomic environment: one places the greatest subjective value on those things that are in relatively short supply.

2. A Socialization Hypothesis. The relationship between socioeconomic environment and value priorities is not one of immediate adjustment: a substantial time lag is involved for, to a large extent, one's basic values reflect the conditions that prevailed during one's pre-adult years.

The scarcity hypothesis is similar to the principle of diminishing marginal utility. And it implies that recent economic developments have significant consequences. During the period since World War II, advanced industrial societies have attained much higher real income levels than ever before in history. Coupled with the emergence of the welfare state, this has brought about an historically unprecedented situation: most of their population does not live under conditions of hunger and economic insecurity. This has led to a gradual shift in which needs for belonging, self-expression and a participant role in society became more prominent. Prolonged periods of prosperity tend to encourage the spread of Postmaterialist values; economic decline tends to have the opposite effect.

But there is no simple one-to-one relationship between economic level and the prevalence of Postmaterialist values. These values reflect one's subjective sense of security, not one's economic level per se. While rich people tend to feel more secure than poor people, one's sense of security is also influenced by the cultural setting and social welfare institutions in which one is raised. Thus, the scarcity hypothesis must be supplemented with the socialization hypothesis: a basic personality structure tends to take shape by the time an individual reaches adulthood, and changes relatively little thereafter.

Taken together, these two hypotheses generate a set of predictions concerning value change. First, while the scarcity hypothesis implies that prosperity is conducive to the spread of Postmaterialist values, the socialization hypothesis implies that neither an individual's values nor those of a society as a whole will change overnight. For the most part, fundamental value change takes place as younger birth cohorts replace older ones in the adult population of a society. Consequently, after a long period of rising economic and physical security, one should find substantial differences between the value priorities of older and younger groups: they have been shaped by different experiences in their formative years.

Our theory of value change generates a number of more specific predictions. It implies that:

1. Postmaterialist values will be most widespread in the richest and otherwise most secure societies. Conversely, the publics of impoverished and inse-

cure societies will emphasize survival values to a much greater extent.

2. Within any given society, Postmaterialist values will be most widespread among the more secure strata: the wealthier and better educated will be most likely to hold a whole range of Postmodern values, including Postmaterialism; the less secure strata will emphasize survival priorities.

3. Short-term fluctuations will follow the scarcity hypothesis: prosperity will enhance the tendency to emphasize Postmaterialist and Postmodern values; economic downturn, civil disorder or war will lead people to emphasize Materialist and survival values.

4. Long-term changes will also reflect the scarcity hypothesis: in societies that have experienced high levels of security for several decades, we should find a long-term shift from survival values toward Postmaterialist values. This shift is not universal: it should occur only in those societies that have attained sufficient existential security so that a substantial share of the population takes survival for granted; but it is not uniquely Western: it should appear in any society that has experienced the transition to high mass security.

5. In those societies that have experienced a long period of rising economic and physical security, we will find substantial differences between the value priorities of older and younger groups, with the young being much likelier to emphasize Postmaterialist values than the old.

6. These intergenerational value differences should be reasonably stable over time: though immediate conditions of security or insecurity will produce short-term fluctuations, the underlying differences between younger and older birth cohorts should persist over long periods of time.

The 1970 European Community surveys were the first to test the value change thesis. The results showed the age group differences that the socialization hypothesis predicts. Figure 3.1 depicts this pattern in a pooled sample of six West European publics. The basic pattern is similar in all six countries: among the older groups, Materialists outnumber Postmaterialists enormously; as we move to younger groups, the proportion of Materialists declines and that of Postmaterialists increases. Thus, among the oldest cohort, Materialists outnumber Postmaterialists by more than 12 to 1; but among the youngest cohort, Postmaterialists are more numerous than Materialists.

The age differences shown here are striking. But does this pattern reflect life cycle effects, birth cohort effects or some combination of the two? Our theory predicts that we will find birth cohort differences; but these differences between the priorities of young and old could reflect some inherent tendency for people to become more materialistic as they age. If so, then as time goes by, the values of the younger groups will eventually become just like those of the older groups, producing no change in the society as a whole. Does aging make one place ever-increasing emphasis on economic and physical security? The only way to answer this question is by following given birth cohorts over time, to see if they become more Materialist as they age. We can do so: the four-item Mate-

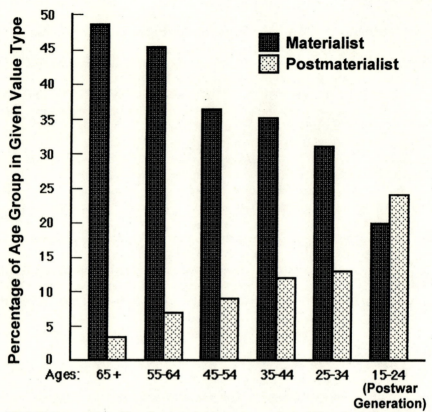

FIGURE 3.1   Value Type by Age Group, Among the Publics of Britain, France,
West Germany, Italy, Belgium and The Netherlands in 1970
Source: European Community survey of February 1970; based on original 4-item Mate-
rialist/Postmaterialist values battery. Reprinted from Inglehart (1990): 76.

rialist/Postmaterialist values battery has been asked in cross-national surveys
carried out by the European Community at least once a year in almost every
year from 1970 to the present.

Figure 3.2 traces the balance between Materialists and Postmaterialists within
given birth cohorts from February 1970 to fall 1994, using the pooled data from
the surveys carried out in Britain, France, West Germany, Italy, Belgium and
The Netherlands (an analysis based on more than 240,000 interviews). Each
cohort's position at a given time is calculated by subtracting the percentage of
Materialists in that cohort from the percentage of Postmaterialists. Thus, at the
zero point on the vertical axis, the two groups are equally numerous (the co-

hort born in 1946-1955 was located near this point in 1970). On this graph, the proportion of Postmaterialists increases as we move up the vertical axis; the proportion of Materialists increases as we move down. If the age differences reflected a life cycle effect, then each of the cohort lines should move downward, toward the Materialist pole, as we move from left to right across this 24-year period.

We find no such downward movement. Instead, the younger birth cohorts remain relatively Postmaterialist throughout the period from 1970 to 1994: given cohorts did not become more Materialist as they aged by almost a quarter of a century—instead, many of these cohorts were slightly less Materialist at the end of this period than they were at the start.

What Causes the Period Effects?

In addition to presenting the results of a cohort analysis from 1970 to 1994, Figure 3.2 shows the current rate of inflation, superimposed as a heavy shaded line. Since the theory predicts that Postmaterialist values will rise when inflation falls, the inflation index runs from low rates at the top of the graph to high rates toward the bottom. This makes it easy to see that (as predicted) inflation and Postmaterialist values move up and down together, bearing in mind that a downward movement of the inflation line indicates rising rates of inflation on this graph.

Striking period effects are evident: there was a clear tendency for each cohort to dip toward the Materialist pole during the recession of the mid-1970s and again during the recessions of the early 1980s and the early 1990s. These effects are implicit in the theory, which links Postmaterialist values with economic security. High inflation rates tend to make people feel economically insecure, and as the graph demonstrates, there is a remarkably close fit between current economic conditions and the short-term fluctuations in Materialist/Postmaterialist values. High levels of inflation depress the proportion of Postmaterialists. But these period effects are transient; they disappear when economic conditions return to normal. In the long run, the values of a given birth cohort are remarkably stable. Despite the fluctuations linked with current economic conditions, the intergenerational differences persist: at virtually every point in time, each younger cohort is significantly less Materialist than all of the older ones. These enduring generational differences reflect differences in the formative conditions that shaped the respective birth cohorts: the older ones were influenced by the hunger and insecurity that prevailed during World War I, the Great Depression and World War II; the younger ones have grown up in an era of historically unprecedented prosperity.

Strictly speaking, these data do not prove that generational change is taking place: one can never distinguish between cohort effects, period effects and aging effects on statistical grounds alone, since any one of them is a perfect linear

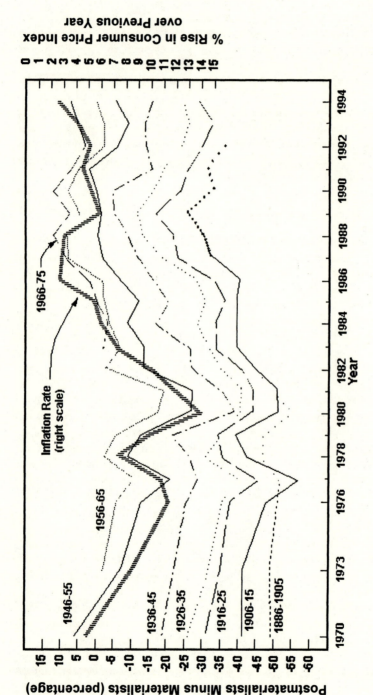

FIGURE 3.2 Cohort Analysis with Inflation Rate Superimposed (Using Inverted Scale on Right): Percent Postmaterialists Minus Percent Materialists in Six West European Societies, 1970-1994

Source: Based on combined weighted sample of European Community surveys, carried out in West Germany, France, Britain, Italy, The Netherlands and Belgium, in given years, using the 4-item Materialist/Postmaterialist values index (N=253,356).

function of the other two. Theoretically, the pattern in Figure 3.2 might reflect a combination of life cycle (or aging) effects plus some mysterious period effect that somehow prevented each cohort from becoming more Materialist as it aged from 1970 to 1994. So far, no one has identified a period effect that might have done this (for a debate on this point, see Clarke and Dutt, 1991; and Inglehart and Abramson, 1994); and if someone did, it would be an ad hoc explanation, designed to fit an existing set of observations.

The generational change hypothesis, on the other hand, was published long before these data were collected—and it predicted both the robust cohort differences subsequently observed, and the period effects. If one agrees that the downward swings toward Materialist values found in the mid-1970s, the early 1980s and the early 1990s were probably due to the economic fluctuations that occurred in those years (and the empirical fit is very good), then the pattern looks like a clear case of intergenerational value change. If this is true, it has far-reaching implications: in the long run the values of these societies should shift in the predicted direction.

Value Changes Observed in Western Countries, 1970-1994

A good deal of intergenerational population replacement has taken place since 1970. The intergenerational value change thesis predicts that in the long run, this should produce a shift from Materialist toward Postmaterialist values among the populations of these societies. More than a quarter of a century has passed since these values were first measured in 1970. Do we find the predicted value shift? As the following evidence demonstrates, we do indeed.

Figure 3.3 shows the overall trend among the populations of the six nations first surveyed in 1970. Like the cohort trajectories in the preceding figure, the trend line shown here dips steeply downward in each of the three recent recessions; but the long-term trajectory shows a clear upward trend, and regression analysis reveals that this trend is statistically significant at the .001 level (see Abramson and Inglehart, 1995: chapter 4). Though each given birth cohort in the preceding figure shows relatively little net movement upward or downward from 1970 to 1994, the line for the total sample shows a strong upward movement, reflecting intergenerational population replacement: by 1994, the two oldest cohorts had almost completely disappeared from the sample, and had been replaced by two younger (and much more Postmaterialist) cohorts. In 1970, the mean position for the sample as a whole was located about halfway between the cohort born in 1916-1925 and the cohort born in 1926-1935; by 1994 this point had moved up more than two cohorts and was located slightly below the position of the 1946-1955 birth cohort. A substantial value shift had occurred in the population as a whole. In 1970, Materialists outnumbered Postmaterialists overwhelmingly in all of these countries, but by 1994, the balance had shifted markedly toward Postmaterialist values. In 1970, within these

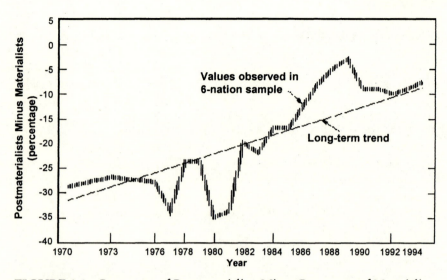

FIGURE 3.3 Percentage of Postmaterialists Minus Percentage of Materialists in Combined Sample of Six West European Societies, 1970-1994
Source: Based on combined weighted sample of European Community surveys carried out in West Germany, France, Britain, Italy, The Netherlands and Belgium in given years (N = 253,356).

six West European nations as a whole, Materialists outnumbered Postmaterialists by a ratio of almost 4 to 1. By 1994, this ratio had fallen to less than 1.5 to 1: Postmaterialists had become almost as numerous as Materialists.

Figure 3.3 shows the trend in six European countries for which detailed time series data are available from more than 40 European Community surveys that were carried out in each of these countries from 1970 to 1994. An almost equally detailed time series is available for Denmark and Ireland, from the surveys that were carried out in each country from 1973 to 1994. Figure 3.4 shows the net shift in these eight countries, plus the U.S. Eight of the nine countries show a shift from Materialist toward Postmaterialist values, with only Belgium remaining unchanged. In the early 1970s, Materialists heavily outnumbered Postmaterialists in all nine of these countries. By the early 1990s, Postmaterialists had increased almost everywhere and had become more numerous than Materialists in the U.S., Denmark and The Netherlands. If one knows the relative proportions of Materialists and Postmaterialists in each birth cohort of a given nation, plus the size of each cohort (obtainable from census figures), one can calculate the amount of value shift that would take place each year as a result of intergenerational population replacement. Abramson and Inglehart (1987) have done so, finding that in Western Europe, the population replacement process

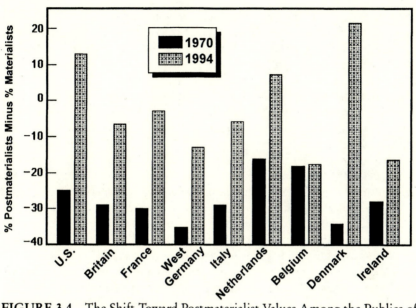

FIGURE 3.4 The Shift Toward Postmaterialist Values Among the Publics of Nine Western Societies, 1970-1994
Source: European Community surveys, February 1970 and fall 1994; and (despite the legend above) U.S. National Election Surveys from 1972 and 1992.

would bring a shift toward Postmaterialism of slightly more than one point per year in the percentage difference index or PDI (this constitutes the vertical axis in figures 5-2, 5-3 and 5-4). This is a relatively modest gain; in any given year, it could easily be swamped by fluctuations in current conditions linked with security or insecurity. But these short-term fluctuations move in both directions: in the long run, they tend to cancel each other out. The impact of intergenerational population replacement, on the other hand, moves in one continuous direction for decades. In the long run, its cumulative effects can be substantial. This seems to be the case with the data at hand. For these nine countries as a whole, over the 24-year period from 1970 to 1994 the PDI shows a mean shift toward the Postmaterialist pole of 23 points: this is almost exactly the amount of change that would be expected to occur solely as a result of intergenerational population replacement.

Economic conditions were not more favorable in 1994 than they were at the start of the series, in 1970; they were worse. The early 1990s were a period of recession, and as Figure 3.2 indicates, the levels of Postmaterialism in most cohorts reached a peak about 1989 and declined during the next few years. Nevertheless, as younger, more Postmaterialist cohorts replaced older ones, the population as a whole showed a long-term shift toward Postmaterialist values in almost every country. Despite substantial short-term fluctuations, and despite the fact that the surveys in our most recent year, 1994, occurred when Western Europe was still recovering from a major recession, the predicted shift toward Postmaterialist values took place—and its magnitude was just about the size that would be predicted by an intergenerational population replacement model. Figure 3.4 shows only the starting point and the end point of each country's time series from 1970 to 1994. In a more detailed analysis of this time series, consisting of at least 33 surveys for each nation, Inglehart and Abramson (1995) examine the trends in each of the eight countries; then, using regression analysis, they demonstrate that Britain, France, West Germany, Italy, The Netherlands, Ireland and Denmark all show large and statistically significant long-term trends from Materialist to Postmaterialist values over this period. In the eighth case (Belgium), they find no trend. But a time series analysis controlling for the joint effects of inflation and unemployment demonstrates that there is a statistically significant trend toward Postmaterialism in all eight of the West European countries for which a detailed time series is available over the past two decades: Belgium showed no shift toward Postmaterialism because it has suffered much higher levels of unemployment in recent years than in the 1970s, which has largely offset the effects of intergenerational population replacement. When they control for inflation and unemployment, Belgium is no longer a deviant case: it too shows a significant shift toward Postmaterialism. Controlling for inflation and unemployment largely explains the period effects: as the theory implies, high levels of inflation and unemployment encourage an emphasis on economic security, rather than on Postmaterialist values. As we have seen, a substantial shift toward Postmaterialist values also took place in the United States. These data come from the six NES presidential election surveys carried out from 1972 to 1992. Six surveys do not provide a sufficient number of time points to test the trend's statistical significance but the net effect in the U.S. seems to be almost as large as in most West European countries. Findings from a wide range of industrialized societies indicate that since 1970, the trend from Materialist toward Postmaterialist values has continued.

4

American Youth Are Becoming More Materialistic

Richard A. Easterlin
and
Eileen M. Crimmins

Although much has been written about the values of today's youth, there is little consensus even on the facts of recent trends. In studies published in the same year, Levine and Yankelovich reached diametrically opposed conclusions. Yankelovich, in an approach influenced by the Maslovian hierarchy-of-needs framework, asserted that personal self-fulfillment was increasingly coming to the fore (Maslow 1954; Yankelovich 1981). Levine, in an almost despairing paean, *When Dreams and Heroes Died*, saw a return to private materialism, along lines suggested by Altbach (Altbach 1974; Levine 1981).

AUTHORS' NOTE: The authors are equally responsible for this article. Lead authorship is alternated in successive articles. The authors are grateful to Donna Hokoda, Christine Macdonald, and Yasuhiko Saito for excellent research and technical assistance. The authors would also like to thank Jerald G. Bachman, David Heer, and an anonymous *Public Opinion Quarterly* referee for helpful comments and Andrew Kohut, Dawn Oberman, and Bickley Townsend for providing unpublished data.

EDITORS' NOTE: This contribution represents an excerpt from a paper originally published in the *Public Opinion Quarterly* Volume 55:499-533 as "Private Materialism, Personal Self-Fulfillment, Family Life, and Public Interest: The Nature, Effects, and Causes of Recent Changes in the Values of American Youth." © 1991 by the American Association for Public Opinion Research. All rights reserved. The excerpt includes text and data from pp. 499-512 in the original publication. We thank the *Public Opinion Quarterly* for permission to reprint.

These conflicting views echo the more general literature on changing values of the American population described by Hammond (1986). Hirschman (1982) and Schlesinger (1986) have claimed, like Levine, that there is an ongoing shift from public concerns to private materialism. Bellah and his associates (1985) see, similar to Yankelovich, a growing emphasis on personal self-fulfillment. Inglehart (1977, 1981, 1985) is able to have the best of both worlds. Although he also sees through Maslovian eyes a long-term trend from materialism to postmaterialism (the latter embracing both public interest concerns and personal self-fulfillment), he allows for materialistic lapses from trend in periods of physical or economic insecurity.

This article draws on two national sample surveys of American youth in an attempt to clarify: (1) the nature of recent trends in private materialism, personal self-fulfillment, family life, and public interest as life goals of American youth, (2) possible effects of these trends on the personal plans and attitudes of American youth, and (3) the causes of trends in life goals. As shall be seen, the evidence suggests a sharp shift toward private materialism from the seventies through 1986-87, with important effects on plans and attitudes. The causes of the shift appear to be linked to the impact on the values of the American population generally of declining real wage rates and rising material aspirations in the post-1973 period.

Concepts, Data, and Measurement

Concepts

Private materialism is taken here to mean the pursuit of one's own material well-being; family life, to mean those goals relating to family formation and welfare; public interest, to mean concerns for the welfare of the broader community; and personal self-fulfillment, to have to do with aspirations for personal development and self-actualization as in Maslow's hierarchy of needs. As in the economic model of preferences, we view these goals as largely competitive with one another. Each person's time is limited, and the more time spent pursuing one goal, the less there is available to achieve others. Pursuit of personal gain is likely to mean giving up time that might have been devoted to societal concerns. Similarly, family goals, such as having children, may be sacrificed to enhance personal material well-being. This conception leads to interpreting life goal statements in a relative sense. Rather than looking at the importance of each goal singly, we are interested chiefly in the set of life goals. If the stated importance of goals A, B, and C remains unchanged but that of D increases sharply, then there has to have been a relative decline in the importance of A, B, and C.

Data

The analysis uses data from two unusually valuable surveys: one of college freshmen, the other of high school seniors. The data on college freshmen are from the Cooperative Institutional Research Program (CIRP), which is an ongoing annual national survey conducted since 1965 that is now under the auspices of the University of California, Los Angeles, Higher Education Research Institute. We use data beginning in 1966 because the questionnaire format was better established by the second year. Each year the CIRP surveys more than 200,000 full-time students, constituting the entering freshman classes at approximately 550 2-year and 4-year colleges and universities across the United States. A subset of the data, amounting in 1985 to 192,000 cases, is weighted to provide a nationally representative sample of all first-time, full-time students entering institutions of higher education in the fall of each year (Astin, Green, and Korn 1987).

The data on high school seniors are from Monitoring the Future, a nationally representative survey of high school seniors that is remarkable for its scope and has been conducted annually beginning in 1975 by the University of Michigan Survey Research Center (Bachman, Johnston, and O'Malley 1987; Johnston, Bachman, and O'Malley 1986). Again, we use data beginning in the second year of the survey, 1976, in order to maintain comparability over time in questionnaire design. While about sixteen thousand respondents are queried each year, the survey comprises five different questionnaires with only partially overlapping questions. Most of the variables of interest here were collected on only one of the five forms; thus, the sample size for each response is usually somewhat over three thousand students. The school drop-out rate has averaged a fairly constant 15-20 percent; hence, this survey covers about 80-85 percent of American youth (Bachman, Johnston, and O'Malley 1987, p. 3; U.S. Department of Education 1988, p. 54).

Because the wording or item order on the CIRP questionnaire was intermittently changed before 1974 and after 1986, the periods selected for the main part of the present analysis are 1974-86 for CIRP and 1976-86 for Monitoring the Future. In addition, available comparable data on the life goals are shown for the CIRP data for 1966-73 and for both surveys for 1987 through 1989. The cross-sectional analysis is based on data for 1985, the most recent year for which data tapes from both surveys are available.

A number of investigators involved in these surveys have produced valuable studies relevant to the present topic (Astin 1985, 1988; Bachman 1987; Bachman and Johnston 1979a, 1979b; Bachman, Johnston, and O'Malley 1986; Green 1989; Green and Astin 1985; Herzog, Bachman, and Johnston 1978). Although their results are generally consistent with those presented here, the present study differs somewhat in conceptual framework, in covering a longer period of time, in adding cross-sectional data, and in fuller consideration of causes and effects of changing values. Also, this study differs from that of Hoge, Luna, and Miller (1981) in that it is based on nationally representative data rather than on data for a few colleges.

In addition, the present study differs from earlier ones in drawing on two sets of data for generalization. Although differences between CIRP and Monitoring the Future in the population sampled, the rating scale, the nature and wording of life goals, and the order of life goals prevent direct comparison of point-of-time responses, the availability of two data sets has the advantage of enabling one to check whether generalizations about patterns of association among life goals and trends over time are consistent between the two. Also, because the range of questions other than those on life goals differs between the surveys, their joint use permits a wider scope of inquiry than either would alone.

Measurement of Values

Both surveys include quite similar questions probing respondents' life goals, and these questions contain individual life goal items that provide fairly direct counterparts of the four concepts of interest. These four "primary indicators" in each survey are the principal focus of the subsequent analysis; however, additional life goal items closely related to the primary indicators provide useful insights that strengthen and expand the interpretation of the data. Table 4.1 lists the primary and subsidiary indicators included here, classified according to their conceptual counterparts.

Nature of Life Goals and Their Trends

Importance of Life Goals in 1985

How important to American youth are the goals of private materialism, family life, personal self-fulfillment, and public interest? In 1985 among college freshmen, all of the goals except personal self-fulfillment evoke substantial support; 63-71% rate them as essential or very important (Table 4.2A, col. 11). Personal self-fulfillment is seen as somewhat less important—the importance of developing a meaningful philosophy of life is placed in the top two categories by 43% of freshmen.

Among high school seniors, all four goals are considered important, but their relative order is different from that for college freshmen (Table 4.2B, col. 11). Personal self-fulfillment is a close second to the family goal, while private materialism and the public interest goal find somewhat less support. The differences between the surveys in ranking and level of support for the four goals are due chiefly to differences in the goals included, their wording, and order. Although the population of youths included among high school

TABLE 4.1 Classification of Life Goals in the CIRP and Monitoring the Future Surveys

Life Goal	CIRP Survey	Monitoring the Future Survey
1. Private materialism	Being very well-off financially[a]	Having lots of money[a]
	Being successful in a business of my own	Being successful in my line of work
		Being able to find steady work
2. Family goals	Raising a family[a]	Having a good marriage and family life[a]
		Living close to parents and relatives
		Being able to give my children better opportunities than I've had
3. Personal self-fulfillment	Developing a meaningful philosophy of life[a]	Finding purpose and meaning in my life[a]
4. Public interest	Helping others who are in difficulty[a]	Making a contribution to society[a]
	Influencing the political structure	Being a leader in my community
	Influencing social values	Working to correct social and economic inequalities
	Participating in a community action program	
	Becoming involved in programs to clean up the environment	
	Helping to promote racial understanding	

Note: In the CIRP survey the instruction is "indicate the importance to you personally of each of the following," and the rating categories are "essential, very important, somewhat important, and not important." In the Monitoring the Future survey the instruction is "How important is each of the following to you in your life," and the rating categories are "not important, somewhat important, quite important, and extremely important." Seven items in the CIRP survery and four items from the Monitoring the Future survey are omitted because they were not considered indicators of the four concepts of interest.

[a] Taken as the principal indicator of the specified life goal in each survey.

TABLE 4.2 Life Goal Correlations ≥ .20, 1985

A. College Freshmen

Life Goal	Own Money[a]	Own Business	Family	Philosophy of Life[a]	Political Structure	Societal	Community	Environmental	Racial	Helping Others[a]	Percent, Top Two Ratings[b]
	(1)	(2)	(3)	(4)	(5)	(6)	(7)	(8)	(9)	(10)	(11)
Very well off financially[a]	...	0.37									71
Successful in own business		...									52
Raising a family[a]			...								70
Developing a philosophy of life[a]				...	0.26	0.30	0.38	0.31	0.37	0.27	43
Influencing political structure				0.26	...	0.50	0.30	0.28	0.29		16
Influencing societal values				0.30	0.50	...	0	0.26	0.32	0.33	33
Community program				0.38	0.30	0.35	...	0	0.47	0.38	23
Environmental program				0.31	0.28	0.26	0.42	...	0	0.26	20
Racial understanding				0.37	0.29	0.32	0.47	0.39	...	0	32
Helping others in difficulty[a]			0.21	0.27		0.33	0.38	0.26	0.37	...	63

(continues)

TABLE 4.2 (continued)

B. High School Seniors

	Money[a]	Success in Work	Steady Work	Good Marriage/ Family Life[a]	Live Close to Parents	Give Children Opportunities	Find Meaning/ Purpose in Life[a]	Leader in Community	Correct Inequalities	Contribute to Society[a]	Percent, Top Two Ratings[b]
Lots of money[a]	...										61
Success in work		...									91
Find steady work		0.30	...								95
Good marriage/family life[a]			0.27	...							89
Live close to parents/relatives				0.20	...						34
Give children better opportunities		0.20	0.27	0.31	0.20	...					86
Find purpose/meaning in life[a]						0.27	...				86
Being leader in community						0.21		...			26
Correct societal/ economic inequalities							0.25	0.33	...		32
Contribute to society[a]		0.21					0.27	0.51	0.37	...	55

Source: Micro-data tapes for 1985.

Note: There are no negative correlations of .20 or less. In panel A, for each bivariate correlation, N = approximately 175,000; in panel B, N = approximately 3,250.

[a] Principal indicator (see Table 4.1).

[b] In panel A, indicates rating of "essential" or "very important"; in panel B, "extremely important" or "quite important."

seniors is considerably greater and less homogeneous, this cannot account for the difference in ratings between the two groups in Table 4.2, because the life goals of high school seniors with no college plans differ very little from those with college plans (Bachman, Johnston, and O'Malley 1987, pp. 36-38).

In general, then, among the goals specified in the two surveys, private materialism, family life, personal self-fulfillment, and the public interest all are quite important to American youth. However, those who rate one goal highly do not necessarily rate the others highly. This is clear from the correlation matrixes in Table 4.2, where, to simplify interpretation, the entries are confined to correlations of .20 or greater, disregarding sign. Note that in both panels there is a virtual absence of correlations between the indicators of private materialism and those of the public interest. Clearly, those who rate one life goal highly usually do not rate the other highly, a result consistent with Hirschman's (1982) and Schlesinger's (1986) contrast between those with private versus public involvements. (This is not to say, of course, that there is an inverse relationship between the two.) In contrast, within the public interest groupings there are consistently high positive correlations among the indicators.

There are other notable consistencies between the two surveys. In both, those who consider personal self-fulfillment important are likely to consider the public interest important, but not private materialism. This is consistent with Inglehart's assimilation of self-actualization to a public interest orientation in his postmaterialist versus materialist groupings (Inglehart 1981, p. 892).

Also in both surveys, the family goal emerges as a distinct one, with only one case out of a possible six of a correlation at the .20 level or higher with the other three primary indicators. Because of the financial requirements of family life, one might have expected a noticeable positive correlation between the goals of family life and private materialism, but in neither survey is this true. This suggests that the goal of private materialism is interpreted by respondents primarily as goods for oneself, not for one's entire family. There is, however, a relationship between giving children better opportunities and the goals of steady work and being a success at work, suggesting that the latter goals may be chiefly seen as instrumental to successful family life, rather than linked to one's own material aspirations.

Trends in Life Goals

What of trends in the life goals of American youth? Again, the two surveys give quite similar results in the period in which they overlap, although the changes are more pronounced in the college freshmen data. The most sizable changes are a sharp increase in private materialism as a life goal and a decline in the importance of personal self-fulfillment (Figure 4.1). This shift appears to date from the early or mid-seventies, although precise dating is difficult because

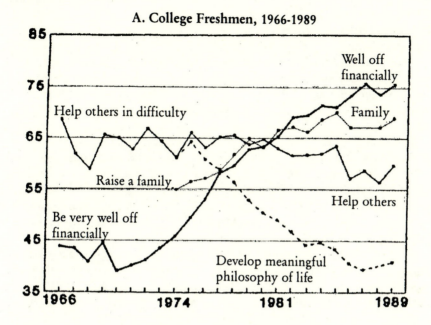

A. College Freshmen, 1966-1989

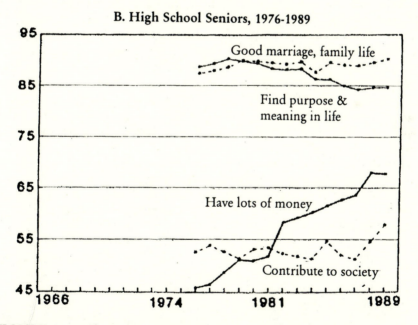

B. High School Seniors, 1976-1989

FIGURE 4.1 Life Goals of College Freshmen and High School Seniors
Source: See Table 4.3. Because of format change *A* data are omitted for "Raise a family" in 1987 and "Philosophy of life" in 1988.

of uncertainties about the reliability of the pre-1974 data. Compared with private materialism and personal self-fulfillment, the public interest and family goals change more moderately. Among high school seniors both remain fairly constant in absolute magnitude. Among college freshmen the importance of family life increases and public interest declines slightly. In relative terms, however, these goals, as well as personal self-fulfillment, have diminished in importance.

This shift in goals appears to have ended in recent years. Particularly in the freshman data, but to some extent also in those for high school seniors, one sees a leveling off in the period starting around 1986-87. (Indeed, newly released freshmen data for 1990, taken together with those in Figure 4.1, hint at a possible reversal [see Astin, Korn, and Berz 1990].) This is an additional reason for focusing the trend analysis here on the period from the mid-seventies through 1986.

If the analysis is expanded to include the subsidiary as well as primary indicators of Table 4.1, a clearer picture emerges of the trends through 1986 suggested by Figure 4.1. Consider, for example, the parameters of simple least squares trend lines fitted to the time series for each life goal for the period from the mid-seventies to 1986 (Table 4.3). Comparing average rates of change as measured by the slope coefficient, b, one finds a similar pattern in both surveys. Private materialism and family life goals increase in importance, with the specific goal of making money having by far the greatest rate of increase. In contrast, public interest concerns usually decrease in importance (though the trends are not always statistically significant), and personal self-fulfillment declines the most.

Within the public interest grouping, there is a similar and instructive pattern in both surveys among the subsidiary indicators. Public concerns relating to specific social objectives—promoting racial understanding, participating in community action or environmental programs, and correcting social and economic inequalities—have statistically significant negative trends of mild or moderate magnitude (rows 7-9, 19). Public concerns of a more general nature—influencing social values, influencing the political structure, and being a community leader—have positive (though not always significant) trends (rows 4, 5, 17). Our primary indicator in each survey, the importance rating of which is considerably greater than any of the subsidiary indicators (see Table 4.2), falls between these two groupings, apparently averaging them in some degree. To the extent one emphasizes commitment to specific social objectives, there has seemingly been a turning away from the public interest, not only relative to private materialism and family life but in an absolute sense as well.

In both surveys the pattern in the trend results of the full set of survey items in Table 4.3 is generally consistent with that in the cross-sectional analysis of Table 4.2—those items that have sizable positive correlations cross-sectionally usually have similar directions of change. Thus items positively correlated with private materialism usually have significant positive trends, while those posi-

TABLE 4.3 OLS Regression Parameters for Importance of Specified Life Goal Against Time

Population and Life Goal[a]	Percent, Top Two Ratings		Regression Statistics		
	1974	1986	b	t	R2
College freshmen (1974-86):					
Private materialism:					
1. Very well off financially[b]	46	73	2.19	14.10	0.94
2. Successful in own business	38	49	0.80	4.90	0.66
Family life:					
3. Raising a family[b]	55	67	1.19	9.40	0.88
Public interest:					
4. Influencing social values	27	33	0.30	4.30	0.59
5. Influencing political structure	13	15	0.06	0.90	0.00
6. Helping others in difficulty[b]	61	57	-0.34	-2.30	0.26
7. Promoting racial understanding	36	27	-0.61	-3.90	0.62
8. Participating in community action program	28	19	-0.82	-7.90	0.84
9. Participating in environmental program	26	16	-0.91	-6.50	0.77
Personal self-fulfillment:					
10. Developing philosophy of life[b]	61	41	-1.98	-17.10	0.96
High school seniors (1976-86):					
Private materialism:					
11. Lots of money[b]	46	63	1.84	14.10	0.95
12. Success in work	88	91	0.40	8.80	0.88
13. Steady work	92	94	0.37	5.60	0.75
Family life:					
14. Live close to parents/relatives	26	33	0.81	6.30	0.79
15. Give children better opportunities	83	88	0.49	8.50	0.88
16. Good marriage and family life[b]	88	89	0.09	1.00	0.00
Public interest:					
17. Being leader in community	21	28	0.43	4.40	0.65
18. Contribute to society[b]	53	52	-0.04	-0.30	0.00
19. Correct social/economic inequalities	33	32	-0.17	-2.00	0.22
Personal self-fulfillment:					
20. Find purpose/meaning in life[b]	89	85	-0.44	-5.10	0.22

Source: For college freshmen data: Astin et al. (1986); Astin, Green, and Korn (1987); and Astin, Korn, and Berz (1989). For high school senior data: Bachman, Johnston, and O'Malley (1980a, 1980b, 1981, 1984, 1985, 1987); Johnston, Bachman, and O'Malley (1980a, 1980b, 1980c, 1982, 1984, 1986).

Note: For college freshmen, N = 13 for each regression; for high school seniors, N = 11 for each regression.

[a] Ranked by b within each life goal category.

[b] Principal indicator (see Table 4.1).

tively correlated with public interest tend to have small or negative trends. In this sense the micro data lend support to the time series analysis.

As regards recent generalizations about values of American youth, the evidence supports the Levine (1981) interpretation over that of Yankelovich (1981)—a growing emphasis on private materialism relative to personal self-fulfillment—and with regard to American society more generally, the Hirschman (1982)-Schlesinger (1986) view over that of Bellah and his associates (1985)—a shift from public concerns to private materialism. Although Inglehart's argument for a postmaterialist trend is not supported here, he might explain the shift toward materialism as due to the emergence of an "environment of insecurity," as in his analysis of European trends in the seventies (Inglehart 1985).

Summary

Since the early seventies there has been a marked shift in the value orientations of American youth. There has been a substantial increase in private materialism as a life goal, a modest turning away from the public interest, and a sharp decline in emphasis on personal self-fulfillment. Compared with public interest and personal self-fulfillment, family concerns have increased modestly, but not nearly as much as has the emphasis on private materialism. Relative to private materialism, the other three goals have all declined in importance. Since about 1986-87, this shift appears to have ended and may even have started to turn around, but the life goals of young people today are still much different from those of their predecessors 15 years ago.

Inglehart Replies:
Postmaterialism Is the More General Trend

In their chapter in this volume, Easterlin and Crimmins (1997) argue that "American youth are becoming more materialistic." Their conclusion seems completely at odds with the findings from a massive body of evidence from representative national surveys carried out in a number of advanced industrial societies. After reviewing their evidence, I will undertake to reconcile the two sets of findings.

Are the Young More Materialist?

The findings on this point are not as incompatible as they may at first seem—for Easterlin and Crimmins' piece might more accurately be entitled "U.S. High School Seniors Are Growing More Materialistic Than They Used to Be." Their findings do not seem to apply to the young in general, as compared with the old; nor is there any indication that they apply to intergenerational differences outside the U.S. And perhaps most crucially of all, their findings are not based on representative national samples, even of the U.S. population; they are based on successive cross-sections of high school seniors and college freshpersons.

This fact has two important consequences. First, the claim that "the young are growing more materialist" immediately raises the question, "More material-ist than what?" More Materialist than the old? Or more Materialist than they, themselves, used to be? The database used by Easterlin and Crimmins does not cover the full range of generations; consequently it cannot be used to answer such questions as whether the postwar birth cohorts are more or less Material-ist than historically older cohorts. Since their database consists solely of per-sons about 18 years old, it does not permit comparisons between the values of 20-year-olds and 60-year-olds—or any comparison between the values of "the young" and "the old" in general. It *can* be used to compare those who were high school seniors in 1970 with those who were high school seniors in 1990, but this is a quite different issue. The claim that "the young are growing more mate-rialist" might easily be understood to imply that the young are more materialist than the old in general. It seems unlikely that they are, and their evidence can-not test this question.

The fact that Easterlin and Crimmins's data are based solely on high school seniors and college freshpersons has another, even more crucial attribute: the composition of this sample has undergone massive changes over the past few decades. The high school seniors of today represent a very different segment of the U.S. public than did the high school seniors of two or three decades ago. The importance of these changes can scarcely be overstated.

In 1970, only 52 percent of U.S. adults had completed high school; in 1994, 81 percent had done so. The high school dropouts are anything but a random cross-section of the population: to a greatly disproportionate extent, they con-sist of those from the economically least secure backgrounds. But in 1970, nearly half of the adult population had dropped out; in 1994 only 19 percent had done so (U.S. Bureau of the Census, 1995: 157). This is linked with a massive change in the composition of high school seniors. Today, this group includes a much larger share of the economically least secure stratum. An equally dramatic shift has taken place in the composition of first-year college students. In 1970, less than 11 percent of U.S. adults had entered college; in 1994 more than 22 percent had done so. Again, the social backgrounds of those who enter college are very different from those who don't. In 1994 the pool of college freshpersons was much less narrowly recruited than it had been in 1970; it contained a larger share of people from economically less secure backgrounds. One of the key hypotheses in our theory of value change implies that this stratum should have a subtantially smaller proportion of Postmaterialists and a much higher pro-portion of Materialists than the most secure stratum, and the empirical evi-dence overwhelmingly confirms this expectation.

In short, our theory implies that a change in the composition of the U.S.

high school seniors and college freshpersons like that which has taken place during the last few decades should produce a shift in values of precisely the type that Easterlin and Crimmins observe. We do not believe that this is the only reason for the differences between the two sets of findings, but it may go a long way in helping to account for it.

Two additional factors are probably also involved in the differences between the two sets of findings. One is the simple fact that, although Easterlin and Crimmins use the same label ("materialist") to describe the phenomenon they discuss as I apply to one of the polar types in my theory of value change, we actually use quite different measures. Their findings are implicitly assumed to refute the idea of a shift from Materialist to Postmaterialist values, but the measure they are using does not necessarily tap the same phenomenon. Simply on the basis of face content, I would assume that there is a fair amount of overlap between what the two measures are tapping, but this assumption has not been tested empirically. If I were to make an educated guess, lacking any empirical results, I'd assume that the two measures would probably prove to be correlated at about the .3 or .4 level. While well above a random relationship, this would still leave a good deal of room for slippage. Insofar as they are measuring different things, they would not necessarily find the same trends.

A third consideration that helps reconcile the two sets of findings is the fact that, under given conditions, we would *expect* to find that "the young are growing more materialist"—*not* in the sense that, at a given point in time, the youngest cohorts are more Materialist than the oldest cohorts, but in the sense that a given birth cohort has become more Materialist than it used to be, in response to current conditions. To see why this is true, let us turn back to Figure 3.2.

As the scarcity hypothesis implies, a given cohort's values respond to current conditions: prosperity will enhance the tendency to emphasize Postmaterialist values; conversely, diminishing economic and physical security will lead people to emphasize Materialist values. Empirical evidence covering the period from 1970 to 1994 supports this expectation. During the recessions of the mid-1970s, the early 1980s and the early 1990s, there *was* a shift toward Materialist values. This did not eradicate the tendency for younger birth cohorts to be less Materialist than older ones—quite the contrary, the intergenerational differences remained remarkably stable. But insecurity did tend to make all cohorts register a higher proportion of Materialist choices; conversely when conditions improved, all cohorts placed more emphasis on Postmaterialist goals. Thus in 1980, the 1946-55 birth cohort was a good deal more Materialist than it had been in 1970; its level of Postmaterialism showed a good deal of recovery subsequently, but again in 1991, this cohort was slightly more Materialist than it had been in 1970. The absolute levels of Materialist/Postmaterialist values within a given birth cohort can and do fluctuate considerably, in response to current conditions. But in the long run, the value priorities of given birth cohorts are relatively stable. Consequently, as the older cohorts in Figure

3.2 have left the sample and been replaced by younger cohorts, there has been a substantial net shift toward Postmaterialist values *in the population as a whole.* The point is simple but important: the absolute levels of given cohorts can and do fluctuate. Period effects are by no means incompatible with intergenerational value change. Quite the contrary, they are to be expected.

Conclusion

In summary, we believe that the differences between the findings from representative national samples of the publics of advanced industrial societies, and Easterlin and Crimmins's findings from surveys of U.S. high school seniors and college freshpersons, can be attributed to three main factors.

First, the composition of the pool that consitutes the high school senior and college freshperson population of the U.S. has undergone dramatic changes in the past few decades. These changes have brought a much larger proportion of the economically less secure stratum into that pool, which theoretically should tend to produce effects of precisely the kind that Easterlin and Crimmins observe.

Second, the two bodies of data operationalize their measures of "Materialist" values in quite different ways. Without empirical measures, it is difficult to determine the extent to which they tap the same phenomenon. Insofar as they measure different things, they would not necessarily show the same trends.

Finally, there is no reason to believe that "the young" have become more Materialist than "the old" in general. Easterlin and Crimmins's findings *do* indicate that the U.S. high school seniors and college freshpersons of 1990 were more Materialist than the U.S. high school seniors of 1970. But this finding is by no means incompatible with an overall intergenerational shift from Materialist to Postmaterialist values. Some degree of fluctuation in the values of given cohorts is a predictable consequence of the scarcity hypothesis.

The findings from successive samples of high school seniors are an interesting and significant phenomenon, and are worthy of further research. But findings based on much more broadly-based samples, from a wider range of societies, indicate that the trend from Materialist toward Postmaterialist values has continued.

Easterlin and Crimmins Reply:
Materialist and Postmaterialist Values: A Comment

It is exciting to engage in serious debate about the evidence regarding values. Thanks to the enormous advance in survey research on subjective attitudes in the past half century, there now exists a substantial database that makes possible empirical testing of a priori generalizations about values. Professor Inglehart has been one of the leaders in the development of this field, and we have benefitted substantially from his pioneering work. Some of our empirical results are consistent with his, notably the point-of-time association between self-actualization goals and public interest orientation. Others seemingly differ significantly, especially regarding his claim of the shift from materialist to nonmaterialist values. We are pleased to have Professor Inglehart's observations on our work, and grateful to the editors of this volume for inviting us to provide a brief response. We focus on the three items in the fine concise summary at the end of Professor Inglehart's remarks.

1. The socio-economic composition of the group that we study has admittedly changed in the past two decades. However, even when the analysis is confined to those of a given economic background, for example, those whose parents both completed college, the pronounced shift toward materialism remains. Put more generally, the shift is common to students from all socio-economic backgrounds. Had we included this observation in our original article, we would doubtless have forestalled Professor Inglehart's justifiable concern about the composition of our two samples.

2. Differences between Professor Inglehart and us in the way of measuring materialist values go to the heart of our seemingly contradictory findings. We would like to feel that the survey questions that we use tap directly into what is commonly understood as material aspirations, while Professor Inglehart's measure is, at best, an indirect one.

3. Our analysis of high school seniors and college freshmen makes no claim that in Professor Inglehart's words, "'the young' have become more Materialist than 'the old' in general." We do, however, suggest that young cohorts of the late 1980s were starting out with more materialistic attitudes than young cohorts of the early 1970s. This is not what one would expect if more recent cohorts were becoming more "postmaterialistic." But the shift we observe is not necessarily a long-term trend. The evidence we have examined suggests that the shift has been caused by increasing economic insecurity among older adults who, in turn, have reshaped young people's values in the course of the socialization process.[1] The rise in economic insecurity among older adults appears to have abated in recent years, and with it, the rise of materialism among the young. There is thus some similarity between Professor Inglehart and us in regard to the mechanisms underlying fluctuations in values. Important differences remain, however, in regard to the measurement of values and the nature and determinants of the long-term trend in values.[2]

Notes

1. The paper in which this analysis is most fully developed is directed more toward the economics profession than a general audience. See Richard A. Easterlin, "Prefer-

ences and Prices in Choice of Career: The Switch to Business, 1972-87," *Journal of Economic Behavior and Organization*, 27 (1995), 1-34.

2. See Richard A. Easterlin, *Growth Triumphant: The Twenty-first Century in Historical Perspective*, Ann Arbor, MI: University of Michigan Press, 1996, chapters 10, 11.

Inglehart's Rejoinder:
How to Reconcile the Findings

Despite the apparently contradictory findings presented by Easterlin and Crimmins, on the one hand, and Inglehart, on the other hand, we do indeed seem to be moving toward converging interpretations. Turning to the same three points as they did, I would sum things up as follows.

1. In my contribution to this volume, I concluded that the dramatic change that has occurred in the last few decades in the social background of U.S. high school seniors and college freshpersons probably accounts for part, but not all, of the shift toward more Materialist values among this respondent pool. This conclusion seems consistent with the findings from both sides.

2. Given the different ways in which we have measured "Materialist" values, we are probably, to some extent, tapping different phenomena. I agree that Easterlin and Crimmins's use of the label "materialist" accords with common-sense usage at least as closely as mine. From the start, I have used the labels "Materialist" and "Postmaterialist" values to refer to a specific shift in the priorities accorded to economic and physical security, on the one hand, versus self-expression and quality of life, on the other hand. This is a special use of terminology, but regardless of how it is labeled, the underlying phenomenon seems to have important implications.

3. The findings based on Easterlin and Crimmins's samples do not indicate that the young have become more Materialist than the old in general. It would be a misreading of the title, "The Young Have Become More Materialist," to conclude that the young have become more Materialist than the old. Period effects within given cohorts are compatible with the thesis of intergenerational value change, and (as Easterlin and Crimmins point out) these findings could be interpreted as a period effect, not a reversal of the generational shift. At the same time, I am convinced that Easterlin and Crimmins have identified an interesting and substantial period effect; and I find their proposed interpretation of this phenomenon quite plausible.

Over the past two decades, these authors have produced many findings that struck me as interesting and significant. Easterlin and Crimmins's most recent contribution adds to that list.

5

The New Political Culture in Japan

Naoyuki Umemori
with
Michael Rempel

This paper examines the degree to which Japan exhibits the "New Political Culture," conceptualized by Terry Clark and Ronald Inglehart (1990) to characterize advanced industrial or "post-industrial" societies. Clark and Inglehart base their "New Political Culture" (NPC) theory largely on data from Western Europe and the United States. They attempt to incorporate non-Western case studies, including Japan, but the data which they present outside of the West tends to be limited to just a few survey years. By contrast, this paper introduces and interprets longitudinal data and analyses accumulated by Japanese scholars since 1945. The results confirm some but call into question other aspects of the NPC, and also of the "post-industrial politics" framework proposed by Rempel and Clark in this volume's introduction. Most importantly, whereas the NPC features a declining influence of traditional political organizations (e.g., parties) and a rise of citizen activism in "new social movements," Japan has not evidenced the latter development. Instead, especially in the youngest generation, the more basic Japanese trend is towards rising political apathy.

In interpreting Japan's political culture, some scholars focus heavily on the influence of "traditional" values in contemporary Japanese society. However, data in this paper indicate that traditional values are waning. Consequently, Japan increasingly features *values* which *do* conform with NPC expectations but political *activities* which do *not*. These patterns challenge the existence of a linkage between developments in values and in political activities. The results indicate that the advent of post-industrial society may give birth to belief in a new political culture, without such belief necessarily involving or provoking a concurrent rise in specifically political interests and forms of activism.

To illuminate Japan's political culture, I pose several alternative hypotheses on trends in Japanese social activities: (1) consumerism, (2) religion, and (3) nationalist ideology.

The New Political Culture

Clark and Inglehart define the New Political Culture (NPC) by seven core components (1990: 2-3; see also Clark 1994: 25-28):
1. The classic left-right dimension is transformed.
2. Social and fiscal/economic issues become explicitly distinguished.
3. Social issues rise in salience relative to fiscal/economic issues.
4. Market individualism and social individualism grow.
5. Questioning of the welfare state rises.
6. Hierarchical political organizations decline; issue politics and broader citizen participation rise.
7. These NPC-related changes are more pervasive among younger, more educated and affluent individuals and societies.

The Social Origins of the NPC in Japan

In elaborating on the social origins of the NPC (summarized in component #7), Clark and Inglehart primarily emphasize macroeconomic changes. Central among these are: (1) the decline of agricultural and small family firms, (2) the early twentieth century rise and subsequent decline of large manufacturing firms, and (3) the mid- to late-twentieth century rise of high-technology, information-based service firms.

Japan has recently undergone each of these changes. Regarding the first, from 1950 to 1993, the proportion of the Japanese workforce in agricultural forestry and fishery declined from 48.3% to just 5.9%. Regarding the second and third, over those same years, the proportion of the Japanese workforce employed in manufacturing and services increased respectively from 21.9% to 33.7% and from 29.7% to 59.9% (Yano Tsuneta Kinenkai 1995: 96). Focusing especially on developments within the service sector, "information industries" employed just under 20% of the Japanese workforce in 1955 but over 35% by 1980 (Tokyo Kogyo Daigaku Joho Shakai Kenkyukai 1988: 29).

Accompanying these sectoral shifts, Japan's aggregate growth and per capita affluence rose over the same period. In 1993, Japan's GNP per capita was $31,450, far in excess of the figure for most Western industrialized countries, including the United States, Germany, and France (World Bank 1995). These accomplishments came with stunning rapidity, exemplified by the doubling of per capita income in the twelve years from 1975 to 1987. Clark and Inglehart emphasize that such rising affluence, measured either by aggregate or individual level growth or income variables, is critical for the NPC to emerge.

Clark and Inglehart also posit that *demographic* shifts towards a "slimmer family" with more egalitarian and flexible role relations contribute to the NPC's emergence (1990: 18-19). In Japan, these demographic shifts are well under way. Compared with earlier in the century, fewer Japanese persons marry, those who do marry later in life, parents have fewer children, more women work, more marriages end in divorce, and fewer adults live with their parents or grandparents in extended families. As a consequence, by 1985, the average age of first marriage rose to 28.0 for males and 25.4 for females, higher than the figures for West Germany, France, Britain or the United States (Yuzawa 1987: 66). Also, from just 1960 to 1980, labor force participation among married Japanese women rose from 8.8% to 29.6%, indicating a substantial weakening in the pre-industrial tradition of a sex-based division of labor (Yuzawa 1987: 86).

In sum, Japan has experienced the macroeconomic and demographic changes which Clark and Inglehart identify as social origins of the NPC. Next, I examine recent value changes.

The Rise of Postmaterialism in Japan

The first five components of the NPC elaborate on different aspects of a shift of political discussion away from *economic* and towards qualitative *social* or *cultural* issues. Similarly, the "post-industrial politics" framework in the introduction to this volume identifies the rise of a left-right cleavage and of organized "new social movements" on social issues like environmentalism, women's equality, and free speech.

Supporting this shift towards social issues is Inglehart's theory (1977, 1990) of the rise of "postmaterialist" values throughout advanced industrial societies. With modern technology and economic development allegedly solving millennium-old problems of food production and physical security, Inglehart reasons that persons are increasingly free to concern themselves not with how to find or pay for their next meal but with how to achieve an intellectually or aesthetically rewarding life. Inglehart speculates that these latter, more "postmaterialist" goals entail a greater emphasis on "new social movement" causes, like promoting a clean environment or global peace.

Clark and Inglehart hypothesize that any political cultural effects of structural changes will be most apparent in the young. (See also Rempel and Clark, this volume.) This is in light of research showing that persons tend to form political outlooks in their youth and to change them little as they age (e.g., Davis 1992; Easterlin and Crimmins 1991; Inglehart 1977, 1990). This implies that older persons, who grow up under earlier structural conditions, will often maintain correspondingly earlier cultural standards. By contrast, younger persons are more likely to be culturally responsive to recent structural changes. Therefore, if the discussed social origins have in fact generated the NPC, this will be most evident in political attitudes of the young.

TABLE 5.1   Postmaterialism Is Rising in Japan

	Most Important		Second Most Important	
(percentages)	*1981-82*	*1990-91*	*1981-82*	*1990-91*
Maintaining Order in Nation	38.5	34.5	19.9	20.8
Giving People More Say	19.3	29.2	26.2	23.1
Fighting Rising Prices	37.2	27.7	37.2	36.7
Protecting Freedom of Speech	5.0	8.6	16.6	19.4

Note: The question reads: "If you had to choose, which one of the things on this card would you say is most important?. . . And which would be the next most important . . . Maintaining order in the nation, giving people more say in important government decisions, fighting rising prices, protecting freedom of speech, don't know."
Source: World Values Survey, 1981-82 and 1990-91 editions.

Inglehart often tests for postmaterialism with a survey question which asks respondents to identify their first and second most important goals among: (1) maintaining order in the nation, (2) giving people more say in important government decisions, (3) fighting rising prices, and (4) protecting freedom of speech. He classifies the first and third of these as *materialist* and the second and fourth as *postmaterialist.* I focus on results for Japan.

In the 1990-91 World Values Survey (WVS), 37.8% of Japanese respondents chose one of the two postmaterialist options as most important. This is lower than for all but three of the eighteen Western European and industrialized North American countries surveyed.[1] Still, viewed more for what it says about Japanese citizens, this figure is large, and represents a 13.5% increase for Japan from the 1981-82 WVS. Table 5.1 displays the Japanese results for both WVS editions.

Also, in 1973 and 1978, Inglehart tested for postmaterialism with a questionnaire which asks respondents to identify their goals from the following twelve:

A. Maintaining a high rate of economic growth;
B. Making sure that this country has strong defense forces;
C. Seeing that the people have more say in how things get decided at work and in their communities;
D. Trying to make our cities and countryside more beautiful;
E. Maintaining order in the nation;
F. Giving the people more say in important government decisions;
G. Fighting rising prices;
H. Protecting freedom of speech;
I.   Maintaining a stable economy;
J. Progress toward a less impersonal, more humane society;

K. The fight against crime;

L. Progress toward a society where ideas are more important than money.

Inglehart classified six as tapping *materialist* needs. Of these, "economic growth," "rising prices," and "stable economy" (A, I, and G) were designed to tap *economic* security, and "strong defense forces," "maintain order," and "fight crime" (B, E, and K) were designed to tap an emphasis on *physical* security. The remaining six tap *postmaterialist* needs. Inglehart's expectation was that the six materialist goals would form one cluster, with the postmaterialist goals forming another.

To test his hypothesis, Inglehart (1990) performed a principal components factor analysis of the rankings of these twelve goals in each of ten countries surveyed in 1973 and 1978. The same five goals in every country cluster on one end of the value continuum, six cluster on the other end, and the last goal falls near the midpoint.

In 1986-1987, a group of Japanese scholars tested Inglehart's hypothesis with the same principal components analysis, just for the Japanese data. Their results strongly support Inglehart's theory, as the six "materialist" goals formed one cluster, and the six "postmaterialist" goals formed another (Shakai Keisai Kokumin Kaigi 1988: 148).

An opinion survey by Sorihu Kohoka provides more long-term evidence of a gradual climb in Japanese postmaterialism throughout the latter part of the twentieth century. The relevant question asks what respondents are most concerned with in their daily life, between: (1) managing to make ends meet, and (2) enjoying emotional satisfaction which cannot be obtained by money and goods. As Figure 5.1 indicates, by 1975, the proportion choosing the former option exceeded the proportion choosing the latter, and postmaterialism has continued to rise since then.

Political Activism in Japan

In component #6, Clark and Inglehart characterize the NPC by (1) reduced support for hierarchical political organizations, and (2) more and broader grassroots political activism. Rempel and Clark pursue the second claim in their introduction to this volume, proposing that there has been a growing "institutionalization of new social movements." I assess these claims separately in the following two subsections.

The Decline in Support for Hierarchical Political Organizations

Clark and Inglehart theorize that voters may indicate distrust of established institutions by refusing to affiliate with major political parties (see also Rempel and Clark, this volume). It is thus relevant that Japan has witnessed a dramatic trend towards non-partisanship. Figure 5.2 shows that from 1960 to 1986, the

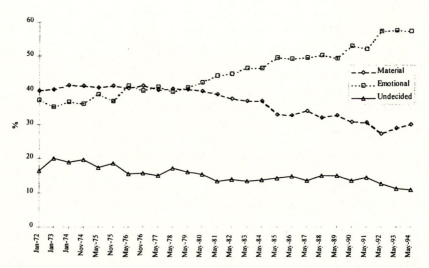

FIGURE 5.1 Japanese Citizens Increasingly Prioritize Emotional Satisfaction over Material Well-Being
Source: Gekkan Yoron Chosa, 10/94: 53.

proportion of Japanese citizens affiliated with either the Liberal Democratic Party (LDP) or the Japanese Socialist Party (JSP) has declined, while the proportion of unaffiliated citizens has risen from under 20% to 38%. This change has most affected the JSP, whose membership declined by over half from 1958. That impact may have occurred in part because the JSP has been closely tied to labor unions, a typical "traditional" or "hierarchical" organization. By contrast, the LDP relies less on its substantive platform or on issue-based ties than on *clientelistic* ties for maintaining its support levels. Still, the LDP's clientelistic and culturally "traditional" emphasis is hardly an effective draw for attracting newly disenchanted holders of NPC values. In fact, Figure 5.3 shows that the LDP is especially unpopular among members of the younger generation. Consequently, with different respective reasons for shunning both major political parties, the young, and other holders of "modern" values, are the strongest candidates for non-partisanship. Figure 5.3 confirms that non-partisanship is greatest among young persons and that the percentage of non-partisan individuals rises when moving successively from each older to the next younger generation (Tokei Suri Kenkyujo 1992: 163; NHK 1991: 144).

Besides political parties, labor unions suffered membership decline. From 1975 to 1994, the estimated organization rate of Japanese labor unions declined by 10% (Yano Tsuneta Kinenkai 1995: 111).

Overall, the Japanese data confirm Clark and Inglehart's expectations that

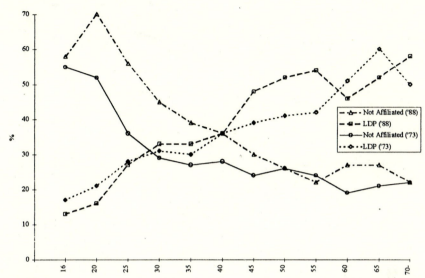

FIGURE 5.2   Non-Partisanship Has Risen Among Japanese Citizens, 1953-1988

Source: Tokei Suri Kenkyujo 1992: 163.

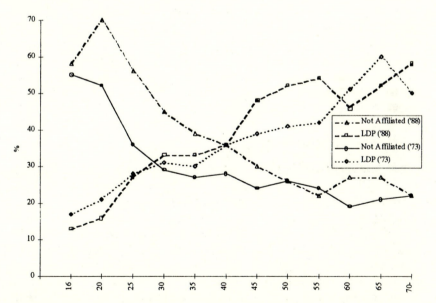

FIGURE 5.3   Non-Partisanship Is Greatest Among Young Persons, 1973 and 1988

Source: NHK 1991: 144.

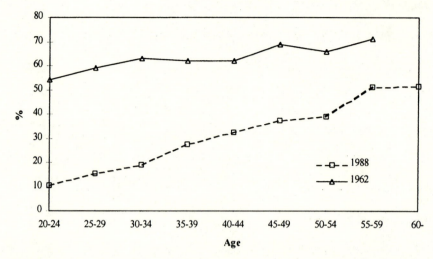

FIGURE 5.4   Interest in Voting Has Sharply Declined, Especially Among Japanese Youth, 1962 and 1988
Note: The question reads: "What do you do in general elections for the House of Representatives?" The answer to which the figure's percentages apply is: "Let nothing stand in
the way of voting."
Source: Tokei Suri Kenkyujo, 1992: 466 and 1970: 475.

citizens have become less supportive of traditional and hierarchical political
organizations.

The Decline in Citizen Political Activism

The Rise of Political Apathy. Importantly contradicting Clark and Inglehart,
and Rempel and Clark, rather than showing a rise of citizen activism in "new
social movements" or in other political groups, Figure 5.4 reveals a marked
decline in the political interests of Japanese youth (Tokei Suri Kenkyujo 1970).
When asked, "What do you do in general elections for the House of Representatives" in 1962, 54% of respondents aged 20-24 answered, "Let nothing stand in the
way of voting." In 1988, only 10% gave that response. Furthermore, the educational level of respondents does not affect this decline in political concern with
voting. Whereas in 1958, 67% of college graduates chose the strongest pro-voting
response, in 1988, only 36.5% did so. Thus contrary to the NPC theory, at least
for voting, there is *not* a trend towards proactive political orientations.
    The decline in voting may simply indicate antipathy toward traditional,

TABLE 5.2   Japanese Participation Levels Have Declined Since the Early 1970s

	1973	1978	1983	1988	1993
Participation in demonstration	4	4	2	2	1
Participation in signature-collecting	24	25	30	32	21
Writing a letter to the mass media	1	1	1	1	0
Petitioning or protesting	5	4	4	4	2
Making a donation	14	13	15	13	9
Attending political meetings	13	12	17	14	12
Buying or reading political publications	11	9	10	8	6
Member of a party or interest group	3	3	4	3	3
Nothing to do	60	61	56	55	64

Source: Hashimoto and Takahashi 1994: 29.

hierarchical political parties. In this sense, more non-voting is not inconsistent with Clark and Inglehart's projections. They do maintain, though, that active and informed citizens disenchanted with traditional political organizations will organize and challenge the old hierarchies by turning to *alternative* forms of political activism:

> New demands are articulated by activist and intelligent citizens, who refuse treatment as docile "subjects" or "clients." They thus organize around new issues of welfare state service provision, like day care or recycling paper. New groups seek to participate in general policy formation (rivaling parties and programs); and may press to participate in service delivery (rivaling government agencies, clientelist leaders, and unions). NPC's are thus seen as "rocking the boat"; they mean to (1990: 3-4).

Yet, this portrayal does not quite apply to Japan. Instead, aggregate Japanese activism levels have *not* risen since the early 1970s. Activism has stagnated, and apathy seems to be replacing it. Table 5.2 shows that from 1973 to 1993, the proportion of Japanese respondents who engaged in many of eight forms of political activism declined. More recently, from 1988 to 1993, the proportion declined for *all* eight forms (Hashimoto and Takahashi 1994: 29).

Figures 5.5A-C present additional evidence, bearing on apathy. The figures reveal that from 1973 to 1993, Japanese citizens increasingly advocated a "wait and see" as opposed to an activist approach towards labor, environmental, and other, unspecified political problems. The shift on environmental problems is especially remarkable. It contrasts with the prevalent view that activism on such an exemplary "new social movement" problem is *rising* throughout the industrialized world. To the contrary, from 1973 to 1993, the evidence reveals an

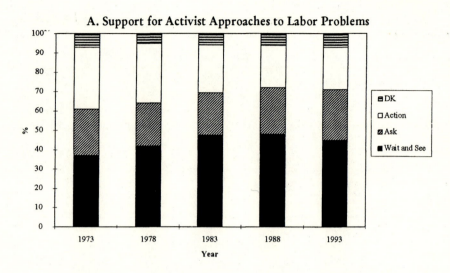

A. Support for Activist Approaches to Labor Problems

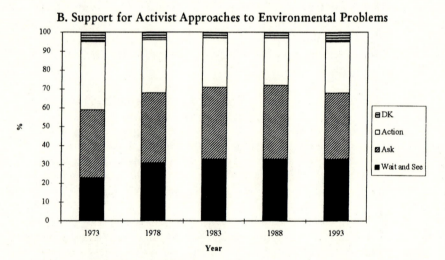

B. Support for Activist Approaches to Environmental Problems

almost 10% *decrease* in the proportion of respondents who said they would "start a civil movement and act to solve the problem" of "environmental pollution," coupled with an over 10% *increase* in the proportion advocating "wait and see" (Hashimoto and Takahashi 1994: 27).

The Decline of Perceived Political Efficacy. Why might people not choose to organize and challenge the old hierarchies which they oppose? One possibility is that people do not believe that available participatory options would be efficacious. Growing cynicism about the possibility for reforming the system

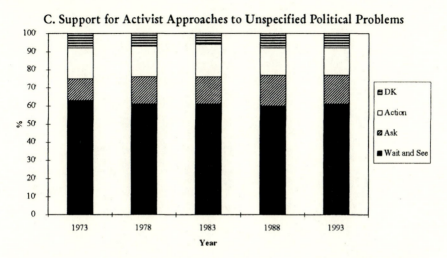

C. Support for Activist Approaches to Unspecified Political Problems

FIGURE 5.5   Support Has Declined for Activist Approaches to Social Problems
Note: The question for Figure 5.5A reads: "Suppose you are employed by a newly established company. If strong dissatisfaction about working conditions arose among employees, what would you do? . . . 1. Wait and see, 2. Ask the boss to improve working conditions, 3. Organize a labor union and act to improve working conditions." The question for Figure 5.5B reads: "Suppose environmental pollution arises in your community. What would you do . . . 1. Wait and see, 2. Ask your boss, politicians or public servants to solve the problem, 3. Start a civil movement and act to solve the problem." The question for Figure 5.5C reads: "On the following list, there are various political activities. Which do you think is the most desirable . . . 1. Choose good politicians and have them act as our representative, 2. If problems happen, ask politicians to solve them, 3. Actively participate in a political party or interest group to realize your aims."
Source: Hashimoto and Takahashi 1994: 27-28.

may engender a general indifference towards *any* type of political activism, even in new, independent citizens' movements. Supporting this assumption, Figures 5.6 A-D reveal a significant decline in the perceived efficacy that citizens ascribe to any political activity (Hashimoto and Takahashi 1994: 25; NHK 1991: 127). Figure 5.6D in particular shows that this feeling is remarkably high in the youngest generation (NHK 1991).

The Decline of Political Knowledge. Cynicism about the existing political system may also breed rising political ignorance. Indeed, Figure 5.7 shows a decline of basic political knowledge among Japanese citizens from 1973 to 1993. Although the percentage of respondents that correctly identified the right to live a humane life as constitutionally guaranteed increased over time, the percentage that so identified freedom of expression or the right to organize decreased by more than 10%.

A. Perceptions of the Political Efficacy of Voting

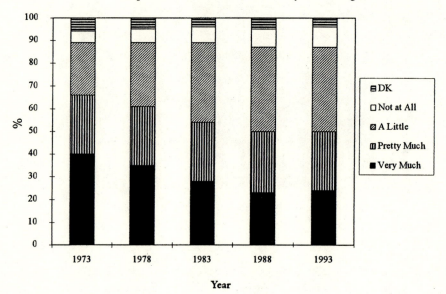

B. Perceptions of the Political Efficacy of Demonstrating or Petitioning

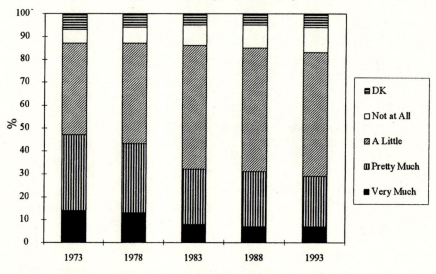

C. Perceptions of the Impact of Public Opinion on National Politics

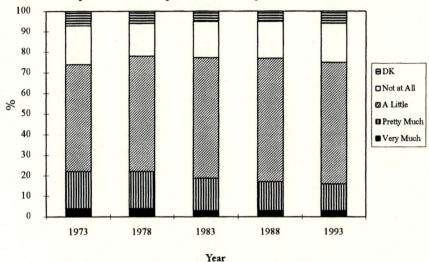

D. Perceptions of the Impact of Public Opinion
on National Politics—Controlling for Age

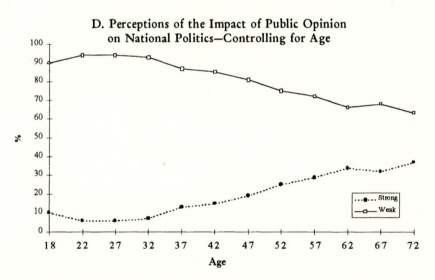

FIGURE 5.6   Japanese Citizens Have Become Increasingly Cynical About the Efficacy of Their Political Activities

Note: (1) The question for Figure 5.6A reads, "How much do you think your vote in general elections affects national politics?" (2) The question for Figure 5.6B reads, "How much do you think such political activities as demonstrating or signing petitions affect national politics?" (3) The question for Figures 5.6C and 5.6D reads, "How much do you think public opinion affects national politics?"

Source: NHK Seron Chosabu 1991: 127.

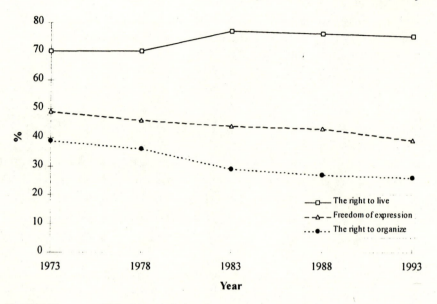

FIGURE 5.7   Political Knowledge Among Japanese Citizens Has Somewhat Declined

Note: The question for Figure 5.7 reads: "Among the following list, which items do you think the Japanese Constitution defines as the people's right, but not an obligation? You can choose as many as you like: *1. to express what you think? 2. to pay taxes? 3. to obey your seniors? 4. to walk on the right side of the road? 5. to live a humane life? *6. to organize a labor union? 7. N.K.? [* = correct answer]."

Source: Hashimoto and Takahashi 1994: 24.

This subsection has provided suggestive evidence for a trend of stagnating Japanese political activism and rising apathy. It can be surmised that if not for the continued increase in NPC or "modern" values, which interact *positively* with participatory orientations and with engagement in participatory acts (Flanagan 1991), there may have been an even greater decline in activism.[2]

The NPC in Contemporary Japan

Although Japan exhibits the social origins hypothesized to generate the NPC, the NPC has emerged only to a limited extent. Postmaterialism is rising, but there is no indication of rising grassroots citizen participation, and some positive evidence of growing apathy. The arrival of NPC values, coupled with the failure of NPC political activities, calls into question Clark and Inglehart's theoretical framework, which groups changes in values and activities together, as coinciding aspects of political development, both driven by the "modernization" process. In place of "modernization theory," I introduce arguments made by Japanese scholars that changes in (1) values and in (2) specifically political interests or activities operate as distinct, independent processes.

The Impact of Japan's Late Modernization

Inglehart (1990) notices Japan's deviation from the NPC and attempts to explain it by referring to Japan's late modernization, compared with the West. Inglehart reasons that Japan's rapid, late industrialization means that a large portion of its adult population will have grown up prior to the onset of the industrialization process. Accordingly, Inglehart hypothesizes that much of Japanese society will remain attached not merely to "materialist" values but, going farther back, to persisting "preindustrial," "prematerialist" values. Illustratively supporting his claim, Inglehart observes that while in the West, young, educated "postmaterialists" tend more than others to prioritize the value of *personal belonging*—"progress towards a less impersonal, more humane society"—in Japan, the opposite pattern holds; older, generally more "traditional" respondents choose that value. Inglehart reasons that this difference results from the unique persistence in Japan of "prematerialist" values, of which qualitative *belonging* to family and community is central:

> This item, dealing with "a less impersonal, more human society," was included in a 1976 Japanese survey. . . . Throughout Western society, the various versions of this item are substantially more apt to be chosen by the young, the affluent, and the well-educated than by their opposite numbers. In Japan, this item is just as likely to be given relatively high priority by the old, the less educated, and those in rural settings (1990: 146) . . . The fact that the decline of traditional Prematerialist values is superimposed on the rise of Postmaterialist values in the Japanese case alters the structure of the Materialist/Postmaterialist dimension in that country. While emphasis on economic and physical security go together in Japan, as elsewhere, emphasis on belonging does not constitute part of a Postmaterialist cluster in the way it does throughout the West. While younger and better-educated Japanese do show a clear-cut preference for having "more say in important government decisions" and "protecting freedom of speech," they may see emphasis on such goals as "harmonious human relations" as implying a paternalistic constraint on individual self-expression (1990: 151).

With such a relatively large proportion of Japanese citizens attached to "prematerialist" values, Inglehart infers that it is not surprising to find that overall, a lower proportion of "postmaterialists" exists in Japan than in other advanced industrial societies. Elsewhere, the slower industrialization process made it more likely for current generations to have grown up at least partially under advanced industrialization's cultural influence. Inglehart concludes that as Japan's transition to advanced industrial society proceeds, it *will* eventually "catch up" to the West culturally (see implications of Ogburn 1961).

However, when taking into account the recent growth of political apathy in Japan, in particular among young persons, Inglehart's "time-lag" hypothesis appears unsatisfactory. His hypothesis assumes that, as in other countries, young persons are relatively more receptive to all aspects of the NPC than older persons and, for that reason, the future influence of the young will eventually lead the NPC to set in. Yet, evidence in this paper reveals that Japan's deviation from NPC activism is especially marked among the young. "Younger and better-educated Japanese" *do not* show a clear-cut preference for having "more say in important decisions" or for "protecting freedom of speech." This phenomenon of growing apathy rather than activism importantly challenges Inglehart's time-lag theory.

The Significance of Sub-Dimensions in "Postmaterialist" Values

Clark and Inglehart explain the emergence of NPC political activities—that is, greater activism in "new social movements"—with a social psychological perspective: "Our explanation for such movements is social psychological: as the family declines in holistic, emotive, and role-defining functions, other groups rise in importance" (1990: 20). Underlying this explanation, Clark and Inglehart implicitly posit two distinct stages of change in people's orientations: (1) when liberated from the confining, role-defining influence of the family, change occurs in people's consciousness from traditional or materialist values towards less materialistic, more libertarian values; and (2) a reorganization of reference group orientations occurs to seek out involvement in politics and politically active groups. But need the second stage necessarily follow the first? Assuming that people increasingly embrace such abstract values as "belonging," "esteem" or "self-realization" *outside* the political sphere, is it necessary that they will demand more participation *in* politics? Or might growing apathy be a *predictable* rather than an *exceptional* outcome?

Some Japanese scholars have tested for a linkage between cultural values and political activities. They divided Inglehart's "postmaterialism" into (1) economic versus post-economic orientations in the private, socio-economic sphere, and (2) order versus participatory orientations in the public, political sphere. They reclassified the 12 goals on Inglehart's questionnaire as in Table 5.3. These scholars then hypothesized that persons who embrace "post-economic" values in the *private* sphere will *not* necessarily support participation in the public, political sphere (Shakai Keizai Kokumin Kaigi 1988: 155).

To test their hypothesis, these scholars conducted a varimax rotation factor analysis on the 12-goal 1986 Japanese survey data. This statistical technique produces clusters of items that tap underlying sub-dimensions in the data. The technique produced precisely the two sub-dimensions and binary goal oppositions that were hypothesized. The first sub-dimension included "economic growth," "stable economy," and "controlling inflation" (negatively), plus the

TABLE 5.3 Revised Classification of Inglehart's 12-Item Value Scale

Private (Economic) Sphere: Economic vs. Post-Economic Values	Public (Political) Sphere: Order vs. Participatory Values
Stable economy Economic growth Fight rising prices	Maintain order Strong defense forces Fight crime
More beautiful cities Less impersonal society Ideas count Freedom of speech	More say in government More say on job

Source: Shakai Keizai Kokumin Kaigi 1988: 155.

postmaterialist goals of "a society where ideas count," "freedom of expression," "less impersonal society," and "more beautiful cities" (positively). The second sub-dimension elicited the remaining goals: "maintain order" and "strong defense forces" (positively) and "more say on the job" and "more say in government" (negatively) (see Shakai Keizai Kokumin Kaigi 1988: 156).

These results thus confirm that Inglehart's "postmaterialism" orientation includes two sub-dimensions: economic versus post-economic values in private, socio-economic life, and order-oriented versus participatory values in public, political life. The trends among the young are as follows. For those over 25, the evidence confirms Inglehart's prediction that younger persons exhibit more postmaterialism than their elders: that is, both more "post-economic" and more "participatory" values. However, among the very *youngest* age group, aged 20-24, support for the two types of postmaterialist values *declines* substantially, especially for *participatory* values, where they rank the same as respondents in their forties. This confirms earlier findings in this chapter that although Japanese youth significantly incline towards NPC cultural or lifestyle concerns, they hold fewer proactive, participatory orientations.

Theories of Contemporary Japanese Political Culture

If political activity in new social movements does *not* substitute for declining involvement in families and traditional organizations, what alternatives have arisen? I consider three: (1) consumerism, or pleasure-oriented lifestyle, (2) religion, and (3) nationalist ideology.

Consumerism: Self-Expression Through "Conspicuous Consumption"

Rather than becoming politically active, one alternative is to cultivate a lifestyle of lavish, private consumption. In this connection, Kojima Kazuhito (1980) argues that "pleasure orientation" values, in which people prefer "current pleasure" over "goals in future," are rising in Japan. People who adopt this orientation tend to prioritize enrichment of their own life and leisure in the private sphere, as opposed to proactive engagement with social problems in the public sphere.

Support for the pleasure orientation has risen especially among Japanese youth. For instance, one Japanese survey indicates for multiple age groupings whether respondents are most concerned in their daily life to: (1) manage to make ends meet, (2) enjoy a rich and pleasant consumption life, or (3) enjoy emotional satisfaction which cannot be obtained by money and goods. Among the youngest respondents, aged 20-29, 30% chose the pleasure-oriented option (the second), nearly double the percentage of respondents choosing that option from any other age grouping (Tokei Suri Kenkyujo Kokuminsei Chosa Iinkai 1992:166).

To summarize the evidence in this chapter on changing values in Japan, younger Japanese citizens are more likely than older ones to prioritize both "post-economic" and "participatory" values; but this tendency faces a substantial setback amongst the very youngest citizens, those in their twenties in the early 1990s. By contrast, there is no similar setback among those in their twenties in the trend towards a "pleasure orientation." Japanese youth may increasingly be compensating for the decline of traditional family and community attachments through consumption rather than political activism.

Japanese Religion

Clark and Inglehart observe that some organized religions retard the NPC. For instance, Catholicism's mandate of personal loyalty to the church and its representatives may heighten personalistic and socially conservative outlooks. In this volume, Paul Butts reports such impact. He finds that "religiosity," not just within Catholicism but of *any* kind, is associated across many advanced industrial societies with holding more traditional, socially conservative political attitudes and with less political activity.

If religiosity has a traditional, conservative impact elsewhere, it would seem reasonable to expect the same in Japan, where Confucian tradition places great emphasis on personal loyalty to family and local community (Ward 1965). Yet, recent evidence suggests that Japan provides a curious exception to the rule. From a comprehensive study, Mita Munesuke (1980) finds that from 1973 to 1978, the most conspicuous change in the cultural orientations of Japanese youth is a rise in religiosity. More critically, Mita observes that the kinds of religious aspects that have become increasingly prevalent are sustainable by *individuals,* apart from attachment to an organized church or traditional doctrine. By contrast, the religious aspects that have become *less* prevalent *do* require a formal allegiance. For example, Mita reports that among 20- to 24-year-old males, the percentage indicating a belief in God in the abstract grew substantially from 8% to 21%, but those indicating a belief in the Bible or the official religious canon declined from 7.8% to 4.8%. Mita theorizes that the apparent disjunction between growing personal religiosity and declining allegiance to formal religious institutions reflects the rise among Japanese youth of a new, highly individualistic form of religious conviction, which he terms "cult," corresponding to Emile Durkheim's ([1897] 1951) "cult of the individual."

From further study, Mita reports that individualistic religious beliefs have become especially prevalent among young urban residents and college students, two subgroups which Western theorists identify as catalysts of liberal new social movements: from 1973 to 1978, belief in "God" increased from 7% to 24% among young urban residents (in cities with more than 100,000 residents) and from 6% to 21% among college students.

The possibly growing prevalence of *individualistic* religious beliefs in Japan may explain why Butts (this volume) finds that Japan is unique in the relationship between religiosity and social conservatism. Of fourteen industrialized countries, Butts reports that his complex measure of "religiosity" is the single strongest predictor of social conservatism everywhere *except in Japan*. There, religiosity does not even reach minimal statistical significance, except among women for one of five conservatism measures. Butts hypothesizes that Japan differs from Western industrialized societies due to some distinct meaning of religion in Japan. When joined with Mita's work, this distinct meaning could consist of the growing prevalence in Japan of an individualistic religious orientation.

Even though religiosity in Japan may not deter formation of socially liberal *values*, it may deter participation in new social movements: because, by pursuing religious activities, socially liberal persons in Japan may remove themselves from the potential pool of otherwise available new social movement activists. This effect would be less likely in other countries, where persons who turn to religious activities are more likely to be socially conservative and hence are *already*, for that reason, ruled out from potential new social movement involvement. In sum, theorizing in this subsection on the impact of growing, individualistic Japanese religiosity evokes predictions both of rising socially liberal or NPC *values* and of declining overt political *activism*: just what the Japanese evidence indicates.

Still, in concluding, it is not apparent that adherence to individualistic religion is significantly on the rise in Japan. The change in that direction which Mita identifies from 1973 to 1978 is hardly sufficient to indicate a genuine, long-term trend. In fact, long-term trend data seem to indicate that younger Japanese citizens are *less* likely than older ones to engage in any religious activities or to believe in any religious tenets (NHK Hoso Bunka Chosa Kenkyujo, unpub-

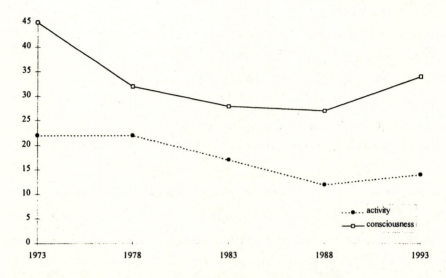

FIGURE 5.8 Religiosity Among Japanese Youth, 1973-1993
Note: The question for the "activity" trend line is, "Are there any religious activities you
do?" The question for the "consciousness" trend line is, "Are there any religious tenets
you believe in?" The trend lines are for those who answered none.
Source: NHK Hoso Bunka Chosa Kenkyujo, unpublished material.

lished material). Still, as Figure 5.8 indicates, these recent data do suggest a
possible reversal towards greater religiosity, when comparing the youngest Japanese citizens with citizens just one generation older. While 22% of respondents
aged 20-24 did not engage in any religious activities in 1973, only 14% did not do
so in 1993. Also, in 1973, 45% of respondents aged 20-24 did not believe in any
religious tenets, whereas in 1993, only 34% had no religious beliefs.

The precise direction and degree of the current trend in religiosity notwithstanding, the hypothesis remains conceivable that the *comparative* proportion of
new social movement activists is *less* in Japan than in Western industrialized
countries, due to the lure of religious pursuits to many Japanese social liberals.
Nevertheless, religious cults have also attracted interest in several Western
countries in recent decades.

Japanese Nationalist Ideology

Some political socialization researchers posit that socialization generates
two types of commitments: (1) "specific support" for select political parties,
policies, or ideologies, such as feminism, environmentalism, or traditionalism,
and (2) "diffuse support," or general feelings of patriotism towards one's nation

(Dawson, Prewitt, and Dawson 1977). Viewed in these terms, the transition to the New Political Culture involves a change in the most popular forms of "specific support." That is, the NPC embraces some specific political values and policies over others, but neither it nor its contrasting alternatives speak to the issue of "diffuse" support, or basic national allegiance. Thus the potential for the NPC to emerge would seem greatest when political discourse focuses more on internal political differences and debate *within* a nation than on a generalized patriotism. If, by contrast, political discourse focuses more on repeated affirmations of the "diffuse support" which binds the nation together and distinguishes it from "foreign" elements, internal political cultural evolution—for example, towards the NPC—might be stunted.

This context heightens the significance of Japanese nationalism. Figures 5.9A-B show the gradual rise of "diffuse," nationalist sentiments in Japan from 1973 to 1993. In 1973, 91% of all Japanese citizens surveyed answered that they are "happy to be born in Japan"; in 1993, 97% gave that response. This increase is mainly due to the much more dramatic changes that have occurred among younger and more educated Japanese citizens. Whereas in 1973, 82% of respondents aged 20-24 answered that they are happy to be born in Japan, in 1993, 95% gave that response (NHK Hoso Bunka Chosa Kenkyujo, unpublished material).

Japan is not unique for nationalist sentiments, as is clear from ethnic rivalries throughout Eastern Europe and the rise of neo-fascist and anti-foreigner attitudes elsewhere. However, the high rate of "diffuse support" among current Japanese youth suggests a new form of nationalism. Indeed, the recent prevalence of *nihonjinron* seems to be a product and producer of this growing "diffuse support." *Nihonjinron* is a name for essays on what it means to be Japanese, particularly in the face of the importation of goods, ideas, and practices from the West. Peter Dale (1986) reports that in the roughly 30 years between 1946 and 1978, approximately 700 *nihonjinron* were published, but a remarkable 25% of those were published in the final three years studied, from just 1976 to 1978. From analyzing the content of the *nihonjinron*, Dale attributes to many of them three core assumptions or motivations. First, they implicitly assume that the Japanese people comprise a culturally and socially homogenous racial entity, whose essence is virtually unchanged from prehistoric times. Second, they presuppose that this fundamental essence differs radically from that of all other known peoples. Third, the essays are consciously nationalistic, displaying a conceptual and methodological hostility to any mode of analysis which appears to derive from non-Japanese sources.

Political leaders have taken up the nationalist mantle as well. Prime Minister Ohira Masayoshi launched the "age of culture" program in 1979 for establishment of a genuinely "comprehensive Japanese culture" and for a new assessment of the "special quality of Japan's culture" (see Harootunian 1989: 80). Prime Minister Nakasone declared that Japan had won an economic and intellectual *victory* over the West, asserting that in no other nation "does information

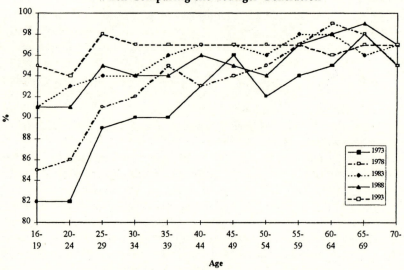

A. Rising Nationalism Is Especially Apparent When Comparing the Younger Generation

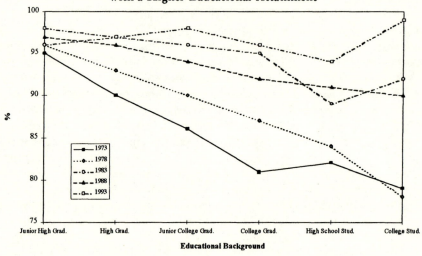

B. Rising Nationalism Becomes More Apparent Among Citizens with a Higher Educational Attainment

FIGURE 5.9 Nationalist Sentiments Are Rising in Japan, 1973-1993
Note: the question for Figure 5.9 is, "Do you think you are happy to be born in Japan?" The trend lines are for those who answered, "Yes, I think so."
Source: NHK Hoso Bunka Chosa Kenkyujo, unpublished material.

come so naturally into one's head. . . . [T]here is no other country which puts such diverse information so accurately into the ears of its people. It has become a very intelligent society—much more so than America" (cited in Ivy 1989: 22).

Why did Japanese nationalism come to the fore in the 1970s, when it had been relatively dormant in preceding decades? Masao Miyoshi (1989) suggests that immediately after World War II, the prospects posed by select, West-supported postwar policies for allowing Japan to catch up to the West economically and a general feeling that Japan needed to atone for "war guilt" stifled openly nationalistic expressions. However, by the mid-1970s, the perception spread that Japan had completed its economic, political, and moral recovery. With the West increasingly a global competitor, and with "Japan bashing" overseas adding fuel to the fire, the time was ripe for nationalism to surface. Interestingly, "Japan-bashing" confirms from outside a key component of the same nationalistic ideas simmering inside Japan, in that *both* tendencies constitute the Japanese as socially and culturally distinct. Adding finally to the self-assurance of nationalistic Japanese authors has been the growing post-1960s ambivalence of many Westerners towards the moral correctness and political effectiveness of the West's own past conduct in international affairs, in particular towards Japan and (for Americans) towards Japanese-Americans intered during World War II.

The "diffuse support" discursive orientation of Japanese nationalism is obvious. Adding to its NPC-deterring effects, it fosters a subtle "specific support" of the politics of tradition. This occurs with Japanese nationalism's reaction against all policies or policy directions perceived to have been imposed during the postwar military occupation. Since those policy directions tended to be towards more progressive, "modern" or NPC political values and policies, the reaction's ideological effect has been to reframe Japan's internal "traditional-modern" value cleavage as pitting Japan as a culturally unified, tradition-based nation against the West. In this context, "traditional" political modes like clientelism can be articulated and praised as integral to Japanese culture, or in other words as a necessary aspect of "diffuse support," rather than as merely one of many "specific" modes. The Japanese media tended in the 1970s to portray clientelism as representing the essence of Japanese culture or a secret underlying Japan's economic success. Thus contrary to how many theorists characterize the media, they may not always have a socially liberalizing or modernizing impact. Instead, the media may primarily reflect the socio-political and socio-cultural direction of powerful and potentially conservative social or political forces.

Conclusion

Japan shares important political cultural characteristics with other advanced industrial societies. High affluence and education among substantial segments of the population, rise of the mass media, proliferation of advertising and growth of consumer pursuits all link Japan with the West. These factors have generated aspects of the NPC in Japan; but perhaps as importantly, they have suppressed others. In this chapter, I aimed to show that the causes of this suppression should not be reduced to specifics concerning "Japanese culture" or "late modernization." Rather, the causes can be found within fundamental conditions of advanced or "post-industrial" society.

Some available theories on the effects of *post-industrial* or *postmodern* society may be instructive. They can be loosely summed up with the aphorism, "Success breeds complacency." Amidst rapid economic growth and affluence, Japanese citizens may increasingly perceive that Japan's major social ills have been cured. That may lead political protest to lose some of its urgency and persons to be drawn increasingly to non-political pursuits, like private consumption or religion. Also, when persons do think of politics, they are less likely to take sides on divisive issues like labor conflict, women's rights, or the environment, and more likely to stress general concerns relating to Japanese unity or to its perceived national interests: for example, "diffuse" as opposed to "specific" forms of political support. Exhibitions of vague, "diffuse," patriotic sentiments can justify a citizen's wish to feel a sense of national belonging and involvement without incurring the time and effort to obtain information or act on specific issues.

Rather than rising religiosity or nationalism, a "postmodernist" account would tend to place more emphasis on the depoliticizing effects of the "consumption" industry: on the first of the three explanations offered in the preceding section. From Daniel Bell (1976) to the critical pessimists Max Horkheimer and Theodor Adorno ([1944] 1991), many twentieth century theorists have seen in the proliferation of informational media, popular entertainment, and advertising promotion of an increasingly non-political, consumption-driven society. Thus increased media access does not necessarily produced rising political knowledge, interest, or activism. Rather than information, persons can use the media for gossip, sensational "news magazine" programs, or sports. As Clark and Inglehart sardonically comment, "It is hard to rouse party militants [note pun] from a comfortable TV and beer (1990: 28)." Just this effect is evident in contemporary Japan; also, at least hypothetically, this outcome can happen in *any* post-industrial society.

Post-industrial society may not bring democratic revitalization, where enlightened, active citizens seize popular control of decaying political institutions, or participate in "new social movements." Lurking underneath is the quite contrary and powerful specter of growing disinterest and depoliticization. Pleasure-oriented lifestyles, the proliferation of new religious cults, or the rise of nationalism may surface. Japan's deviation from the NPC, therefore, should not be interpreted as an indication of its "unique" historical experience or cultural background, but as a manifestation of one possible consequence arising from post-industrial society itself. The Japanese case effectively illustrates post-industrial society's ambivalent character.

Notes

1. The Western European countries are France, Britain, West Germany, Italy, the Netherlands, Denmark, Belgium, Spain, Ireland, Northern Ireland, Norway, Sweden, Iceland, Finland, Portugal, and Austria. With the United States and Canada, this produces a total of eighteen Western industrialized countries. Japan brings the total to nineteen. Among those, Japan would rank sixteenth in postmaterialism, using the specified measure. The only countries below it would be Denmark, Norway, and Portugal.

2. Flanagan (1991) uses the antinomy of "modern" versus "traditional" values. He considers as "modern" values: (1) "libertarian" versus "authoritarian" values concerning respect for authority, (2) open political participation and an active political opposition, (3) "universalistic" versus "personalistic" criteria for allocating jobs or other socioeconomic benefits and for relating to government officials, and (4) "cosmopolitan" versus "parochial" attitudes concerning the prioritization of national versus local political issues. While these dimensions vary somewhat from the NPC, it is likely that holders of "modern" and NPC values are similar in overall political outlook.

Part 3

The New Middle Class Politics:

What Is Special About the Politics of
Professionals and Other Middle Class Persons?

6

The Politics of Professionals in Five
Advanced Industrial Societies

Steven Brint,
William L. Cunningham,
and
Rebecca S. K. Li

Professionals have been a fast-growing stratum in the late twentieth century, making analysis of their political inclinations especially valuable, with implications for citizen politics generally. Before World War II, less than 1 percent of all employed people in the United States were college graduates and classified by the Census Bureau as "professional, technical, and kindred" workers. Today, the comparable group is more than fourteen times as large. There has been similar growth of the professional population in other advanced industrial societies. Theories of political change emphasizing the rise of "the information age" or "post-industrial society," like that in the introduction to this volume, have been constructed largely in response to the growth of the professional stratum (Bell 1973; Reich 1991). Social scientists who see the potential for a politically "progressive" orientation note that professional elites have often held ideologies promoting "social responsibility," opposing the more purely individualistic utilitarianism of "classical liberalism" (or "economic conservatism" in contemporary usage) (see, e.g., Haskell 1984; Brint 1994: chs. 1-2). Still, professionals have often clearly inclined towards the right of the political spectrum.

When we consider the variety of professional occupations—doctors, lawyers, professors, engineers, computer scientists, architects, accountants, writers

AUTHORS' NOTE: We would like to thank Thomas Boje, Rogers Brubaker, Terry Nichols Clark, James A. Davis, Seymour Martin Lipset, Misagh Parsa, Linda Brewster Stearns, and Frederick D. Weil for comments that improved earlier drafts of this paper.

and editors, policy analysts—we may at first be overwhelmed by their evident differences. The commonalities that professionals share come out only when we compare them to other kinds of workers. Professional occupations tend to require high levels of education and are based on the cultivation of problem-solving skills and judgment. Through the credentialing process, professionals obtain some protection from the free-for-all of unregulated labor markets. Also, professionals usually have a great deal of autonomy over how they go about their work; they are frequently less intensively supervised than other workers. At the same time, they are not bosses in the same way that top executives and even middle managers are. (See the discussions in Derber 1983; Freidson 1986: chs. 4 and 7; and Brint 1994: ch. 2.)

For all of these reasons, if a new kind of class politics is developing in the more advanced or "post-industrial" societies, professionals are a strategic group to examine. But *is* such a politics developing? And, if so, is it a new conservatism, a new liberalism, or something in between? Are the basic political tendencies of professionals evident across the developed world, or do professional politics take different forms in different societies?

We address these questions by analyzing survey data from several industrial societies. We will show that professionals generally tend to be conservative on economic issues and liberal on issues related to social tolerance and to the protection of individual civil liberties. We will also show that some consistent bases of political division also exist among professionals—and that those in the *growing* professional occupations are the *most* conservative on economic issues and the most liberal on civil liberties issues. At the same time, we will show that national contexts greatly matter in explaining the politics of professionals—indeed, specific national contexts matter more than cross-national, common tendencies. Countries whose overall political culture embraces conservative norms have professionals with views on the right, while countries with social democratic norms have more liberal-minded professionals. However, this general tendency notwithstanding, the range of individual country-based differences is striking. Distinct national patterns of cleavage in the professional and managerial classes are also evident in the data.

We will additionally argue that if by "class politics" one means a definable political orientation among people in a social stratum, then the "new class" of educated professionals can be plausibly described as promoting a class politics. In the United States, this politics would be ideologically close to "neo-liberalism" or socially liberal Republicanism. If by "class politics," however, one requires a distinctive class-based *economic* interest that is opposed to the interests of dominant social groups, then professional "knowledge workers" *cannot* be described as promoting a class politics. The development of such a political orientation among professionals would, in all likelihood, require high levels of populist social unrest and an updating of the "social responsibility" ideologies characteristic of turn-of-the-century professionalism.

The Changing Portraits of Professional Politics

Let us begin with a brief history of efforts by social scientists to characterize the politics of professionals in the wealthier industrial societies. Taken together, the differences suggested by social scientists over the last 30 years show just how historically contingent are major images of professional politics, and how these images reflect broader political changes.

Before 1960, when professionals were still a small part of the labor force, there were two common images of their political views. They were most often described as a *conservative middle class group*—more highly educated than business people, but not significantly more liberal politically (see, e.g., Anderson and Davidson 1943; Campbell, Gurin, and Miller 1954; Lipset 1960: ch. 9). As an advantaged group, they naturally inclined toward conservative parties and policies that supported the established order. There is also a hint in the social scientific writing of the period that some well-established professionals, in alliance with members of the upper classes, acted as a kind of *social balance wheel*, using reasoned analysis to moderate the passions evoked in democratic politics (Lipset 1960: 318-22). *Intellectuals*, by contrast, had a reputation for being attracted to reformist and radical politics (Shils 1958; Lipset 1960: ch. 10); but intellectuals were considered as distinct from the *professional* stratum. In the Mannheimian tradition, they were considered a quite distinct and more socially "unattached" status group.

These images of conservatism and moderation seemed unable to account for the apparently liberal turn in the politics of professionals in the later 1960s and early 1970s, a time of social conflict when highly educated people often seemed to be more critical of their societies than accepting of them. During this period, two new theories of political change emerged. These were the theories of "postmaterialist politics" and of the "new class." In both, professionals played an important role—this time as a distinctively *liberal* group.

The idea of *post-materialist politics* is associated with the work of the political scientist Ronald Inglehart (1973, 1977). He argued that the "materialist" conflicts of the industrial age were resolved in favor of institutionalized wage bargaining and the social safety nets established by the welfare state. As contention over the materialist issues of the industrial period faded, new issues came to the fore. These post-materialist issues had to do with "higher-order" social needs (an idea borrowed from the psychologist Abraham Maslow's "needs hierarchy")—that is, needs beyond those related to sheer survival. They included "quality-of-life" needs (such as needs for a beautiful and well-preserved environment), "expression" needs (such as needs for greater democratic participation in social life), and "belongingness" needs (such as needs of previously disadvantaged groups to gain full social inclusion). Inglehart anticipated that younger and more highly educated people would be in the vanguard of post-materialist politics, because they would be more likely to be future-oriented rather than oriented to present material satisfaction—and because, in an age of affluence, they were more likely to have had their material needs already satisfied.

The *new class theory* also gained currency during the 1970s. Two new class theories emerged—one encompassing the broad stratum of highly educated professionals (Ehrenreich and Ehrenreich 1977; Gouldner 1979) and the other focusing only on the most "intellectually oriented" professions, located in the public and non-profit sectors (Kristol 1972, 1975; Bruce-Briggs 1979). The broader version included engineers and scientists as much as artists, writers, and professors, while the narrower version focused on those latter occupations. The broader version concentrated on a group that looked more like a "class" in the sociological sense of the term, while the narrower version concentrated on a group that looked more like a class in the politically self-conscious and active sense of the term. Both versions of the theory argued that, as conflict between labor and capital subsided in mature industrial societies, a new kind of class conflict developed, this time dividing a newly powerful class of professionals, rich in "cultural capital," from the old dominant class of business owners and executives, rich in "economic capital." The distinctive interests of the new professional class were considered to be (1) improving the wage situation of people with high educational qualifications and (2) protecting the autonomy of professional work from rationalization by bureaucratic authorities. This class was also portrayed as interested in gaining power through advancing cultural values, associated with what was learned in an advanced education, that were distinctly more liberal than the values of the old dominant class. According to the new class theory, the "middle class" thus divided into a traditionally conservative business-oriented wing and an "oppositional intelligentsia" (Ladd 1979). A cognate view was developed in the work of the French social theorist Pierre Bourdieu (1984 [1979]: ch. 5). For Bourdieu, professionals who rank higher in education than income are a "dominated fraction of the dominant class" and are expected to adopt more left-of-center politics than upper-income professionals and managers, who are the "dominant fraction of the dominant class."

Predictably enough, as politics in advanced industrial societies swung to the right beginning in the mid-1970s, new images of professional politics again developed.[1] A full-fledged theory of professional politics for this more conservative age was introduced in the *cumulative trends* theory of the senior author of this paper (Brint 1984, 1985). Brint argued that the relatively privileged economic circumstances of professionals encouraged conservatism on economic issues, while their relative cosmopolitanism and lack of anchorage in socially conservative moral communities encouraged liberalism on social issues. The theory interpreted professional class liberalism as based, in large measure, on compositional and historical changes in the post-World War II period. In the first place, the composition of the professional class changed in the 1960s and 1970s. Those locations that grew fastest—academe, government, and others—were those traditionally more supportive of liberal politics. Also, the political emphases of the 1960s and early 1970s, particularly the salience of non-economic issues (such as war, civil rights, and protest) highlighted the kinds of issues on which professional class liberalism is greatest. These trends largely reversed in the later 1970s and 1980s. During this period, private sector employment and applied technical occupations grew faster than public sector employment and the social and cultural occupations. Moreover, the issues axis shifted dramatically toward a focus on the stagnating economy, highlighting issues on which professionals tend to be conservative rather than liberal.

Research on the Political Orientations of Professionals

The various theories prompted many empirical investigations (see, e.g., Brint 1984; Inglehart 1977; Kriesi 1989; Ladd 1979; Lamont 1993; Lipset 1981: 503-23; Clark and Ferguson 1983; Hout, Manza, and Brooks 1994; Martin 1994). The characterization of professionals as economic conservatives and social liberals has been widely supported in empirical studies (Clark and Ferguson 1983; Brint 1984). However, some intriguing counter-indicative findings can also be found. For example, Brint (1994: 177-84) showed that on select economic issues, professionals are now more liberal than blue-collar workers, who have traditionally been the most liberal on economic issues. For example, Hout, Brooks, and Manza (1994) provided evidence that professionals have shifted toward a stronger preference for candidates of the Democratic Party in the recent national elections in the United States, while blue-collar workers have tended to shift away from the Democrats. On the basis of these findings, Brint distinguished between "redistributive" and "regulatory" forms of liberalism on economic issues—the first more attractive to lower-income groups like blue-collar workers and the second more attractive to professionals.

Perhaps the major weakness of the research thus far is that it has lacked a comparative focus. Many studies have been based on American data alone. With rare exceptions, cross-national studies have been primarily interested in revealing similar trends across several industrial countries (e.g., Inglehart 1977, 1987), rather than in revealing ways that the specific national context can also shape professional politics. For instance, the introduction to this volume proposes a framework which characterizes "post-industrial politics" as a multinational phenomenon; but this framework may not be sufficiently sensitive to the differences that distinguish various post-industrial societies from each other. Perhaps the most national context-sensitive comparative work to date has been that of the senior author of this paper (Brint 1994: ch. 9). That work suffers, however, from being limited to data collected at one point in time. Snapshots at one point in time make it difficult to determine whether moods of the moment or deeper structural forces are at work.

Survey Evidence from the
International Social Science Program

In this paper, we use citizen survey data to characterize the dominant tendencies in the political attitudes and identifications of professionals in contemporary advanced industrial societies. We undertake two major sets of analyses. The first aims to show common, cross-national patterns in the politics of professionals, including common patterns of internal division. Within the limits of the available data, these analyses attempt to answer the question: Is there a common form of professional politics across the more advanced industrial societies? The second set of analyses aims to compare the strength of these common patterns of professional politics with the strength of forces emerging out of the distinctive national political contexts in which professionals from different countries are situated. These analyses attempt to answer the question: Are common structural forces or distinctive national contexts more important determinants of the politics of professionals?

We would not want to claim too much for what can be known from public opinion data alone. This type of data cannot probe the inner life or deepest psychological impulses of respondents. It cannot help to understand the thrust-and-parry of real political conflict—or how events and policies shape those conflicts. Survey evidence provides a broad bird's-eye view of public opinion at a given point in time. In real life, this continually changes in response to new forces in the environment, new messages that generate a following, and new kinds of elective affinities that come into play. Survey evidence provides important clues and indications about where we are and where we might be heading. This, of course, remains important.

The data in this paper are drawn from the International Social Science Program's 1985 and 1990 "Role of Government" surveys. We look at responses from five countries—Australia, Great Britain, Italy, the United States, and West Germany—whose populations were surveyed in both years. We will examine those questions repeated word-for-word, or nearly word-for-word, in both years. There were 33 items that satisfied two additional criteria for inclusion: (1) that significant levels of variation in response existed in each of the countries, and (2) that the responses to the items could be arranged uncontroversially on a liberal-conservative or left-right continuum.[2] This set of 33 included 31 attitude items and two items that measured identification with parties of the right and left.

We were unable to develop scales to provide summary measures for the survey items, because of the certainty that the error variance for scales developed in two survey years would be substantially different. The analyses were, therefore, based on the individual items rather than summary scales. To aid interpretation, we group items into three broad categories: (1) civil liberties, (2) government social welfare responsibilities and welfare state spending, and (3) government economic policies and regulation of business. The party identification items are grouped with items concerning welfare state policies, since they seemed to be most closely related to this set. Issues of freedom of speech and assembly and other civil liberties protections are, of course, only one part of the issues conventionally included under the heading of "social issues," but unfortunately, these are all we have in the ISSP.[3]

Table 6.1 provides detailed information on the dependent variables in the analysis (the 33 political survey items). The numbers to the right of the table are the percentages of the total pooled responses from the five countries that take the more liberal positions in each of the two years. This includes everyone in the surveys, both professionals and nonprofessionals.

Table 6.1 indicates that responses were relatively stable over the five-year period. None showed very sharp shifts and about half changed by five percentage points or less. It is particularly interesting that overwhelming majorities—in the neighborhood of 80 percent or more in all five societies—favored weaker labor unions, higher levels of deregulation of industry, further cuts in government spending, and increased spending on law enforcement. (Items concerning law enforcement are not included in Table 6.1 because we did not conduct further analyses of these questions. See endnote 1.) These items might be considered the core of the contemporary conservative orthodoxy in the world's richer industrial societies, an orthodoxy that arose in the years following the "slumpflation" of the mid-1970s. (We discuss the trends in political attitudes and party identifications in greater detail in the appendix.)

Cross-National Commonalities in the Politics of Professionals

We first assess common aspects of the politics of professionals across the five societies. Table 6.2 does this by comparing the attitudes of professionals with the attitudes of blue-collar workers. Blue-collar workers have been stalwarts of the "old politics" of welfare state expansion in industrial societies, so they make a useful reference group. Table 6.2 displays: (1) the number of items in each of the three attitude domains in which professionals gave more liberal responses than blue-collar workers; (2) the number of items on which blue-collar workers gave more liberal responses; and (3) the number on which no significant differences were found between the two groups. The data can be summarized as follows. Professionals in all five countries were consistently more liberal than blue-collar workers on civil liberties issues.[4] Professionals were sometimes more liberal, sometimes more conservative than blue-collar workers on welfare state issues. Finally, professionals were generally (though not exclusively) more conservative than blue-collar workers on economic policy and business regulation issues.

If we look a little more carefully at the data on attitudes about welfare state programs, clearer patterns emerge. Professionals and blue-collar workers most

TABLE 6.1 Information on Dependent Variables, Five ISSP Countries

	1985 Total Liberal %	1990 Total Liberal %
Civil Liberties Variables (N = 11):		
OBEY (Should citizens obey laws without exception?) Value 2 (follow conscience) coded as liberal; value 1 (obey without exception) coded as conservative.	66	66
PROTEST (Should protest demonstrations be allowed?)	62	78
STRIKE (Should anti-government strikes be allowed?)	36	35
REVMEET (Should revolutionaries be allowed to hold public meetings?)	54	62
REVBOOKS (Should revolutionaries be allowed to publish books?)	63	70
RACMEET (Should racists be allowed to hold public meetings?)	40	44
RACBOOKS (Should racists be allowed to publish books?) Values 1 and 2 (definitely and probably allow) coded as liberal; values 3 and 4 (probably and definitely not allow) coded as conservative.	49	50
TAPCRIM (Should police be allowed to tap the phone of a known criminal?)	44	52
MAILCRIM (Should police be allowed to open the mail of a known criminal?)	62	71
HOLDCRIM (Should police be allowed to detain a known criminal?) Values 3 and 4 (probably and definitely not allow) coded as liberal; values 1 and 2 (probably and definitely allow) coded as conservative.	40	48
MISTAKE (Which is the worse type of judicial mistake?) Value 1 (convict innocent) coded as liberal; value 2 (let guilty person go) coded as conservative.	79	77
Welfare State Variables (N = 11):		
CUTSPEND (Should government spending be cut?) Values 4 and 5 (against and strongly against) coded as liberal; values 1, 2, and 3 (strongly favor, favor, and neutral) coded as conservative.	17	12
CREATJOB (Should government be responsible for creating jobs?) Values 1 and 2 (strongly favor and favor) coded as liberal; values 3, 4, and 5 (neutral, oppose, and strongly oppose) coded as conservative.	82	75
NATENVIR (How much should government spend on the environment?)	51	73

(continues)

TABLE 6.1 *(continued)*

	1985 Total Liberal %	1990 Total Liberal %
NATEDUC (How much should government spend on education?)	63	68
NATAGED (How much should government spend on old age pensions?)	62	61
NATUNEMPL (How much should government spend on unemployment benefits?)	35	30
NATARTS (How much should government spend on culture and the arts?) Values 1 and 2 (spend much more and spend more) coded as liberal; values 3, 4, and 5 (neutral, spend less, and spend much less) coded as conservative.	17	20
GOVJOBS (Is government responsible for providing jobs for all?)	69	61
GOVUNEMP (Is government responsible for the unemployed?) Values 1 and 2 (definitely should be and probably should be) coded as liberal; values 3, 4, and 5 (neutral, probably should not be, and definitely should not be) coded as conservative.	75	69
RGTPARTY (Does respondent identify with a political party of the right?) Conservative, Christian Democratic, Nationalist, Australian Liberal, and American Republican parties coded as conservative; all others coded as nonconservative.	38	31
LFTPARTY (Does respondent identify with a political party of the left?) Communist, Socialist, Social Democratic, Labour, Green, Free Democrats, Alternative List, British Liberal, and American Democratic parties coded as liberal; all others coded as non-liberal.	42	39

Economic Policy and Business Regulation Variables (N = 11):

TAXRICH (How much income tax should the rich be required to pay?) Values 1 and 2 (much larger and larger proportion) coded as liberal; values 3, 4, and 5 (same, smaller, and much smaller proportion) coded as conservative.	76	77
REDUCE (Is government responsible for reducing income differences?) Values 1 and 2 (strongly agree and agree) coded as liberal; values 3, 4, and 5 (neutral, disagree, and strongly disagree) coded as conservative.	52	51

(continues)

TABLE 6.1 *(continued)*

	1985 Total Liberal %	1990 Total Liberal %
PRICES (Should government be responsible for keeping prices under control by law?) Values 1 and 2 (definitely and probably should be) coded as liberal; values 3 and 4 (probably and definitely should not be) coded as conservative.	67	56
WAGES (Should government be able to control wages by law?) Values 1 and 2 (strongly favor and favor) coded as liberal; values 3, 4, and 5 (neutral, oppose, and strongly oppose) coded as conservative.	45	39
LESSREG (Should there be less government regulation of business?) Values 4 and 5 (oppose and strongly oppose) coded as liberal; values 1, 2, and 3 (strongly favor, favor, and neutral) coded as conservative.	18	22
CLOSINGS (Should government support declining industry?) Values 4 and 5 (oppose and strongly oppose) coded as liberal; values 1, 2, and 3 (strongly favor, favor, and neutral) coded as conservative.	57	56
LABINFL (Do trade [labor] unions have too much or too little power in society?) Values 4 and 5 (too little and far too little power) coded as liberal; values 1, 2, and 3 (far too much power, too much power, and about right) coded as conservative.	9	11
BUSINFL (Does business have too much or too little power in society?) Values 1 and 2 (far too much and too much power) coded as liberal; values 3, 4, and 5 (about right, too little power, and far too little power) coded as conservative.	46	47
STEEL (What role should government have in the steel industry?)	56	52
BANKING (What role should government have in the banking industry?) Values 1 and 2 (own or regulate) coded as liberal; value 3 (neither own nor regulate) coded as conservative.	59	60
GOVPRICES (Is government responsible for keeping prices stable?) Values 1 and 2 (definitely or probably should be) coded as liberal; values 3 and 4 (probably or definitely should not be) coded as conservative.	88	80

TABLE 6.2 Bivariate Comparisons of Professionals and Blue-Collar Workers on 33 Political Attitude and Identification Items, Five ISSP Countries, 1985–1990

	Australia	Germany	Great Britain	Italy	U.S.A.
A. 1985 Data					
11 Civil Liberties Items:					
# of Items on which Highly Educated Professionals were more Liberal than Blue-Collar Workers	9	7	8	5	8
# of Items on which Blue-Collar Workers were more Liberal than Highly Educated Professionals	0	0	0	0	0
# of Items on which No Significant Difference* was found between the two Groups	2	4	3	6	3
11 Welfare State Items:					
# of Items on which Highly Educated Profesionals were more Liberal than Blue-Collar Workers	2	2	1	2	0
# of Items on which Blue-Collar Workers were more Liberal than Highly Educated Professionals	2	3	5	1	7
# of Items on which No Significant* Difference was found between the two Groups	7	6	5	7	4
11 Economic Policy Items:					
# of Items on which Highly Educated Professionals were more Liberal than Blue-Collar Workers	0	0	0	1	0
# of Items on which Blue-Collar Workers were more Liberal than Highly Educated Professionals	6	6	7	7	9
# of Items on which No Significant Difference* was found between the two Groups	5	5	4	3	2

(continues)

124

TABLE 6.2 *(continued)*

	Australia	Germany	Great Britain	Italy	U.S.A.
B. 1990 Data					
11 Civil Liberties Items:					
# of Items on which Highly Educated Professionals were more Liberal than Blue-Collar Workers	11	11	8	NA	9
# of Items on which Blue-Collar Workers were more Liberal than Highly Educated Professionals	0	0	0	NA	0
# of Items on which No Significant Difference* was found between the two Groups	0	0	3	NA	2
11 Welfare State Items:					
# of Items on which Highly Educated Professionals were more Liberal than Blue-Collar Workers	4	4	3	3	3
# of Items on which Blue-Collar Workers were more Liberal than Highly Educated Professionals	4	3	1	0	5
# of Items on which No Significant Difference* was found between the two Groups	3	4	7	6	3
11 Economic Policy Items:					
# of Items on which Highly Educated Professionals were more Liberal than Blue-Collar Workers	1	0	0	1	1
# of Items on which Blue-Collar Workers were more Liberal than Highly Educated Professionals	7	7	4	3	7
# of Items on which No Significant Difference* was found between the two Groups	3	4	7	7	3

* Chi-square significance measured at p < .05.
Note: Italy is missing all civil liberties items in 1985 and missing on party identification items in both 1985 and 1990.

favor different *types* of welfare state programs. Professionals showed significantly stronger support for what might be called "middle-class" entitlement programs— such as government spending on the arts and education—while blue-collar workers showed significantly stronger support for spending on job-creation and economic security programs—such as unemployment benefits and old age pensions. For the most part, self-interest appears to override any broader conceptions of "social responsibility" in both groups. One possible exception: professionals in Australia, Germany, and Italy were more likely than blue-collar workers to oppose continued cuts in government spending on social welfare programs—though it must be said that this was not a popular position in any country, including these three.

In both years, blue-collar workers were the more liberal stratum on a majority of the economic policy and business regulation issues. They were particularly more likely to be interested in the reduction of income inequalities and to think that government should intervene to save declining industries. The explanation is clear: having less economic security, by and large, than professionals, they were more security-conscious. One possible base of professional class liberalism did emerge on these items, however. This had to do with the extent of business power in society. In 1990, professionals showed propensities across the five countries to oppose the further deregulation of business—in three countries they were more opposed than blue-collar workers by a statistically significant margin. Similarly, they were as worried as blue-collar workers about the power of business in society—indeed, in Great Britain, Italy, and the United States, they were in percentage terms more worried about business power.

In sum, we have clear support for previous characterizations of professionals as social liberals and economic conservatives. Additionally, we have mild and partial support for the thesis that liberalism on economic issues is becoming differentiated by social class, with professionals more likely to favor positions related to middle-class entitlements and the regulation of business, while blue-collar workers are more likely to favor positions related to economic redistribution and ensuring economic security for the less well-off (such as policies aimed at reducing income differences between rich and poor).

It is important to emphasize that in some areas in which professionals were *relatively* liberal, they were far from liberal in an absolute sense. In absolute terms, they were clearly part of the conservative majorities of the era. At the same time, on virtually all issues, professionals were more liberal than business owners and executives. Differences of 10 to 15 percent were common between highly educated professionals and high-income businesspeople on a wide range of social spending and policy issues. In our opinion, this is not large enough to represent serious class tension or class conflict, but it is large enough to be noteworthy.

Common Patterns of Internal Division Among Professionals

This leads to the next question: If professionals overall are not liberal, are any segments of professionals more likely than others to hold views of a sharper liberal or oppositional character? And, if so, why do we find these patterns? Some writers (e.g., Kristol 1972; Berger 1986) have argued that professional people in creative and public welfare occupations are particularly prone to look at their society's elites with a skeptical eye and to rally under the banner of equality. To examine this notion, we looked separately at highly educated social and cultural specialists. The category "highly educated" was defined as the top fifth in education in each country. "Social and cultural specialists" were defined to include artists, writers, journalists, editors, professors, other teachers, nonacademic social scientists, urban planners, government social policy specialists, and psychotherapists.

The findings indicate that social and cultural specialists were, by no means, a "vanguard" of political liberalism in the later 1980s. At most, such professionals were a little more liberal than managers and professionals in technical fields on issues central to the emerging form of professional class liberalism in general: support for civil liberties, for government spending on middle-class entitlement programs, and (moderate) concern about the influence of business in society. On virtually all *economic* issues, those having to do with the influence of labor unions, unemployment insurance, old age pensions, wage and price controls, and regulation of specific industries, social and cultural specialists were conservative and closer to other professionals than to blue-collar workers in both the 1985 and 1990 surveys.[5]

More sophisticated questions about the internal divisions among professionals require treatment using multivariate techniques. To study the social bases of cleavage among professionals, we created ten variables: four related to employment circumstances and six related to demographic and cultural background. These include most variables discussed as specific social bases for liberalism and conservatism among professionals. The employment variables include occupation, sector, income, and employment status (i.e., self-employed or salaried). The demographic and cultural variables include age, education, sex, marital status, religion, and religiosity. We expanded the sample population base in these analyses to include not only professionals but also *managers* to provide a large enough group for meaningful statistical tests. The ten variables are described in Table 6.3.[6]

For these analyses, we relied on logistic regression, because of the large number of dependent variables in the data sets violating the assumptions of normality required for ordinary least squares regression. This problem, which is serious when the data are pooled across countries, becomes still more serious when the data are looked at in a country-by-country fashion. We have, therefore, dichotomized all dependent variables into "liberal" and "conservative" answer categories, using the independent variables to predict liberal responses.

TABLE 6.3 Information on Independent Variables, Five ISSP Countries (Professional-Managerial Subsample only)

	1985 Professional/ Managerial Sample Proportion	1985 N	1990 Professional/ Managerial Sample Proportion	1990 N
Employment-Related Characteristics:				
SOCIAL & CULTURAL PRO-FESSIONALS (artists, writers, social scientists, journalists, editors, teachers, social workers, clergy)	29%	404	39%	679
*TECHNICAL PROFESSIONALS (natural scientists, mathematicians, engineers, doctors, lawyers, accountants, marketing specialists, consultants, computer specialists)	24%	330	27%	464
MANAGERS (all business owners and salaried managers)	47%	653	34%	595
PUBLIC SECTOR (includes non-profits)	34%	351	28%	488
FAMILY INCOME (divided into into three categories: top 40%; middle 40%; bottom 20%)	65% (Hi)	704	50% (Hi)	874
SELF-EMPLOYED	26%	359	22%	374
Demographic and Cultural Characteristics:				
AGE (six categories from "under 25" to "65 and older")	30% (<35)	415	28% (<35)	487
SINGLE (single people separated from all others)	17%	233	18%	304
HIGHLY EDUCATED (coded from highest level of education to obtain similar relative proportions)	44%	616	45%	783
FEMALE	37%	507	43%	747
PROTESTANT	41%	568	48%	831
CATHOLIC	37%	512	26%	452
*OTHER/NO RELIGION	22%	310	26%	455
RELIGIOSITY (five categories, ranging from "weekly or more frequent church attendance" to "never attends")	38% (mo.+)	346	32% (mo.+)	553

(continues)

TABLE 6.3   *(continued)*

	1985 Professional/ Managerial Sample Proportion	1985 N	1990 Professional/ Managerial Sample Proportion	1990 N
Country Variables:				
AUSTRALIA	22%	310	28%	494
*GERMANY	13%	180	25%	430
GREAT BRITAIN	30%	415	19%	335
ITALY	19%	267	21%	364
UNITED STATES	16%	218	7%	115

* Reference category in regressions.
Note: Data include professionals and managers in five ISSP countries—Australia, Germany, Great Britain, Italy, and the United States.

Our findings are based on over 300 logistic regressions—regressions on each of the measured dependent variables in each of the five countries in both time periods. The two variables most closely associated with the theory of post-materialist transformation (i.e., youth and higher education) are clearly important in the explanation of liberalism on civil liberties issues, but religious variables, not mentioned in the theory, are also highly important. The major variables associated with the new class theory (i.e., social and cultural professions, public sector employment, and high levels of education) perform poorly. The first two variables are relatively important on economic issues (at least in several countries) and the third is often important on civil liberties issues. But none of the three variables are predictive of liberal attitudes across all three attitude domains. Further, income, a variable not discussed by the new class theorists, is the most important influence on welfare state and economic policy issues. Finally, the cumulative-trends theory, with its interest in employment-related variables as predictors of economic attitudes and demographic variables as predictors of social issues, fits two of the countries (Australia and the United States) relatively well in the 1990 data, but it too fails as a general model. The variables in the cumulative trends theory are at best inconsistent predictors, and in a few cases (i.e., marital status and gender) show little predictive power at all. Country-specific models also do not perform well. National patterns found in the 1985 data are often not repeated in the 1990 data.

Yet we do find several moderately strong patterns across the five countries. Liberalism on civil liberties items was most often related to four variables: (1)

youth, (2) high levels of education, (3) low levels of identification with the major religions, and (4) low levels of religiosity.[7] The explanation here is straightforward: At least since the 1950s (Stouffer 1955), these circumstances have shown a connection to tolerance for nonconformity and support for civil liberties, because they are associated with less dogmatism.

The variables in our analyses predicted attitudes among professionals on economic issues less well. Nevertheless, four variables showed significant net associations with economic liberalism with at least moderate frequency: (1) lower income, (2) work in the social and cultural professions, and (3) employment in the non-profit and public sectors. Again, the explanation is straightforward: These are spheres most distant from the core of the private sector market economy and the free market norms prevailing there. In addition, (4) younger people—whose economic circumstances are usually less secure—showed high levels of liberalism on most economic issues.[8] Where economic circumstances are more insecure, professionals are likely to have more critical views of business leaders and the working of the market economy.

These variables, contained within the larger set highlighted in the cumulative-trends model, appear to be those of decisive importance. Therefore, modifying the cumulative-trends model to draw attention just to these core variables appears warranted. However, methodological considerations recommend exercising caution before substantially revising the model. In particular, this study's use of dichotomous dependent variables may result in a reduction of information, leading to a reduction in the number of significant relationships that such an analysis can uncover, as compared to analyses based on ordinal or interval level data. After taking into account these possible limitations in the analyses, the amount of scaling-back required to make the cumulative trends model fit cross-national opinion data may in fact be less than the findings suggest is necessary.

Comparing the Influence of Structural Forces and National Contexts

To date, social scientists have found very strong country effects on a variety of attitude and party support measures (see Wilensky 1981; Weil 1985; Harding, Phillips, and Fogarty 1986; Verba et al. 1987; and Dalton 1988). It is reasonable to suppose that professionals, too, will hold opinions that vary considerably from country to country. The question is whether common structural forces (as discussed in the preceding section) or specific national contexts are *more* important influences on the politics of professionals.

To investigate the relative importance of structural and national context variables, we conducted a second set of logistic regressions on the 33 dependent variables. In addition to the 10 employment-related and demographic/cultural variables, we added the five ISSP countries as additional dummy-coded independent variables. (In this analysis, West Germany was used as the reference category for the other country variables.)

In Table 6.4, we report the number of times the logit "R" statistic reached the level of .1 or above for the dependent variables in each of the three broad political attitude domains for each of the two survey years. The "R" statistic is a close approximation to a partial correlation coefficient in OLS and can be used as a measure of the relative strength of a net association. The cutoff we have selected is arbitrary and meant simply to isolate relationships that are very strongly significant in the data. (Other variables showed significant but weak net associations.) This analysis gives a sense of whether employment-related, demographic, or country variables are the most influential in the differentiation of attitudes among professionals.

The analysis shows the overwhelming importance of national political context. As Table 6.4 indicates, age and education were comparatively strong predictors on the civil liberties items, but the country variables were otherwise unrivalled in their strength as predictors. The unmistakable conclusion is that professionals and managers are creatures of national political cultures to a greater degree than they are influenced by cross-national circumstances in their employment or social situations.

Some of the specific country patterns are of particular interest. In both survey years, professionals and managers in Germany were more oriented to the protection of civil liberties than were professionals and managers in the other countries. This may reflect a sensitivity among educated elites there to civil liberties violations, as a reaction to the breakdown of civil society during the Nazi period. Country differences were also pronounced on welfare state and economic policy issues. Political attitudes on income redistribution and the social welfare responsibilities of governments tended to be more conservative in Australia and the United States, and more to the left in Italy. The British joined the more conservative Australians and Americans during the Thatcher period (1985), but began to support social security programs more strongly in the post-Thatcher era (1990).

Brint's distinction between business-oriented and social democratic political cultures helps to explain the latter national patterns (see Brint 1994: 187-92). In Louis Hartz's famous phrase, the United States and Australia were "born bourgeois" and remain that way, while the European countries have experienced a long history of statism and working-class rebellion that has left its mark on the national norms of political culture in the age of mass democracy.[9] The British have long struggled with the contrasting implications of classical liberalism and Labour Party communitarianism/collectivism (Beer 1959). This struggle is seen in the ISSP data in the individualist certainties of the Thatcher period and the second thoughts of the post-Thatcher period (Kavanagh 1987: chs. 9-10; Riddel 1989: ch. 9).[10]

TABLE 6.4 Frequency of Strong Net Associations for Employment-Related, Demographic, and Country Variables on 33 Political Attitude Items (R > .1)

	11 Civil Liberties Items	*11 Welfare State Items*	*11 Economic Policy Items*
A. 1985 Data			
Employment Variables:			
Soc/Cult Profs.	0	1	0
Managers	0	0	0
Technical Profs.	Ref.	Ref.	Ref.
Public Sector	0	0	0
Income	NA	NA	NA
Self-Employed	0	0	0
Demographic Variables:			
Younger Age	6	2	0
Single Status	0	0	0
High Education	5	0	2
Female	0	0	0
Protestant	1	1	1
Catholic	0	0	0
No Religion	Ref.	Ref.	Ref.
Highly Religious	0	0	0
Country Variables:			
Australia	6	4	5
Great Britain	7	6	3
Italy	7	4	7
USA	5	5	3
West Germany	Ref.	Ref.	Ref.
B. 1990 Data			
Employment Variables:			
Soc/Cult Profs.	0	0	0
Managers	0	0	0
Technical Profs.	Ref.	Ref.	Ref.
Public Sector	0	0	0
Income	NA	NA	NA
Self-Employed	0	0	0
Demographic Variables:			
Younger Age	4	2	0
Single Status	0	0	0
Highly Educated	3	0	2

(continues)

TABLE 6.4   *(continued)*

	11 Civil Liberties Items	11 Welfare State Items	11 Economic Policy Items
Female	0	0	3
Protestant	1	0	0
Catholic	1	0	0
No Religion	Ref.	Ref.	Ref.
Highly Religious	0	0	0
Country Variables:			
Australia	3	6	6
Great Britain	7	4	3
Italy	NA	2	4
USA	3	5	3
West Germany	Ref.	Ref.	Ref.

Note: These results are only for professionals and managers in the five ISSP countries.

Distinctive National Patterns of Intra-Class Division

National context is important in a second way: Different lines of cleavage are *salient* in different countries. To see these patterns, it is necessary to return to the country-by-country regressions. We will call attention to two patterns in particular: one which helps to define politics in the United States (and, to a degree, also in Australia), and another which colors political life in Great Britain and West Germany.

The first pattern has to do with the special importance of religion in the United States (and, in a similar but weaker way, in Australia). In the highly religious United States, both Protestant and Catholic identifications are strongly associated with conservative views on civil liberties issues—and also on welfare state issues.[11] The latter connection is particularly noteworthy, since this is not a domain with an obviously logical relationship to religious belief. Religion in the United States tends to have an anti-government temper, in addition to its more intuitively obvious support for the traditional authority of a religiously conditioned prescriptive morality.

The second pattern has to do with the special importance of high levels of education in England and Germany. Net of other significant variables, the highly educated were conservative on issues of economic policy in most countries, but they were either liberal or not politically definable in Germany and Great Britain.[12] Although university education is not as elite as it once was in these countries, it appears to remain rooted to some degree in the status ideals of a cultural aristocracy historically hostile to the expansive aspirations of economically conservative utilitarian ideas (see, e.g., Williams 1962; and Rothblatt 1968). By contrast, higher education in the United States and Australia is relatively free of this "spiritual" import. It is seen as an advantageous credential and, net of other variables, it is now associated, not surprisingly, with conservative views on economic issues. Something similar was true with respect to the social and cultural specialists. In Great Britain and West Germany, they did tend to identify with the more conservative political parties and to worry about the dangers of civic disorder (as measured by the civil liberties items). Still, they also show an evident concern about the welfare of the poor. It seems likely that this pattern of "Tory" or "Bismarckian" reformism is similarly rooted in the self-consciously elitist humanistic education systems in those two countries, an institutional legacy not found to the same degree in the other ISSP countries.

· Conclusion

We are now in a position to answer the questions with which we began this paper. Neither professionals generally nor the presumably more intellectually oriented social and cultural specialists express a new left-of-center politics. Like the other classes and strata of advanced industrial societies, professionals are instead overwhelmingly conservative on issues related to economic distribution, the role of the welfare state, and crime control. The picture that emerges from our analyses is of a stratum that is conservative on economic issues, although relatively tolerant and non-authoritarian on social issues. A degree of economic liberalism is evident only on issues related to middle class entitlements and (to a lesser degree) on issues related to the regulation of business. In addition, where professionals work and their demographic characteristics exert a large effect in differentiating their views: Social and cultural professions, nonprofit and public sectors, and lower income levels are centers of such economic liberalism among professionals. By contrast, relative youth, higher levels of education, and weak religious identifications are clearly associated with liberalism on social issues.

Those who see a general tendency in professional politics across the wealthier industrial societies wish to emphasize the importance of evolutionary trends and of those social groups which comprise the "vanguard," driving those trends forward. It is from an essentially evolutionary perspective that generalizations about the "coming of post-industrial society," the emergence of "post-materialist politics," "new-class liberalism," and other similar formulations arise. Based on the ISSP data and other cross-national studies (see Brint 1994: ch. 9), it is our view that the possibilities of meaningful cross-national generalizations about professional politics are limited. Professionals do show a relatively consistent profile across the five industrial societies studied in this paper, and the same lines of internal division do also show up with reasonable frequency. At the same time, the political culture of the nation-state remains a very important determinant of the politics of professionals. Indeed, we would go so far as to say that professionals are far more creatures of their national political cultures than they are of any presumed general trends in technological, economic, or social structural changes. Professionals are more conservative in countries with business-oriented political cultures, and more social welfare-oriented in countries with social democratic political cultures. Also, distinctive national cleavage lines affect professionals as much as other groups in society. We have, for instance, discussed the special significance of religion in the United States and Australia, and the special significance of the highest levels of education in England and West Germany.

It is more difficult to answer the first question we raised in the introduction to this paper. Do professionals express a new kind of class politics in the more advanced industrial societies? If by "class politics," we mean that they express political views that reflect the distinctive circumstances of a "class situation," the answer is at least in large measure "yes." They are relatively privileged, but more reliant on cultural resources than on strictly economic or on office-holding resources. Their level of privilege encourages economic conservatism, while their reliance on cultural resources encourages the protection of institutions supporting open cultural life on social issues, and perhaps also a degree of distance from pure business considerations. Professionals generally work in less supervised and (in Durkheim's sense) less "morally concentrated" circumstances (Collins 1988: 208-23). They are usually exposed to a number of unconventional ideas in higher education. These experiences further encourage a degree of distance from absolutist, socially conservative moralities.

The current political affinities of professionals are, at the same time, strongly reinforced by contemporary historical circumstances. The economic conservatism of professionals is reinforced by pressures common to all industrial economies that have made it more difficult to support high rates of taxation and, therefore, also the services that taxes purchase. Something similar is true in the area of morality. The liberal views of professionals on these issues are strongly reinforced by broader social forces favoring pluralism and individual choice in contemporary, heterogeneous, and highly differentiated industrial societies—as elaborated in this volume's introduction.

A distinction is sometimes made between outlooks that reflect class conditions and class opposition (Mann 1973). Professionals clearly do *not* express a class politics, if by this we mean a distinctive ideology or set of interests *opposed* to dominant elites or a dominant class. Business elites need not beckon professionals toward a market-oriented vision unfettered by broader community commitments: Most professionals in wealthier industrial societies already endorse this vision. Even the much-touted liberalism of professionals on non-economic issues may be much in keeping with a more comprehensive version of laissez-faire—that is "hands-off" on moral and well as economic matters.

Historically, it is true that professionals have at times advanced ideas about "social responsibility" that do not fit in as easily with the more strictly market-oriented ideology of business elites. As R. H. Tawney, a theorist of the older form of "social trustee professionalism," put it:

> (Professionals) may, as in the case of the successful doctor, grow rich; but the meaning of their profession, both for themselves and for the public, is not that they make money, but that they make health, or safety, or knowledge, or good government, or good law. . . . (Professions uphold) as the criterion of success the end for which the profession . . . is carried on, and (subordinate) the inclination, appetites, and ambition of individuals to the rules of organization which has as its object the performance of a (socially valuable) function" (Tawney 1948: 94-5).

These ideas by now show only traces of influence in the professional stratum at large. Today, professionalism forges a connection between skills and markets, not between cultural authority and community functions (Brint 1994: ch. 2). Still, if middle-class professionals come to play a truly distinctive political role in the future, it will almost certainly be in coalition with groups negatively affected by laissez-faire, and built on revised and updated ideologies of social responsibility carried by new solidary networks and organizations, rather than from their current political positions and major professional associations. Changes in the economic and class structure of advanced capitalist societies could at some point lead professionals to represent a truly significant, left-of-center political force. They are, after all, a substantial and growing part of the labor force. Many have the education and confidence that encourage a sense of political efficacy. For the time being, however, they are supporters of a business and market-dominated social order. They are clearly not an important independent interest.

It seems unlikely that professionals will generate a new, independent political outlook if left to their own devices. Just as the middle-class-led Progressive Movement at the turn of the twentieth century was spurred by populist and labor revolt, a future "Neo-Progressive" movement could emerge from discontent of displaced and insecure workers faced with harsh new economic realities. However, this is only one among many possibilities.

Notes

1. Although not specifically concerned with professionals, the work of Terry Clark (Clark and Ferguson 1983: ch. 7) introduces a new vision of the politics of urban elites, a group that clearly includes urban professionals. For Clark, urban elites are divided into four groups: (1) economically and socially liberal "New Deal Democrats," (2) economically and socially conservative "New Deal Republicans," (3) economically liberal but socially conservative "ethnic politicians," and (4) economically conservative but socially

liberal *"new fiscal populists."* This fourth group was regarded by Clark and Ferguson as the ascendant group of urban leaders.

2. Altogether, eight items replicated in 1985 and 1990 were not included in the analysis. Four did not yield significant levels of variation in response. These items related to: (1) government's responsibility for insuring adequate health care; (2) government's responsibility for protecting the aged; (3) governmental spending on law enforcement; and (4) governmental involvement in the electrical power industry. Nearly everyone surveyed felt that government had responsibility for insuring adequate health care, protecting the aged, and spending more to fight crime. Similarly, nearly all respondents favored some governmental regulation of the electrical power industry. Three of the items were excluded because they did not map onto conventional liberal-conservative or left-right scales. An item concerning (5) whether government had a role in assisting industrial growth did not clearly differentiate left and right. Some from both groups thought that government had such a role, and some from both also felt that it did not have such a role. An item asking (6) whether government had too much power in society was dropped for similar reasons: Some people on the left felt that government was too powerful (on behalf of the dominant groups), while many on the right felt that it was too powerful as an inefficient user of tax monies. An item concerning (7) whether governments should fight inflation or unemployment was dropped because responses were much more closely tied to prevailing rates of inflation and unemployment than to any abstract left-right categorization. The final excluded item had to do with (8) governmental spending on defense and the military. The special circumstances of the fall of the Soviet Union and the Eastern bloc in 1988-89 complicated analysis of this item.

3. It is important to note that some clear variations exist in the kinds of sentiments evoked by different items within the three category groupings. For example, civil liberties issues that concern the rights of accused and suspected criminals stimulate a different (and often less liberal) set of responses than questions that have to do with the rights of political protestors and dissidents (as elaborated in the Introduction to this volume). And, as we emphasize below, certain spending items in the welfare state category help to differentiate the interests of the new middle class liberalism from that of traditional working-class reform. Therefore, we will sometimes pick out particular items within the three broad categories for special attention.

4. Professionals in Great Britain and the United States were no more likely than blue-collar workers to insist on protecting the rights of accused criminals; but, otherwise, they joined professonals elsewhere as decidedly more liberal on civil liberties issues.

5. In the attitudes of social and cultural specialists, substantial variation did exixt between the two survey years and also from country to country. Social and cultural specialists fit the image of a *vanguard* of professional class liberalism reasonably well in Australia and the United States in both years. However, they were notably cautious on civil liberties issues in England and Germany in both years, and they were at least as conservative as other professionals on welfare state spending issues in each of the three European countries in 1985.

6. We faced two major problems in the preparation of the ISSP data for these analyses: the problem of the missing data, and the problem of comparability in coding schemes. The problem of missing data was relatively minor. In 1985, information on religion, church attendance, and sector of employment was missing for Italy. Because of these missing data, cross-national regressions were run on the ISSP data both including and

excluding Italy. Where Italy was included, church attendance and sector were dropped from the analysis, and religion was coded as Catholic. Certain variables that we would have liked to have included as independent variables—supervisory status, region, and city size—were also dropped due to missing data, or inconsistencies in coding across countries. In coding cross-national data, it is possible to provide a country-specific meaning for the coding of independent variables, such as high income or high education, or to create categories based on a principle of equalizing proportions across countries. Because the second method has substantial methodological advantages and is not necessarily conceptually less justifiable, we have chosen to use it in these analyses where the variables were not obviously comparable across countries. Thus, we created three-category income variables, separating the top 40 percent of respondents in each country as "high income," the middle 40 percent as "middle income," and the bottom 20 percent as "low income." A similar measure based on equalized proportions was created to discriminate high levels of education from lower levels of education.

7. We found 38 positive net positive associations for youth on the civil liberties items in the nine country and year samples available. (Civil liberties items were missing for Italy in 1990.) We found 25 positive net associations for higher education; 19 negative net associations for Protestant identification; and 11 negative net association for Catholic identifications. (Religion was missing in both years for Italy.) These were, by some measure, the most consistent patterns for the civil liberties items. Business managers were next most frequent with eight negative net associations. It should be emphasized that even these variables were inconsistent predictors. Age, for example, showed net associations in slightly less than half of all possible instances (38 of 99).

8. We found 42 significant positive associations for lower income on the two sets of economic items. (Income was not available in Germany in 1985.) We found 41 significant positive associations for younger age on the two sets of economic items; 30 significant positive net associations for social and cultural specialists on the two sets of economic items; and 22 significant positive net associations for public sector on the two sets of economic items. (Sector was not available for 1985 in Italy.) Self-employment was the next most frequently significant variable on the economic items with 11 significant net negative associations. Clearly, the fit on the economic items is less good than that on the civil liberties items. Income, the most consistent predictor, showed up as significant (and in the expected direction) less than one-quarter of the time net of the other variables.

9. The United States and Australia also have large racial minority populations, which could plausibly influence the political center-of-gravity in these countries. More comparative research would be useful on this point.

10. The particularity of Italian egalitarianism, another noteworthy feature of the data, also has deep cultural roots in, among other things, a virtually society-wide antipathy to inefficient and (frequently) corrupt political authorities. It is one of the hidden balance wheels that allows the country to survive and prosper even in the face of constant government crises and divisive regional and subcultural cleavages (Spotts and Weiser 1986: ch. 14; La Palombara 1987: ch. 10).

11. On the welfare state items, religious identification showed 12 significant net associations and religiosity another 3 in the United States. The pattern was similar though weaker in Australia where religion showed 7 significant net negative associations. Religious effects on the welfare state set of variables were almost nonexistent elsewhere.

12. Compared to five significant net associations in Australia and six in the United States, high levels of education showed only one net negative association in Germany and a balance of two positive and two negative net associations in Great Britain.

Appendix:
Trends in Political Attitudes on the ISSP, 1985-1990

To study attitude change in the five ISSP countries, we looked at percentage changes in liberal and conservative views between 1985 and 1990 for the total populations and for the professional-managerial subsamples in each country. The comparisons are based on 33 items in Table 6.1. Our analysis is based on the number of items in three attitude domains (civil liberties, welfare state spending, and economic policy) that changed significantly between 1985 and 1990. We look first at all five countries together and then each country separately. The magnitude of change is measured in five spans: (1) greater than 10 percent more liberal, (2) 5 to 10 percent more liberal, (3) a change of less than 5 percent in either direction, (4) 5 to 10 percent more conservative, and (5) more than 10 percent more conservative. Results are in Appendix Table 6.A1. (It is important to keep in mind that it is more difficult for the professional-managerial subsamples to achieve statistically significant levels of change, because of the smaller size of the subsample. Therefore, direct comparisons between the professional-managerial subsamples and the total population samples should be made with caution.)

Appendix Table 6.A1 indicates that the later 1980s were a period of considerable stability in the political attitudes of national populations in the five countries. Over half of the items (17 of 33) showed a shift of five percentage points or less between the two survey years, when all five countries are grouped together. Of the remaining items, all civil liberties items shifted in a liberal direction, as did party identifications and attitudes about spending on the environment. It is particularly interesting that, during this period that is so commonly described as conservative, left parties picked up support in Australia, Germany, Great Britain, and the U.S. (albeit, in the case of the U.S., not as fast as the conservative party). One item not included in the formal analysis is of interest: Citizens also no longer felt that too little was being spent on defense and the military, no doubt reflecting an adjustment to the end of the Soviet Union and the Cold War. Attitudes on crime control and "economic issues" involving extension of the welfare state and intervention of government in the regulation of business moved in a conservative direction—but again not sharply. On certain issues, a sharp conservative shift would have been out of the question, since national norms were already very conservative. Overwhelming majorities of citizens in the ISSP countries—in the neighborhood of 80 to 90 percent—felt that labor unions should not have more power, that business should not be subjected to more regulation, and that government should make further cuts in social spending.

National Trends and the Professional-Managerial Stratum

Do professionals and managers lead, follow, or reflect national trends? Professionals and managers can be characterized as slightly "ahead of the pack" with respect to the generally liberal trends on civil liberties issues, and they can be characterized as a moderating "brake" in several countries with respect to the generally conservative trends on

TABLE 6.A1 Attitude Change, 1985-1990, Five ISSP Countries, Total
Population and Professional-Managerial Subsample

	More Than 10% More Liberal	Between 5 and 10% More Liberal	Less Than 5% Difference	Between 5 and 10% More Conservative	More Than 10% More Conservative
A. Total Five Countries					
11 Civil Liberties Items:					
Total Sample	1	5	5	0	0
Profs.-Mgrs.	2	3	6	0	0
11 Welfare State Items:					
Total Sample	1	2	3	5	0
Profs.-Mgrs	2	2	6	1	0
11 Economic Policy Items:					
Total Sample	0	0	8	2	1
Profs.-Mgrs.	0	1	7	3	0
B. Australia					
11 Civil Liberties Items:					
Total Sample	2	2	7	0	0
Profs.-Mgrs.	2	2	7	0	0
		(1 non-sig.)			
11 Welfare State Items:					
Total Sample	1	1	7	1	1
Profs.- Mgrs.	1	2	6	1	1
		(2 non-sig.)			
11 Economic Policy Items:					
Total Sample	1	1	6	2	1
Profs.-Mgrs.	0	1	7	2	1
				(1 non-sig.)	
C. Germany					
11 Civil Liberties Items:					
Total Sample	1	0	6	3	1
Profs.-Mgrs.	1	1	4	4	1
		(1 non-sig.)		(2 non-sig.)	
11 Welfare State Items:					
Total Sample	2	3	4	2	0
Profs.- Mgrs.	6	2	3	0	0
11 Economic Policy Items:					
Total Sample	0	0	10	1	0
Profs.-Mgrs.	2	5	4	0	0
		(2 non-sig.)			
D. Great Britain					
11 Civil Liberties Items:					
Total Sample	0	0	7	2	2

(continues)

TABLE 6.A1 *(continued)*

	More Than 10% More Liberal	Between 5 and 10% More Liberal	Less Than 5% Difference	Between 5 and 10% More Conservative	More Than 10% More Conservative
Profs.-Mgrs.	0	2 (2 non-sig.)	6	2 (1 non-sig.)	1
11 Welfare State Items:					
Total Sample	1	2	3	5	0
Profs.- Mgrs.	3	1 (1 non-sig.)	6	1	0
11 Economic Policy Items:					
Total Sample	0	4	5	2	0
Profs.-Mgrs.	2	4 (3 non-sig.)	2	1	2
E. Italy					
11 Civil Liberties Items:					
Total Sample	NA	NA	NA	NA	NA
Profs.-Mgrs.	NA	NA	NA	NA	NA
11 Welfare State Items:					
Total Sample	1	2	5	1	0
Profs.- Mgrs.	4	2 (1 non-sig.)	2	1 (1 non-sig.)	0
11 Economic Policy Items:					
Total Sample	0	2	9	0	0
Profs.-Mgrs.	0	4 (4 non-sig.)	7	0	0
F. United States					
11 Civil Liberties Items:					
Total Sample	1	4	5	0	0
Profs.-Mgrs.	2	3 (2 non-sig.)	5	0	0
11 Welfare State Items:					
Total Sample	2	3	5	0	1
Profs.- Mgrs.	2	3	5	1 (1 non-sig.)	0
11 Economic Policy Items:					
Total Sample	0	1	9	0	1
Profs.-Mgrs.	1	4 (1 non-sig.)	6	0 (1 non-sig.)	0

Note: Numbers in parentheses for professional-managerial subsamples indicate non-significance at $p < .05$.

welfare state issues. Indeed, in Germany, professionals and managers tended to move in a more liberal direction on welfare state issues, rather than simply resisting conservative trends. (See also Brint 1994: ch. 9.)

Nevertheless, patterns were impressively similar to those found in the larger national populations. Citizens in the five countries, and professionals and managers, typically showed greater concern about protecting civil liberties (though less for people accused of crimes), greater concern about unemployment, and greater support for environmentalism in 1990 compared to 1985. They were also increasingly libertarian—strongly favoring more market-oriented views—on issues involving wage and price controls, regulation of specific industries, and support for declining industry. Similarly, they showed at least a slightly lower level of support for many job- and social security related-programs of the welfare state.

Distinctive National Patterns of Attitude Change

Distinctive national patterns of change reflected either particular, highly publicized problems affecting a society during this period or pre-existing country trends. For example, respondents in Germany and England showed particular sensitivity to unemployment and racism, two issues of public concern given rising levels of job competition and anti-immigrant feeling in those countries. Professionals and managers in the United States were significantly more likely to favor more regulation of the banking industry in the wake of the savings and loan scandals of the later 1980s.

The inertial principle can be seen in differential trends of Italians and Australians. The Italians, European outliers in egalitarianism and skepticism about the market, showed more pronounced shifts to the left on items moving in a liberal direction, and somewhat less pronounced shifts to the right on items moving in a conservative direction. The reverse pattern is found among the Australians, the most conservative of the five.

7

Partisan Alignments of the "Old" and "New" Middle Classes in Post-Industrial America

Clem Brooks
and
Jeff Manza

A central topic in recent controversies over post-industrial political change has been whether traditional social cleavages—especially those based on class or religion—are declining in influence (e.g., Franklin et al. 1992; Dalton and Wattenberg 1993; Manza, Hout and Brooks 1995). A number of analysts (including some contributors to this volume) have argued that "the political expression of class interests has declined," as the editors put it in their introduction (see also Clark and Lipset 1991; Clark, Lipset, and Rempel 1993; Rose and McAllister 1986; Inglehart 1990; Franklin et al. 1992; Pakulski and Waters 1996a, 1996b). Other analysts have claimed that class differences remain as salient as in previous decades (Heath, Jowell, and Curtice 1985, 1987; Heath et al. 1991; Hout, Brooks, and Manza 1993; Goldthorpe 1996; Evans 1998).

In our own research on class voting in United States presidential elections since World War II, we have characterized *overall* change in class-based political divisions as a pattern of trendless fluctuation. However, we have found evidence of a *realignment* in the voting tendencies of several specific classes (Hout, Brooks, and Manza 1995; Brooks and Manza 1996; Manza and Brooks 1996a). In particular, we have found a shift among professionals from being the most *Repub-*

AUTHORS' NOTE: Authors names are arranged in alphabetical order; both contributed equally to this paper.

lican (of the six classes we analyzed) in the 1950s to the second most *Democratic* in recent elections, and a shift of the self-employed class from an essentially centrist posture to an increasingly strong alignment with the Republican Party (Brooks and Manza 1997; Hout, Brooks, and Manza 1995).

Figure 7.1 documents the trends in relative[1] voting among three "middle class" groups since 1952: professionals, the self-employed, and managers.[2] Professionals were in a solidly conservative alignment during the 1950s, but then exhibited progressively greater support for the Democratic Party. By contrast, from 1952 to 1972, managers became more Republican in their vote choice. Since 1972, managers' vote has varied, but they remain solidly aligned with the GOP. Finally, starting with the 1980 election, the self-employed have gone from a position close to that of the average voter to a strongly Republican political alignment.

These findings warrant reopening classical debates over the political alignments of the "old" and "new" middle classes in post-industrial America.[3] We extend the analysis of middle-class politics by investigating the sources and internal differences in the partisan identification of the self-employed, professionals, and managers. We focus on partisan identification, because partisanship constitutes the most enduring form of political affiliation, and one that is typically independent of the popularity of particular candidates.

Theoretical Background

The "Old" Middle Class

Small business owners and other self-employed persons constitute the "old" middle class.[4] To a greater extent than most employed persons, the self-employed face direct exposure to market pressures. Many social scientists hypothesize that such pressures can elicit distinctive political attitudes and behavior. Although systematic research on the political alignments of the self-employed in post-industrial societies has been fairly limited, the political trajectory of this group has been the subject of an extraordinarily wide range of contradictory hypotheses. Many interpretations of right-wing movements have suggested that these usually draw disproportionate support from the "frustrated" petty-bourgeoisie (for the claim that the petty bourgeoisie provided strong support for National Socialism in Weimar Germany, see Lipset 1981 [1960], chap. 5; for projected conservatism of the self-employed in the United States, see, e.g., Corey 1935, chaps. 6, 7; Mills 1951, chaps. 1-3; Lipset 1963 [1955]; Lo 1990; for other sources, see Hixson 1992). However, reviewing evidence about the politics of the self-employed in the United States in the mid-1970s, Hamilton (1975) argued that "independent businessmen" were much more likely than other groups to be politically centrist. Hamilton explains that although some independent business people are relatively privileged and affluent (and presumably conserva-

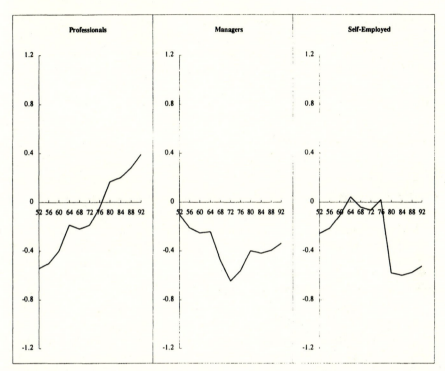

FIGURE 7.1   Professionals Have Grown More Democratic, and Managers and the Self-Employed Have Grown More Republican, 1952-1992
Note: Scores are maximum likelihood estimates of middle class vote choice for each presidential election year, 1952-1992. Data are from the National Election Studies.

tive), that is offset by the more liberal politics of many others, who come from working-class origins and receive only modest incomes (cf. Form 1985, chap. 4).

Debates over the political alignments of the self-employed have been heated, in part because of sharp disagreements about who belongs in the group.[5] Some analysts have suggested that post-industrial capitalism is creating new openings for small entrepreneurs, especially in the less-proletarianized industrial sectors (Bechhofer and Elliot 1985; Steinmetz and Wright 1989; Kellner and Heuberger 1991; Reich 1991). These entrepreneurs are sometimes seen as playing crucial roles in the generation of a new form of knowledge capitalism (see especially Kellner and Heuberger 1991). But this fairly optimistic conception of the growth of self-employment may neglect the growing number of persons turning to self-employment out of economic desperation (e.g., Linder 1994). Not only are wages typically low among this segment of the self-employed, but self-employment also typically bars an individual from access to a variety of government transfer programs, including unemployment insurance (see, e.g., Linder 1989).[6]

The heterogeneous economic situations of the self-employed (cf. Aronson 1991; Linder and Houghton 1991) make our earlier results on their sharp right turn in presidential voting all the more notable. One might have expected, given the difficulties of using survey data to adequately measure the self-employed, that we would find random fluctuations rather than systematic trends among this group.[7]

The "New" Middle Classes

The "new" middle classes—defined here to consist of professionals and managers—have also elicited contradictory assessments as they have grown and changed over the 20th century. Different scholars have viewed the NMC as (1) a conservative bastion of the status quo, closely aligned with capital (e.g., Derber, Schwartz, and Magrass 1990; Goldthorpe 1982, 1995; Kellner and Heuberger 1992); (2) an internally divided stratum, with some wings having liberal attitudes on social issues (Brint 1994); (3) a potentially liberal or radical force, drawn to the left out of material interests in the maintenance or expansion of the public sector (Gouldner 1979; Bruce-Biggs 1979).[8]

Our detailed voting analysis extends these debates (see Figure 7.1). Since the early 1960s, voting trends among professionals and managers have situated them in divergent political alignments. In a previous study, we explained these differences as a function of the increasingly liberal views of professionals on social issues, which drive them towards electoral support for the Democratic Party (Brooks and Manza 1997). We found that without the powerful effects of social issue liberalism, Democratic presidential candidates would have lost considerable ground among professionals. Indeed, the net effect of the change in all other variables would have actually led to a *reversal* of professionals' pro-Democratic voting trend in the post-1972 period. This finding cuts against the bulk of the existing social science literature, which has tended to ignore or downplay evidence of the political salience of social issues for the middle class (e.g., Jackman and Muha 1984; Kuttner 1987, p. 112; Himmelstein 1990, pp. 107-18).[9]

Our earlier research suggested that party identification plays a mediating role in the effect of social liberalism on professionals' vote choice. It also suggested that differences in the levels of social liberalism between professionals and managers have contributed to differences in their patterns of party identification. In the current study, we directly take up questions about the partisanship of old and new middle classes by examining the *sources* of their partisan differences.

Data and Measures

We use National Election Study (NES) data from the six presidential election year surveys from 1972 through 1992. Prior to 1972, the National Election Studies did not field all of the items we have found necessary for an analysis of middle class partisanship (see Brooks and Manza 1997). However, since the sharpest political differences between our three middle class segments emerged during and after 1972, this limitation is largely irrelevant for this.

Class Categories

Our analysis distinguishes three middle class segments among labor force participants employed more than 20 hours a week:

- Professionals, both salaried and self-employed (including lawyers, physicians, engineers, accountants, architects, educators and teachers, public administrators, scientists, researchers, writers, publicists, computer programmers, librarians, health professionals and nurses, and persons working in related fields);[10]
- Salaried managers (including all private sector administrators and non-retail sales managers); and
- The self-employed (including all non-professional business owners, sole proprietors, and independent consultants and contractors).[11]

Details about the coding schemes used to derive these schemes are in Brooks and Manza (1996) or Hout, Brooks, and Manza (1995).

Independent Variables

The independent variables we analyze represent four types of mechanisms of middle class politics, relating to (1) sociodemographic attributes; (2) economic assessments; (3) attitudes towards the state; and (4) attitudes towards social issues. We have extracted a number of items from the NES to measure these variables. Most of the sociodemographic covariates included in the analysis—gender, race, cohort, and employment sector—are coded as dummy variables (see Table 7.1). Education is coded as a continuous variable.

An indicator of subjective economic well-being is an item asking if the respondent is better off than a year ago. Insofar as negative economic assessments encourage a vote against the incumbent president—a Republican in five of the six elections considered—economic dissatisfaction may help explain Democratic partisanship among professionals. For this variable, higher scores indicate greater levels of dissatisfaction.

The next block of variables concern welfare state/government issues and social issues. The state item asks whether the government should ensure the provision of jobs and a guaranteed minimum standard of living for all citizens. The resulting seven-point scale is coded as a continuous variable. We consider three specific social issues: abortion, the civil rights movement, and gender equality. The abortion item is a dichotomy, coded "1" for the most pro-choice response and "0" otherwise.[12] The civil rights and gender equality items are

TABLE 7.1   Average Social Background Characteristics and Political Attitudes
of Professionals, Managers, and the Self-Employed

Independent Variables	Professionals	Managers	Self-Employed
Gender (Women = 1)	.466	.295	.292
Race (African-American = 1)	.061	.027	.038
Birth Cohort (Sixties Generation = 1)	.525	.455	.403
Years of Education	15.370	14.210	12.970
Region (South = 1)	.219	.243	.287
Employment Sector (Public = 1)	.346	.091	.000
Household Income (scaled to constant 1992 dollars)	50,742.30	54,939.95	48,304.14
Economic Satisfaction (higher scores ⇒ greater dissatisfaction)	.730	.640	.860
Welfare State Attitudes (higher scores ⇒ greater support)	2.600	2.060	1.910
Abortion Attitudes (extreme pro-choice = 1)	.481	.428	.383
Civil Rights Movement (higher scores ⇒ greater support)	.950	.800	.660
Gender Equality (higher scores ⇒ greater support)	4.960	4.610	4.270

Source: Data are from the National Election Studies pre- and post-election surveys, 1972
through 1992; figures in columns are sample means.

seven-point scales, which we analyze in our regression models as continuous
variables. Using these items, we have pooled data from the six election studies
into a single data set covering the entire 1972-1992 period.

Measuring Partisanship

The dependent variable in our analyses is one's identification with the Democratic versus Republican Parties, which we measure using the Michigan School's
classic seven-point scale reproduced in the NES series (Campbell, Converse,
Miller, and Stokes 1980 [1960]; see also Wattenberg 1994). The categories range
from strong Democrat to strong Republican.[13] To facilitate the analysis, we
collapsed this scale into a dichotomy, coded "1" for Democratic or Independent
identification and "0" for Republican identification.[14]

Statistical Model

Given that our partisanship variable is a dichotomy, we use a logistic regression model in the analyses. Table 7.1 summarizes the independent variables.

Once we have obtained the model's coefficients, we then use the coefficients to derive estimates of the causal contributions of each independent variable to explain partisan differences among professionals, managers, and the self-employed.[15]

Results

Table 7.1 shows the sample means and proportions for the independent variables in the analysis (over the entire 1972-1992 period). Several significant differences between the three groups are evident. Women are much more highly represented in the professions (46.6%) than among managers (29.5%) or the self-employed (29.2%). African-Americans are similarly more often professionals than managers or self-employed, although they are significantly underrepresented among all three classes. As might be expected, professionals have somewhat more education than managers and considerably more than the self-employed. Managers have the highest household incomes (averaging $54,940 in 1992 dollars over the 1972-1992 period), with professionals at $50,742. Despite the evidence of increasing numbers of low-income self-employed persons in the post-industrial economy, self-employed respondents in the NES reported an average household income not much below professionals ($48,304).

The subjective economic and attitudinal items also reveal several key sources of differences between the groups. As predicted by theories suggesting that the self-employed are more likely to support the political right, the self-employed express significantly more economic dissatisfaction than professionals or managers (with professionals somewhat higher than managers). Although their attitudes towards the welfare state are more conservative than workers (cf. Brint 1994; Brooks and Manza 1996), and grew more conservative from 1972 to 1992 (Brooks and Manza 1997), professionals are nonetheless considerably more moderate on issues of social welfare provision than are managers or especially the self-employed. Professionals also express more liberal attitudes than managers towards abortion rights, the civil rights movement, and gender equality, while on those issues the self-employed is the most conservative group.

In Table 7.2, we present the results of our regression analysis of party identification. The coefficients of the initial model (model 1) represent the effect of whether one is a professional or a manager, as distinguished from being self-employed. The negligible < .001 coefficient for managers shows that managers have essentially the same (pro-Republican) party identification as the self-employed. By contrast, the .407 coefficient for professionals shows that professionals are much less likely to identify with the Republican Party than either of the other two classes.

The coefficients of the preferred model (model 2) show the effects on Democratic versus Republican party identification of the other social background and attitude variables. Although many individual effects are interesting, the most

TABLE 7.2 Logistic Regression[a] of Party Identification[b] on (1) Social Class, (2) Changes over Time (Year Main Effects), (3) Other Structural Characteristics, and (4) Political and Social Attitudes Among Middle Class *(N = 1727)*

Independent Variables	Initial Model		Preferred Model[c]	
Constant	−.096	(.10)	.537	(.44)
(1) Impact of Social Class Location (within the middle classes):				
Professionals	.407*	(.12)	—	
Managers	<.001	(.14)	—	
(2) Impact of Year:				
1976	—		.113	(.21)
1980	—		−.143	(.27)
1984	—		−.515*	(.25)
1988	—		−.980*	(.25)
1992	—		−.744*	(.25)
(3) Impact of Social Structural Characteristics:				
Female	—		.137	(.11)
African-American	—		1.929*	(.49)
Sixties Generation	—		.178	(.12)
Education (in years)	—		−.135*	(.03)
Household Income (in 1992 dollars)	—		−.00001*	(<.01)
Region (South = 1)	—		.421*	(.13)
Public Sector Employee	—		.115	(.14)
(4) Impact of Political and Social Attitudes:				
Economic Satisfaction	—		.247*	(.08)
Economic Satisfaction	—		−.429*	(.17)
Welfare State Attitudes	—		.323*	(.04)
Abortion Attitudes	—		−.425	(.27)
Abortion Attitudes: * Year(linear constraint)	—		.198*	(.06)
Civil Rights Movement Attitudes	—		.350*	(.11)
Gender Equality Attitudes	—		.110*	(.04)
Civil Rights Item x Professionals	—		.323*	(.11)
STATISTICS[c]				
-2LL (d.f.)	2371.83 (1724)		2025.42 (1705)	
BIC	−10,479		−10,684	

Note a: Logistic coefficients are presented in columns (s.e. in parentheses); an asterisk indicates significance at the .05 level (2-tailed test).

Note b: Party identification is coded "1" for independent/weak/strong Democrats and pure Independents, and "0" for independent/weak/strong Republicans.

Note c: -2LL for model 3 (including the two dummy variables for professionals and managers) is 2024.28 (d.f. = 1703); BIC = −10,670.

relevant result is that when all these variables are included in the model, respondents' location as a professional, manager, or self-employed *no longer* influences their party identification. In other words, it is only because professionals possess, on average, different social background characteristics and political attitudes from managers and the self-employed that professionals' party identification differs from the two other classes. If all three classes were the same in social background and political attitudes, they would support the same political parties.[16]

Why are professionals more Democratic than managers in their partisanship? Table 7.3 contrasts the sources of partisan difference between professionals and managers (in the first column), and between professionals and proprietors (in the second column). The (average) predicted logit difference in Democratic/Independent identification for professionals versus managers during the 1972 through 1992 period is .609. Taken as a whole, social-structural factors cancel each other out, resulting in a trivial estimate for their overall impact (.005) and thus explaining little of professionals' and managers' divergent patterns of partisanship (less than 1%). Similarly, differences in personal economic satisfaction have a small impact, explaining less than 4% of partisan differences.

Views of the welfare state are of greater political consequence for partisan differences among professionals and the self-employed, explaining roughly 29% of their partisan differences. However, it is primarily the greater social liberalism among professionals that disposes them more than managers towards Democratic identification. Attitudes towards abortion, civil rights, and gender account for 67% of the differences in partisan identification (with most of this coming from attitudes towards civil rights).

The second column of Table 7.3 indicates the sources of partisan differences (.467) between professionals and the self-employed. Results for the social-structural variables actually predict that professionals will be more *Republican* than self-employed persons. The greater proportion of African-Americans, women, sixties generation members, and public sector employment all predict greater Democratic identification among professionals, but these factors are more than offset by professionals' greater relative education, affluence, and regional location relative to self-employed persons (predicting a net –.247 logit difference). The impact of differential rates of economic satisfaction on the two groups is minimal. Differences on attitudes towards the welfare state are predicted as raising the log-odds of Democratic identification by .223, and differences in social issue attitudes raise the log-odds by .501. Similar to the earlier analysis of professionals and managers, most of the impact of social issues stems from divergent views of race, which accounts for 87.4% of partisanship differences. In the NES data, professionals' greater willingness to endorse the goals of the civil rights movement is a key to understanding their partisan differences with both groups.

TABLE 7.3 Liberal Views on Social Issues Best Explain Partisanship Differences Among Professionals, Managers, and the Self-Employed

Independent Variables	Estimates[a] for Comparing:			
	Professsionals vs. Managers		Professionals vs. Self-Employed	
Social-Structural Variables:				
Gender	.023	(.038)	.024	(.051)
Race	.066	(.108)	.044	(.094)
Birth Cohort	.012	(.020)	.022	(.047)
Education	−.157	(−.258)	−.324	(−.694)
Income	.042	(.069)	−.024	(−.051)
Region	−.010	(−.016)	−.029	(−.062)
Employment Sector	.029	(.048)	.040	(.086)
ALL SOCIAL-STRUCTURAL	.005	(.008)	−.247	(−.529)
Economic Variables:				
Personal economic satisfaction	.022	(.036)	−.010	(−.021)
Ideology Variables:				
Welfare State Attitudes	.174	(.286)	.223	(.478)
Abortion Attitudes	.010	(.016)	.017	(.036)
Civil Rights Attitudes	.359	(.589)	.408	(.874)
Gender Attitudes	.039	(.064)	.076	(.163)
ALL SOCIAL ISSUE ATTITUDES	.408	(.670)	.501	(1.073)
TOTAL LOGIT DIFFERENCE IN PARTY IDENTIFICATION 1972-1992	.609	(1.000)	.467	(1.001)

Note a: Estimates in columns are the predicted difference in the log-odds of Democratic identification attributable to differences in row-specific factors (figures in parentheses are the proportion of this difference explained by row specific factors).

Making Sense of Partisan Change and Stability Among the Middle Classes

This study has considered the sources of the emerging differences in partisanship among the "old" and "new" middle classes over the past two decades. Our key finding is that the relatively greater moderation of professionals' attitudes towards the welfare state and their greater liberalism on social issues (especially race) account for the divergence of their partisan alignment from the other NMC segment (managers) and also from the self-employed.

The disproportionate extent of socially liberal attitudes among professionals makes them politically distinctive, drawing them out of what would otherwise be a stable and conservative partisan alignment (exemplified by the other two middle class segments). In addition, professionals' partisan differences with managers and the self-employed result partly from their less conservative views of the welfare state.

Partisanship Change and Post-Industrial Politics

What are the implications of these findings for broader questions about postindustrial political trends among the U.S. middle class? First, at least with respect to professionals, they lend some support for the "new political culture" thesis of Clark (1994; see also Clark and Inglehart 1988; Rempel and Clark, this volume), at least with respect to professionals. Among professionals, social issue-based evaluation of parties and presidential candidates appears to be the key to understanding their partisan distinctiveness. Further, the fact that it is *issues*, rather than class location or economic attitudes, that matter suggests that class-based explanations do not identify the relevant causal mechanism. Economic and social-structural approaches by themselves provide an insufficient basis for understanding contemporary middle class political alignments.[17]

We caution, however, against jumping to the premature conclusion that the changing political behavior of U.S. professionals provides evidence for the declining significance of class in American politics in general. First, the shifting alignments of the self-employed in recent elections are strongly influenced by class factors. Second, even among professionals, class factors exert an important *constraint* on their political behavior. In the absence of their social issue liberalism, class factors would lead professionals to be a politically conservative class. This can be inferred from Table 7.3's results, which show that the partisan differences between professionals and managers shrink by two-thirds when we ignore the impact of social issues. In other words, the comparable socio-demographic and economic characteristics of professionals and managers would by themselves situate them in similar (conservative) partisan alignments. It is not that class or social-structural forces do not affect professionals' politics, but the effects of these forces have been blunted by the powerful effects of social liberalism (see also Brooks and Manza 1996; 1997).

Finally, we emphasize that the changing political proclivities of a group such as professionals—while rooted in non-class factors—may nonetheless have important *class consequences.* As the proportion of the Democratic Party made up of professionals has risen in recent years, that party has gradually become responsive not only to the spread of social liberalism but also to a more conservative, anti-redistribution stance which serves, *de facto,* the material interests of a middle (or upper-middle) class constituency (see also Edsall 1984; Kuttner 1987; Phillips 1991). It is thus not surprising that some critics have increasingly viewed the Democratic Party as a vehicle for the advancement of an economically prosperous segment of the electorate. Seen from this perspective, a seemingly non-class process of political change (driven by social issues) may generate new forms of political division that implicate class cleavages. As these trends mature over time, how class cleavages interact with those based on (non-class) ideological factors and with party strategies will merit close attention.

Notes

1. Our measure of "relative" class voting distinguishes between changes that affect all class categories equally (what we term "absolute" change) and changes that have differential effects on certain categories of a cleavage variable (which we term "relative" change). For example, when support for Democratic candidates among *all* classes declines at the *same* rate, the absolute level of support for Democrats declines but the *relative* differences in Democratic support among classes remains stable. If the Democratic candidate receives 50% of the total vote in election A and 40% in election B, and 45% of the vote of managers in election A and 35% of their vote in election B, the relative alignment of managers is unchanged in the two elections, even though their absolute level of support has declined. Measures that fail to distinguish absolute and relative types of change in voting behavior can lead to serious biases because they provide no way of differentiating shifts in party or candidate popularity that reflect preferences among all classes and shifts in party popularity that stem disproportionately from particular social classes (or groups more generally). For further discussion, see especially Heath, Jowell, and Curtice (1987); Hout, Brooks, and Manza (1995); and Manza and Brooks (1996a).

2. These analyses are based on National Election Study (NES) data. For the derivation of these results, see Hout, Brooks, and Manza (1995) and Brooks and Manza (1996, 1997).

3. The distinction between the "old" and "new" middle class has its roots in classic debates over the possibility that capitalist development was (or would) produce a "new class" standing between labor and capital (cf. Gouldner 1979; Szelenyi and Martin 1988). Over the course of this long debate, scholars and political intellectuals have contested the likely political trajectory of the NMC, in particular whether it is likely to line up with capitalists and the petty bourgeoisie or develop its own distinctive politics. For the intellectual history of the concept of the NMC and its roots in the new class debates, the sociologist Daniel Bell's treatment in *The Coming of Post-Industrial Society* remains unsur-

passed (1973, chap. 2); see also Burris (1986). The principal American popularizer of the concept of the NMC was the sociologist C. Wright Mills in *White Collar* (1951). Mills, however, considers virtually the entire range of white-collar occupations as part of the NMC, including sales workers and routine clerical workers. In the schema developed here, we limit our conception of the NMC to managers and professionals.

4. In their definition of this group, which they refer to as the "petty bourgeoisie," Steinmetz and Wright (1989, p. 979) define self-employment as "literally, being employed by oneself and is primarily contrasted to two other conditions: being employed by someone else (a wage earner) and earning an income without being employed at all. . . . A self-employed person is someone who earns an income at least in part through his or her own labor but not by selling his or her labor power to an employer for a wage." In the conception of self-employment utilized here, we adopt a deliberately broad and inclusive definition, including self-employed persons who both employ others and work by themselves.

5. Simply, defining who is, and is not, self-employed is often very arbitrary. The Census Bureau's instructions to its interviewers are sufficiently broad that someone renting a chair in a hair salon, or a domestic worker who contracts directly with an employer, or even a sixteen-year-old schoolchild with a paper route will likely end up being coded as self-employed (see discussion in Linder 1994, pp. 16-20). Other confusions arise in cases of someone with no functional difference in their job coded as "self-employed" in one context but not in another (e.g., a partner in a hierarchical law firm vs. a salaried associate in that same firm). These confusions have led some analysts to propose abandoning the concept altogether. In sociologist Eliot Friedson's (1986, pp. 124-25) view,

> Owning property, whether a professional practice or a shop, owning the means of production, can hardly be important in and of itself in assuring one control over one's economic fate and one's work. Surely the more critical matter is the relationship one has to the market, capitalist or otherwise. When one's goods or services are so valuable on the market as to make consumers supplicants, then one can exercise considerable control over the terms, conditions, content, and goals of one's work.

In this argument, it is the extent of market power rather than employment status that constitutes the key division among the contemporary middle class.

6. The research literature on the "second" or "underground" economies has explicitly investigated this category of nominally "self-employed" but economically marginalized persons (see, for example, Portes, Castells, and Benton 1989; Portes 1994; and MacLeod 1994).

7. Although we discuss our operationalization of the class categories in more detail below, the self-employed category includes some large employers operating successful large and medium-size businesses, sole proprietors or small employers of various sorts, as well as people in working-class occupations who have become independent contractors of one sort or another. At the bottom end, analyses of Current Population Study data suggest that as much as 13% of the self-employed working full-time earn only poverty wages (compared to approximately half the proportion of all full-time workers). See especially Bauman (1987, p. 340), Evans and Leighton (1989), and Linder (1994, p. 47).

8. To conserve space, a more complete overview of the theories that have been put forward to explain middle-class political trends is not presented here. For a fuller sum-

mary of these models—including "new class," "cumulative trends," "economic voting," and "new political culture" approaches—see Brooks and Manza (1997).

9. Even the important research on the politics of professionals by Steven Brint (1984, 1994), while acknowledging higher levels of social liberalism among professionals, nonetheless claims to find a conservative counter-trend during the 1980s based on attitudes towards economic issues and changes in their demographic composition. Commenting on our own work, Brint argues that

> . . . it is true that social issues can have an explosive potential in a society where liberty is a fundamental principle, because they are so much rooted in the constitutive values of the society. . . . The recent history of the United States provides many illustrations of the explosive potential of social issues. In the United States, during the civil rights and Vietnam eras, social issues were of great importance and so, by extension, was the force of professional and middle-class liberalism. The same applies for the more recent debates about abortion, homosexuality, and the rights of protestors. Professionals have, since the mid-1960s, become more like the rest of the country in their voting, while managers have remained predictably more conservative. Some recent research argues that the Democratic voting trend among professionals can be largely explained by the importance of liberal views on social issues to voters in the professional middle class. . . . My own evidence suggests that a large part of the reason why professionals now vote more like the rest of the country is because they *are* (demographically and economically) more like the rest of the country. (1994, pp. 102-3)

10. We maintain that it makes little analytical sense to distinguish between employed and self-employed professionals, most of whom have similar kinds of jobs, mobility patterns, and life chances. Results from an analysis of the collapsibility of the class categories utilizing the Goodman (1981) test showed that with respect to voting, self-employed and employed professionals could be combined into a single class category. See Brooks and Manza (1997) for further details.

11. Some scholars have developed class schemas which distinguish large and medium employers from self-employed persons without employees (e.g., Wright 1985, 1989). While such a distinction might be preferable to collapsing all self-employed persons into a single category, the NES data used in this study do not provide sufficient detail to permit such distinctions. Further, as Marshall et al. (1988, pp. 54-60) have demonstrated, many of the survey respondents who end up in Wright's "bourgeoisie" category at best operate quite modest businesses such as gas stations or fast food restaurants or are merely part owners of firms where they also work.

12. The abortion item is the one item in our analysis with a change in question wording during the 1972 to 1992 period. We have attempted to minimize any measurement biases this wording change may introduce by recoding the item as a dichotomous contrast between the most pro-choice position versus all other positions.

13. The seven categories are as follows: strong Democrat, weak Democrat, independent Democrat, pure Independent, independent Republican, weak Republican, and strong Republican.

14. While it is possible in principle to analyze this seven-category variable as a set of six dummy-variable contrasts in a multinomial logit model, the subsequent presentation of six sets of results tends to be unwieldy. To consider the validity of simplifying the partisanship scale, we use Goodman's (1981) collapsibility test to analyze the two-way table formed by the trichotomous middle-class segment variable and the seven-category

party identification variable. A key result of the Goodman test is that the difference in fit for the model of statistical independence—fitted first to the original $I \times J$ table, and then to a simplified (recoded) $I' \times J'$ table—tests whether a specific recoding strategy results in a significant loss of information about the association (i.e., the non-independence) between the two variables. If this loss is negligible, it will show up in a suitably small value of the partitioned likelihood-ratio chi-square statistic. Conversely, if the partitioned likelihood-ratio statistic is significant for the relevant degrees of freedom (calculated as the difference in the independence model's degrees of freedom for the two tables), it shows that too much information about the non-independence between I and J has been lost by collapsing their categories.

The results of the collapsibility test of recoding the party identification variable as a dichotomy show that information loss is statistically negligible ($L^2_{Goodman}$ = 14.82 @ 12 d.f.). The same holds true, *a fortiori*, for inference based on Raftery's (1986, 1996) Bayesian Information Criterion: $BIC_{difference}$ = -75. In the current analyses, we thus analyze party identification as the following dichotomy: coded "1" for Democratic/Independent identification (Independent and independent/weak/strong Democratic response categories) and "0" for Republican identification (independent/weak/strong Republican response categories). This dichotomous coding should not be interpreted as meaning that being a Democratic versus Independent identifier has the same political meaning. Instead, it indicates that the three middle-class categories in our analyses differ mainly in terms of their likelihood of identifying with the Republican Party (rather than with the Democratic Party, or as an "independent"). The result obtained from the Goodman test is itself of substantive interest, showing that the latent differences in party identification for the three middle-class segments can be succinctly captured as a dichotomous contrast. Political independents—whether partisan "leaners" or "pure" independents (see Keith et al. 1992; Wattenberg 1994)—can be classified as either Republicans or Democrats for these two segments of the middle class.

15. In our previous research on voting differences between professionals and managers (Brooks and Manza 1997), we used a regression decomposition strategy (see also Clogg and Eliason 1986; Firebaugh 1995; Firebaugh and Davis 1988; Teixeira 1987) to make inferences about the relative contributions of the independent variables to explaining trends in professionals' voting behavior and their differences with managers over the entire 1972 through 1992 period. We utilize a similar strategy here to explore *partisan* differences among professionals, managers, and the self-employed. For the decompositions, we multiply the sample means for the relevant group in the analysis by the appropriate regression coefficient. By translating this product into a percentage of the total predicted logit, we can directly compare the respective contribution of each explanatory factor as a means of answering the question at hand (see Brooks and Manza [1997] for additional discussion of these procedures).

16. This can be seen by considering the fit of the preferred model when we add the two dummy variables for managers and professionals. As noted in footnote c in Table 7.2, the fit of the model worsens considerably according to both $-2LL$ (the non-significant improvement in fit is 1.14 @ 2 d.f.) and BIC ($BIC_{difference}$ = 14) when we add the two dummies. We can thus delete these two terms from our preferred model.

17. We should also note that decomposition of the voting trend among managers also shows that increasing levels of social liberalism among that class offset what would be an even stronger turn towards the Republican Party.

## Part 4

New Issues, Ideologies, and Cleavages:

What Mobilizes Citizens?

8

New Fiscal Populism:
Innovations in Political Candidates and
Campaigns in Illinois, 1956-1992

G. Allen Mayer

Let government step back, let people step forward.

—Governor Dan Walker (D-IL)
Inaugural Address, January 1973

New Fiscal Populism?

New Fiscal Populists (NFPs) are fiscally conservative and socially liberal "good government" types. Their stereotypical representative is an upscale, well-educated, white suburbanite. The national press has dubbed them the "Volvo Vote." They were inclined to vote for candidates like Senator Paul Tsongas in the 1992 Democratic presidential primary.

However, NFP is not *merely* a "yuppie" phenomenon. Younger, educated, suburban, ticket-splitting voters do play an important role in NFP's rise, but the support of non-yuppie voters for NFP candidates is essential for electoral success.

There can be no firm litmus test for determining who is an NFP candidate. However, a general characterization of the species becomes possible through observing words and deeds on the campaign trail and in office. Terry Clark and Lorna Ferguson (1983: 184-87) identify five characteristics of the NFP candidate: fiscal conservatism, social liberalism, populism, Democratic party affiliation, and new ideology and policies. Later formulations by Clark and Inglehart (forthcoming) of the New Political Culture and Rempel and Clark's Post-Industrial

Politics (introduction to this volume) similarly extend the NFP conception. I build on the original NFP conception of Clark and Ferguson in part because of its stress on fiscal conservatism more than later formulations. While Clark and Ferguson expand on their five characteristics, their discussion is not exhaustive.

A clearer understanding of NFP can be added through observing critical situations such as political campaigns; after all, it is in campaigns that new ideas are repeatedly tested against voters. Also, we can learn more about changes in *political culture* by analyzing the more "pure" or "extreme" candidates who have appeared in past elections.

I theorize that NFP candidates have some or all of the following characteristics in their rhetoric and actions:

- Political "outsiders" who claim to oppose "politics as usual" in the political power structure—i.e., exhibiting signs of an "anti-hierarchical" political culture.
- Not rigidly ideological, but issue-specific; focus on government as a problem-solver and facilitator—i.e., willing to experiment and "tinker" with government programs, often using "conservative" means to "liberal" ends and vice versa.
- Emphasize public goods and the general welfare more than separable goods such as patronage jobs and contracts; this creates a more positive predisposition towards alternative public service delivery methods, including privatization, public-private cooperative ventures, and the use of volunteers.
- Emphasize reform of the political system and government operations to improve efficiency, openness, and public involvement.
- Appeal to individual citizens or the public at large, not to organized groups and their select constituencies, by running "grassroots" or media-based campaigns instead of focusing on elite or group-based bargaining.
- More fiscally conservative than New Deal liberals, rejecting "tax and spend" policies and embracing government austerity—aim to control spending before raising taxes.
- More tolerant of "nontraditional" lifestyles—this can be exhibited in support for gay rights, reproductive choice, no-fault divorce, and other individual lifestyle choices.
- Progressive on social issues such as race, the environment, women's rights, and criminal justice, usually moving beyond traditional "left vs. right" positions—e.g., supporting market-based environmental regulation, alternative sentencing for nonviolent offenders, or promoting diversity without resorting to quotas.

Traditional Democrats and Republicans claim that NFP candidates try to "have it both ways" by embracing these positions. The old-fashioned "pols" seek to squeeze NFPs into the traditional left-right continuum of the New Deal. But why insist on lumping "social" and "fiscal" issues together? Even these two categories are misleading. No domino effects of policy implications link citizen policy preferences from issue to issue. Instead, the electorate has long held "conflicting" opinions (Converse 1975). Information-age politicians will thus reflect this as government becomes more responsive to the demands of individual citizens.

Some NFP candidate characteristics have little to do with policies. The rhetorical and decision-making *styles* of NFP candidates differ markedly from other candidate "types"; neither "liberal" nor "conservative" labels accurately describe these styles.

As with many labels in social science, NFP itself is a term for a dynamic, far-ranging phenomenon. No litmus test can determine who is and who isn't one. This does not imply that their study is impossible, but similarities in NFP candidates, and the "evolution" of NFP over time can appear more sharply by observing the phenomenon in its natural habitat, on the campaign trail.

The Downsian Model of Voter/Candidate Choice

A conceptual framework of voter and candidate choice is essential to understanding the rise of NFP. The Downsian median voter model provides a powerful and elegant framework from which to work. Downs (1957) applies the analytic tools of microeconomic research to elections. He assumes that voters and politicians are rational, conscious maximizers of personal utility. Individual voters base their voting decisions on a personal cost-benefit analysis (a utility function) of the expected policy bundle(s) that each party and candidate advocates; voters seek to maximize their own personal benefits (and thus utility) from the political system. Politicians (i.e., candidates and political parties) seek to maximize their tenure in elective office. To do this, politicians in a competitive democracy must react in turn to the distribution of policy preferences in the electorate. To maximize their share of the vote, politicians thus fashion their public policy proposal "bundles" after the median voter's policy preferences. The expected (and observed) result is the "clustering" or "Hotelling" of politicians near the median voter's preferences.

The median voter is not the same in every election. Therefore, political elites must respond to change in the locations. This can be quite a feat if a candidate must go through the double barriers of an open primary election with the possibility of multiple candidates, and a general election with usually two candidates. A primary election may have a distinctly different median voter than the general election. This makes choosing the optimal (i.e., vote-maximizing) policy bundle distinctly more complex. A candidate who appeals to the median voter in a partisan primary can emerge as "extreme" in the general election: for example, Barry Goldwater in 1964 or George McGovern in 1972, two classic cases.

In an earlier era in America, and in many countries today, strong political parties eliminate this problem. Political elites held the power to nominate candidates; elites focused on getting elected and staying elected. Therefore, party elites would pick candidates for their perceived ability to win their election. However, the open primary and decline of political machines has severely limited the ability of party elites to dictate who nominees will be. In the American political system, all politics is essentially a state or local affair. Candidates fight presidential races state by state; no truly national political system exists. This paper applies the Downsian model to explain the rise of NFP in Illinois politics; however, the same model should apply to other political systems as well (states, counties, cities, etc.). Politics centers on a geographic and cultural balance of power within a system. When the balance of power changes, so must the politics.

Party machines throughout the nation are declining, and younger voters especially have weak partisan ties; consequently, political elites must formulate new strategies to win elections. NFP candidates are a logical next step in America's "consumerist," media-driven society. In an age of weakening partisan attachments, NFP makes perfect sense.

Background in Illinois Politics

People saw me on television talking to people and they realized that I was communicating, to use that overworked word, I was relating to real people out there. Not to politicians but to real people . . . I was an outsider. I was not a member of the club. I was not a politician . . .
                                                        —Governor Dan Walker (D-IL)

The state of Illinois, like a handful of other states, is a microcosm of America. The state's racial, socioeconomic, regional, and cultural diversity closely resembles the national breakdowns. Illinois is more of a bellwether than a trendsetter. This makes Illinois an ideal laboratory to explore NFP.[1]

Illinois politics is not for the faint-hearted. There is no overwhelming consensus to guide its leaders. Political fiefdoms and feuding power barons are continuing elements of Illinois politics. Political and cultural clashes are the norm, not the exception. Each region of the state has its own flavor. Within the various localities throughout the state, different people, parties, and cultures flourish. (See political region map of Illinois in Figure 8.1.)

Traditionally, Chicago is an impenetrable bastion of Democrats, although both machine and "reform" strains flourish there. Southern Illinois has likewise long been a Democratic stronghold; "yellow dog" Democrats survive and thrive in a southern culture in "copperhead country" at the bottom of the state. The Chicago suburbs and the rural parts of northern and central Illinois have voted Republican since the days of Abraham Lincoln. An informal division of the spoils and respect for spheres of influence maintain the balance of political power in the state. Local offices and the accompanying patronage in Chicago

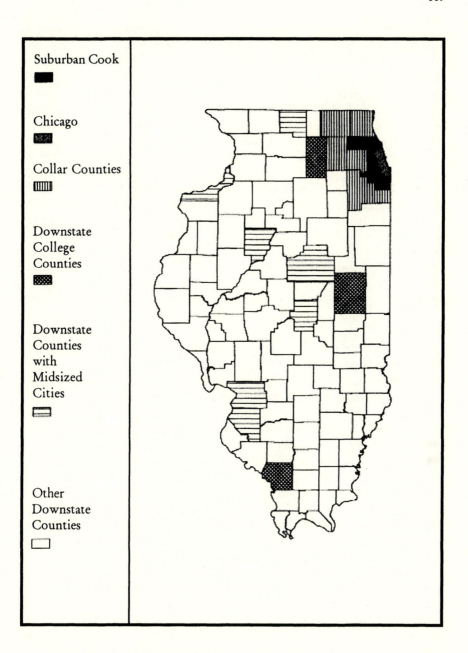

FIGURE 8.1 Map of Illinois by Political Regions

and southern Illinois are Democratic. "Collar county" offices are typically Republican. The two parties usually divide state government, as patronage armies sweep in and out of various Springfield offices. Chicago Democrats and suburban Republicans compete for greater metropolitan area Cook County offices. The offices of clerk, treasurer, and assessor are valuable because of their ability to raise funds for the Cook County Democratic Party; therefore, machine Democrats have usually held those offices.

These main divisions date from the New Deal realignment in the 1930s. However, since the ill-fated year of 1968, and continuing to the present, the system has come dangerously close to breaking down completely. Republicans have made inroads in a handful of Chicago wards (which the late Richard J. Daley's machine had turned Democratic). Independent "split-ticket" voting has increased dramatically in the suburbs. New actors and forces have disrupted the universe that was Illinois politics. The New Deal coalition is fractured and hemorrhaging.

Before this modern anarchy, there was only one game in Chicago—the Democratic machine. "Machine" became synonymous with Richard J. Daley after the 1950s, when he was Chicago's mayor and Cook County Democratic Party chair. Mayor Daley came to power as a part of the "liberal" New Deal Democratic coalition. He belonged to the old school of ethnic patronage politics, but gave his full support to the liberal fiscal programs of the New Deal, Fair Deal, New Frontier, and Great Society.

The common conception of Mayor Daley presiding over a corrupt, authoritarian, all-powerful political machine with an iron fist is bunk. It is the view from the outside. As the most detailed insider's analysis reports, "The party is not a monolithic, totalitarian dictatorship, but rather a feudal structure . . . [Daley's] power rests on a foundation of a shifting coalition of power groups and powerful figures" (Rakove 1975: 106).

The machine under Daley was a consensus-building structure. Its power came from spoken and unspoken contracts between individual voters and their local ward organization, and then from coalitions of ward organizations and organized groups. The machine provided what the people wanted, "the patronage jobs, the honors, the favored treatment, the deals," and the people provided the votes that won the elections for the machine (Kahn 1984: 47).

The machine was non-ideological. Therefore, it had no problem supporting corrupt, racist city council persons on the one hand, while supporting liberal reformers like Senators Paul Douglas, Adlai Stevenson III, and Paul Simon on the other. Loyalty to the Democratic party and its slate was the ultimate litmus test (Kahn 1984: 52). This is perhaps why NFP candidates have perturbed many Democratic party regulars—they are highly independent, often running without supporting other members of the ticket or directly challenging party slates in primaries.

The strength of the machine was such that effective opposition was rare.

Since the time of Mayor "Big Bill" Thompson in the 1920s, the Republican party in Chicago has been unsuccessful at best. The only sustained opposition to the machine has come from the educated, white, liberal reformers who congregate in the lakefront wards (on Lake Michigan); however, with the exception of a handful of city council races, they could claim little success in local politics. The machine was simply too powerful and too popular. Daley had forged a strong coalition of poor African-Americans and various white ethnic groups. In his tightest races, against Polish Democrat-turned-Republican Benjamin Ada-mowski and liberal reform Democrat-turned-Republican Robert Merriam, it was the overwhelming support of south-side African-Americans that put Daley over the top.

The machine started to unravel after 1968 and the disastrous Democratic National Convention that the mayor hosted. Daley switched from New Deal "liberal" to ethnic "conservative" by emphasizing law and order. He depended more on the white ethnic vote than the African-American machine vote.

This change in issue cleavages opened the door for NFP. A new generation of voters, with no personal experience of the Great Depression, was polarizing over issues different from those that had shaped their parents. New Deal structures failed when challenged by race relations, "law-and-order," the Vietnam war, and the social liberalization of the 1960s. The era of "social uprising" had the ironic effect of bringing conservatives out of the woodwork and into power for the first time in a generation. After 1968, few doubted the fragmentation and political exile of the national Democratic party. The New Deal Democratic coalition was breaking up.

In 1972, Chicago politics started moving "from ethnic accommodation to racial politics" (Kahn 1984: 220). The city was polarizing over issues of race. The foremost example of the new politics disrupting the old machine coalition came in the election for Cook County state's attorney. A coalition of African-Americans and white reformers exhibited unusual strength by defeating the machine candidate, Edward Hanrahan, and electing Republican Bernard Carey as the county's chief prosecutor. An unacknowledged alliance of suburban Republicans with the liberal Chicago coalition beat back the Democratic machine. Qualified candidates with machine backing had never lost local elections. They did now.

While Mayor Daley was busy trying to salvage vital local elections, New Fiscal Populism emerged in statewide politics.

Case Studies

Dan Walker's Revolution

In 1972 the incumbent governor, Republican Richard Ogilvie, understood the Chicago machine. Previously, when he was Cook County board president, he had worked with Mayor Daley. Indeed, he was a strange breed of Republican. In his first year in office he pushed through legislation creating the first state-wide income tax, raising the beer, cigarette, and hotel taxes, and increasing state spending by a whopping 45%! It is more than likely that a certain amount of the new state funds went into a new Republican patronage machine; however, the Ogilvie administration launched progressive social programs. He was not the typical New Deal Republican (Howard 1988: 309-16).

By a quirk in state election law, his lieutenant governor was Democrat Paul Simon. Simon won in 1968, although his Democratic running mate and acting governor, Samuel J. Shapiro, lost the governor's race. The Chicago machine knew a surefire vote getter when they saw him. It was no surprise that Simon was the slated candidate for governor in the March 1972 primary election. Simon had served with distinction in the General Assembly as a liberal reformer from southern Illinois. The bow-tie-clad Democrat was backed by the machine, admired by liberal reformers, and beloved by the media (he was formerly a crusading newspaper publisher). He should have been a shoo-in for the nomination.

What no one expected was the advent of NFP in Illinois politics. After the November 1970 elections, a young, charismatic corporate lawyer by the name of Daniel Walker launched his quixotic campaign for the Democratic nomination. Walker had dabbled in politics for years. He had held various appointed positions, but had never run for office himself.[2] He was a leader of the Democratic Federation of Illinois, a statewide group of independent Democrats. In 1970 he was the campaign manager of Adlai Stevenson III's successful U.S. Senate bid. He was the democratic precinct committeeperson for his suburban Deerfield home. He was not a political neophyte, but he was not a professional politician.

Dan Walker was best known for the "Walker Commission Report" on the violence associated with the 1968 Democratic National Convention in Chicago. It was in Walker's summary of the report that the phrase "police riot" was coined. The fallout of the report gave him national notoriety and earned him the respect of young liberals and the enmity of "law-and-order" ethnic Democrats. This age factor is especially significant for NFP. Many of the protesters who admired Walker would go on to become the non-poor, well-educated, non-urban independent voters that support NFP. The ethnic Democrats of the Chicago machine would become the Reagan Democrats in the "outer wards" of Chicago.

Walker launched his bid for the statehouse with a tactic never since repeated. Starting in July of 1971 he took a "walk" across Illinois. He started at the Kentucky border and crisscrossed the state for several months working his way north towards Chicago. He received some coverage of his walking campaign from the mass media, but received a great deal of local attention when he arrived in the small towns and villages he passed through. This was important: ". . . Norton Kay, the campaign press secretary, had made it clear that Walker only was walking in the eyes of the public if the media said he was doing so" (Pensoneau

1993: 47). Altogether, he walked over a thousand miles, staying in the homes of
ordinary people, listening to their concerns.

> . . . the great alienation, the great movement away from the programs of the
> 1960's . . . started in the early 1970's and I picked it up. People realized that you
> can't throw money at problems and solve them . . . And I picked that up because
> of the "Walk" (Walker 1984: 46).

Walker's low-budget, volunteer-based, people-oriented campaign showed his
populist style.

Throughout the campaign, Walker was the underdog. Popular and overconfi-
dent, Simon proposed a restructuring of the tax code so that the state income tax
would bear the full cost of education. It was a fortunate break for Walker. He
drew attention to the dramatic increase Simon was advocating in the income
tax. There was no assurance of a property tax reduction of an equivalent amount.
He asserted that Simon's plan increased the total tax burden on Illinois citizens.
Walker's more fiscally conservative position placed him at odds with many
liberal Democrats. He kept with the classic NFP mantra of fiscal restraint. This
message played well in the more conservative "downstate" and suburban areas
of Illinois.

Walker hammered away on the tax issue, corruption in state government,
and his status as an outsider. ". . . I was not a politician . . . I struck out against
politics as usual" (Walker 1984: 69). In the days before the March primary, only
one poll showed him with a small lead over Simon. He had narrowed the gap,
but it appeared that he had not pulled ahead.

On election day his campaign staff worked feverishly to get out their voters
and minimize the vote fraud in machine precincts. The results astounded everyone. Although Walker lost decisively in Chicago, he held Simon's margin to a
level smaller than expected. Independent and Republican-leaning wards gave
him winning margins. Downstate provided mixed returns. Walker won in university counties, populous urban counties, and many smaller southern counties.
He racked up an impressive 61,000 vote plurality outside Cook County. His
victories in the previously ignored suburban townships of Cook County stunned
the machine. He carried every suburban township. He made up for Simon's
85,000 vote plurality in the city of Chicago, and squeaked by with a 40,000 vote
margin of victory (*Chicago Tribune*, March 23, 1972; *Illinois Issues*, May 1976).

A rough-and-tumble general election campaign followed the primary win.
Dan Walker defeated Richard Ogilvie by over 85,000 votes in the November
general election, bucking a Republican landslide in the presidential and Senate
races. He carried the city of Chicago and "downstate" while making a respect-
able showing for a Democrat in the suburbs (see analysis below).

Conventional wisdom dictates that Walker won on the tax issue. Walker
takes issue with this, asserting that he "did not find the income tax to be a big

issue"; alienation of people from politics and political leaders was what put him over the top (Walker 1984: 45-46). This lends credence to the assertion that the NFP brand of "fiscal conservatism" is different from traditional "tax-hating" Republicanism. Not a rigid anti-tax, anti-government ideology but a desire to reform the system drives NFP. Its leaders do not oppose the use of government to cure social ills. However, they are skeptical about how effective and efficient traditional, bureaucratic government programs will be in solving the problem. Neither a callous conservative nor a free-spending liberal, an NFP leader is a populist, not an ideologue.

Governor Walker served for four fractious years, receiving support from neither the Democratic machine nor the Republicans in the state legislature. He made many changes in the way state government operated. "I said that I would end the evils of the patronage system and did so," said Walker (1984: 47). He championed the Equal Rights Amendment, stronger ethics legislation, abortion rights, reform of the criminal justice system, and "holding the line" on spending and taxes (*Illinois Issues*, March 1976). He focused, however, not on new legislative initiatives, but on a reform of government. Walker felt that innovation in government "does not only mean creating new programs. It also entails devising new ways to make government more efficient" (Pensoneau 1993).

In 1976 he ran his own slate of independent Democrats for the state legislature, statewide offices, and Democratic national convention delegates. The enmity between the Chicago machine and the independent-minded NFP governor and his supporters was greater than the fiercest partisan bickering of the era. The machine sought to destroy NFP in its political infancy. Likewise, the governor could not and would not seek accommodation with the mayor and his supporters. Everyone on the governor's slate went down in defeat—including Walker. Mayor Daley put an all-out effort into Secretary of State Mike Howlett's primary defeat of Dan Walker. Walker gained ground downstate but was overwhelmed by the Chicago machine in the city and in the Cook County suburbs (*Illinois Issues*, May 1976).

Dan Walker entered private practice as an attorney and faded from the political scene. The specter of Daniel Walker hangs over Illinois politicians to this day. Many of Walker's top aides went on to continue in successful political careers. He forever changed the geography and culture of Illinois politics. He brought New Fiscal Populism into competition with the traditional partisan politics.

The Decline of the Chicago Machine

After seeing to Dan Walker's defeat and the election of a Democratic president, Mayor Richard J. Daley died in December of 1976. Eleventh ward city council member Michael Bilandic became acting mayor. In 1977 the people of Chicago elected Bilandic to serve out Daley's term. He was not as adept, however, at running the city and its political machine as his predecessor. He alienated many of his constituents by his failure adequately to prepare the city for the devastating blizzards of 1979. The "city that works" wasn't working anymore.

In 1979, Jane Byrne, a former top Daley aide, defeated Bilandic in the Democratic primary by assembling an "anti-machine" coalition of African-Americans and white reformers. Byrne, however, was not a reformer. She seized control of the machine with a vengeance and proceeded to bloody her political rivals (cf. Fermin and Grimshaw 1992).

Richard M. Daley, son of the late mayor, entered the 1983 Democratic primary to regain control of the machine and city hall. The intra-party fighting opened the way for African-American Member of Congress Harold Washington to mount an effective challenge. After a massive voter registration drive in predominantly African-American wards, Washington won the three-way primary with 36.5% of the vote. He edged out white, liberal Republican Bernard "Before It's Too Late" Epton in the general election with 51.5% of the vote—almost all of which came from the African-American and Latino communities.

Harold Washington's election forever changed the face of Chicago politics. "The race thing" (as his arch-foe, City Council Member Edward Vrdolyak, called it) became a defining issue in local elections. Washington, however, also brought a semblance of "good government" to city hall. If he didn't bury overt patronage, Washington drove nails into its coffin. Never again would the excesses of the machine be deemed acceptable. All candidates for major office, African-American and white, have been held to a higher ethical standard ever since. Washington's election as mayor did for Chicago what Watergate did for the nation. Harold Washington opened an era of reform politics.

The Rapid Rise of Richard Phelan

Richard Phelan's political career began in 1988. Bored with his high-powered law practice, he became active in Senator Paul Simon's presidential campaign. He raised over $100,000 for Simon and was chosen as one of his delegates to the Democratic National Convention. Phelan resigned his delegate slot when approached about the possibility of becoming an outside counsel to the House Ethics Committee. In Washington, D.C., and in political circles in Illinois, Phelan's political stock shot through the roof. He used his expertise in litigation to transform the position of outside counsel into chief prosecutor. He manufactured the case against Jim Wright (D-TX), the embattled Speaker of the House. As Wright's fortunes declined, Phelan's increased. Phelan mastered the use of the media in driving Wright from office. By the time he returned to Chicago, he was a significant force in Illinois politics. He was a giant-killer (Barry 1989: 678-756). Though he had never run for public office, he was mentioned as a possible Democratic candidate for governor. Phelan was "very ambitious" and made no secret of it.

For reasons never made completely public, Phelan declined to run for governor. Instead, he set his sights on a local political giant—Cook County Board President George Dunne. Several high-priced Democratic campaign consultants came onboard.

> It was clear from the research that someone with [Phelan's] profile could be a formidable candidate for that office. An outsider, a reformer, someone who would rationalize a government that was out of date and crack down on the abuse of taxpayer dollars (David Axelrod in *Chicago Tribune*, June 27, 1993).

George Dunne had been president of the Cook County Board since 1969. He was elderly, he had alienated parts of the machine by backing Harold Washington for mayor, and was in a front-page "sex for jobs" scandal. Realizing he could not win, Dunne did his duty as a machine loyalist; he announced his retirement.

The machine slating and Dunne's blessing went to State Senator and 30th Ward Committeeperson Thaddeus "Ted" Lechowicz. A loyal machine soldier since his days as a member of the Young Democrats, he had risen from the rank of precinct captain to Assistant Majority Leader in the Illinois State Senate. Also entering the race was Cook County Clerk Stanley Kusper. Although a career machine politician, Kusper had won the respect of reformers for his efforts at reducing government waste and abuse at the County Clerk's office, a former patronage haven of the machine. Perhaps most significant was the entrance of Appellate Judge R. Eugene Pincham. Pincham was an African-American leader whose liberal judicial philosophy won him the respect of many progressive whites. He entered the race not so much as a reformer, but as the champion of continued African-American empowerment. With the loss of the 1989 mayoral primary and general election races to Richard M. Daley, the African-American community had lost political momentum. Pincham sought to reverse this by taking the second highest office in local politics—the Cook County Board presidency. He sought to reunite and re-energize the African-American community.

The makeup of the primary field produced several "pure" electoral types. Phelan was the NFP. Ethnic Democrat voters had two options in this race, the party-backed candidate, Ted Lechowicz, and the more familiar Stanley Kusper. Radical liberals and anti-machine African-American voters had Judge R. Eugene Pincham. If one assumes no back-room deals and intra-machine fighting (an assumption definitely not perfect in any Chicago race) then Phelan's supporters should have been NFP supporters. The four-way primary provides a wonderful case study of NFP in action.

Richard Phelan kicked off his campaign on Tuesday, September 26, 1989, more than five months before the March 1990 Democratic Primary. His initial campaign emphasized that he was "not a career politician"; he "sees taxpayers as victims of an unresponsive, inefficient county government that puts political interests ahead of people's needs." "I'm not questioning [the] need [for County services] . . . I'm questioning the easy answer to every problem, as I hear it—spend more, tax more," said Phelan (*Chicago Tribune*, September 27, 1989). Phelan started his campaign with the classic NFP efficiency in government mantra, and focused his media hits on appeals to individual taxpayers. As the campaign progressed, Phelan emphasized his support for reinstating abortion on demand at Cook County Hospital, a practice which President Dunne, a devout Roman Catholic, had ended. Phelan's support for a county-wide human rights ordinance codifying equal protection for gays and lesbians was not a prominent campaign theme, but it further illustrates his social liberalism.

Phelan did not overtly court the ward bosses and power brokers who were the traditional king-makers in county politics. This election was not, however, a traditional machine versus liberal reformer campaign. Phelan's campaign will go down as the first truly capital-intensive, mass media effort in Cook County politics. GOTV didn't imply precinct captains ringing doorbells ("Get out the vote"); it meant "Get on TV." That is precisely what Phelan did. He had political and media guru David Axelrod and several hundred thousand dollars. Phelan's war chest bought commercials that created his public image. He ran on media imagery, not on a record of past political accomplishments. Axelrod's commercials "spindoctored" the millionaire, suburban attorney into a major political force. He wasn't a politician or a wealthy snob—he was just a "regular guy" trying to clean up government.

Altogether, Phelan raised over $1.4 million (more than any other candidate) to spend on his campaign (*Chicago Tribune*, March 7, 1990); paid media, not a patronage army, was his weapon of choice on the political battlefield. The mass media carried his campaign into thousands of living rooms. The Phelan campaign made little attempt to forge a coalition of disparate ethnic groups; in place of group-based appeals, it tried to win a plurality of individual voters by reaching them in their homes.

Richard Phelan won the primary decisively. He garnered a majority of the suburban Cook County vote and 34.5% of the Chicago vote, carrying 22 of the city's 50 wards. The reasons for his victory and who voted for him are unclear. An open endorsement from several southwest-side white ethnic committeepersons (most notably the 23rd ward powerhouse Member of Congress Bill Lipinski) and possible covert Irish/Daley machine support muddle the results.

Phelan's victory clarifies the social base of NFP's politics. He received support from a broad range of voters. He garnered high vote totals in areas of educated, non-poor whites. He ran best in suburban and "reformist" districts but more than held his own in working-class, white ethnic wards. He captured 82.8% of the vote in his own suburban New Trier township. He received over 60% in 11 out of 30 suburban townships in the four-way race. In Chicago he garnered 70.4% support in the "independent" 43rd ward, and 59.3% in the "ethnic" 41st ward. His lowest vote totals came in poor African-American wards, as little as 4% in the south-side 6th ward (*Chicago Tribune*, March 1990). This "ward-level" analysis lends credence to the image of NFP as a product of educated, middle-class whites. The significant support of blue-collar ethnic whites, however, dents the notion of NFP as an exclusively "yuppie" phenomenon.

Neil Hartigan—Walker II or Machine Pol?

As Democratic nominee for lieutenant Governor in 1972, Neil Hartigan had at best a chilly relationship with his running mate. For Hartigan had beaten Dan Walker's chosen running mate in the March primary. He represented everything Dan Walker was running against. Neil Hartigan was a Chicago machine politician. He had worked for Mayor Richard J. Daley in City Hall. Like his father, Hartigan was a ward committeeperson and dispenser of machine patronage. He had never worked in the private sector.

Dan Walker didn't like Neil Hartigan and wasn't shy about letting people know it. After the election, Hartigan spent four agonizing years as lieutenant governor in an administration that wanted nothing to do with him. Hartigan had little to do but endure the insults and antagonism between Governor Walker and Mayor Daley.

In 1976 he was renominated for lieutenant governor, again defeating Walker's candidate. This time, however, his running mate was Secretary of State Michael Howlett—Daley's handpicked candidate. Together they lost the November election. Not long afterwards Hartigan's political mentor, Richard J. Daley, died. Hartigan spent the next few years outside politics, earning an "honest" living as a banker. The private sector, however, was not the place for a politician in the prime of life.

In 1982 he made a successful run for attorney general of the state of Illinois. As attorney general, he streamlined his budget and redirected the energies of the office. He placed new emphasis on protecting the rights of senior citizens and the disabled. He was an activist Democrat. In 1986 the party passed him over in slating for governor. They gave former senator Adlai Stevenson III another crack at Republican "Big Jim" Thompson. Stevenson lost. Hartigan won reelection. In 1990 the Democratic party's endorsed candidate was Neil Hartigan. He faced no primary opposition.

The Republican party's candidate was Secretary of State Jim Edgar, a native of central Illinois. Edgar's claim to fame was using his office to launch a crusade against drunken drivers. He was a downstate Republican who had spent his entire life working in government. Now that Governor "Big Jim" Thompson was retiring, he would have the chance to reach the culmination of a career in state government—the governor's mansion.

Edgar and Hartigan displayed prototypical median voter "Hotelling" on social issues. They both came out as pro-choice and pro-death penalty. Both kept their positions on gun control and other regionally divisive issues fuzzy. They both favored higher spending on education and lower property taxes. For all but the best informed voters, it was almost impossible to tell the difference in their positions—except on one issue.

In early 1989, Governor Thompson proposed another hike in the state income tax. House Speaker Mike Madigan (D-Chicago) forced Thompson to accept budget cuts in his patronage army and a temporary tax surcharge that would expire on July 1, 1991—after the 1990 governor's race. Thompson chose not to run for reelection.

In December of 1989, Secretary of State Jim Edgar announced that he would favor making the tax surcharge permanent. Since voters perceived Governor Thompson as "lying" about the actual need for taxes in his 1982 and 1986 races, Edgar hoped that voters would reward him for his candor. Coupled with his pro-choice stand, this sparked two conservative candidates—Dr. Robert Marshall and Steven Baer—to challenge him in the Republican primary. The conservatives ran underfunded "grassroots" campaigns and still took over one-third of the primary vote.

Attorney General Hartigan, at first, took no position on the tax surcharge. When Edgar came out strongly for extending the surcharge and faced significant opposition from his party's right wing, Hartigan seized the issue and ran with it.

> . . . I said I would not support the local government portion of the surcharge because it was not used for property tax relief as intended. With respect to education's portion of the income tax, I indicated that I will only support its extension if, and only if, five measurable improvements occur . . . (AARP Vote).

Hartigan took the New Fiscal Populist, results-oriented approach to the issue of extending the income tax surcharge. Edgar the Republican sounded much more like a fiscally liberal Democrat:

> . . . I strongly believe we cannot roll back the income tax without seriously jeopardizing our education system and putting those who rely on human services into no-win competition with the school children of our state (AARP vote).

Early polls showed Edgar with as much as a twenty-point lead over Hartigan. The Secretary of State was well known—every driver's license printed since 1980 bore his name. Edgar had distanced himself from the scandals and tax hikes of the Thompson administration. Polls showed that many voters did not believe Hartigan on the tax issue; however, they were still willing to vote for him.

"Playing the prairie populist, Hartigan rode the tax issue back into a dead heat with Edgar by Labor Day" (Wheeler 1990: 6). Hartigan began blasting Edgar as a big-spending waster of government money. "I've shown where we can cut $573 million in government waste and inefficiency while still maintaining critical human services . . . His first response is to tax you more, while I know I can manage Illinois better with the money we spend today" (Hardigan campaign literature; see Figure 8.2). While Hartigan contrasted his fiscal conservatism with Edgar's support of the income tax surcharge, he also emphasized his socially liberal record as attorney general of fighting for environmental and consumer protection. Hartigan's campaign literature illustrates how a Democrat, indeed a "New Deal liberal" throughout his career, could shift policy emphasis in a changing political context. Both candidates ran traditional campaigns, mixing volunteers with paid media and campaign appearances. Edgar ran as an honest candidate who pledged not to raise taxes in the future. Hartigan ran with an "anti-tax, anti-insider message" that played well in southern Illinois (Wheeler, 1990: 6). The leading reform organization, Independent Voters of Illinois (IVI), even endorsed Hartigan, the former machine pol. Conversely, the teacher and public employee unions endorsed Edgar, the Republican.

When the dust settled, Jim Edgar pulled out a narrow victory. The returns looked similar to Dan Walker's 1972 victory over Richard Ogilvie. Hartigan did significantly better in the suburban collar counties than Stevenson four years earlier. Edgar made significant inroads in Chicago.

> In the 96 counties that constitute Downstate . . . Hartigan ran like a house afire. Edgar took just a 45,000 vote plurality out of what should have been his base region, nearly 180,000 votes less than Thompson received in 1982 . . . (*Chicago Tribune*, Nov. 8, 1990).

Many pundits attribute Hartigan's rapid rise in the polls to his populist rhetoric and fiscal conservatism. He did better in the suburbs and in downstate than any Democratic gubernatorial candidate since Dan Walker.

His narrow loss resulted from the low voter turnout in the African-American wards on Chicago's south side. Hartigan's poor showing among African-Americans stemmed from his ties to the regular Democratic organization (which had opposed African-American mayor Harold Washington) and likely cost him the election. His NFP style, however, convinced suburban and "downstate" voters to back a Chicago Democrat—putting him within striking distance. If voters see NFP Democrats moving "to the middle" and "away" from the traditional left, then NFP candidates not only reap the gains of increased moderate support, but also can suffer losses among traditional liberal voters.

Neil Hartigan's strong downstate showing indicates the strength of NFP outside its traditional suburban realm. The "swing voters" in the "other 96" counties of Illinois were vital to Hartigan's coalition. Unfortunately, downstate demographics cannot be examined as closely as hyper-segregated Chicago wards. Whether increased levels of education, relative youth, and income correlate with support for NFP cannot be determined from election returns. Still, the increased Hartigan support in non-metropolitan areas helps extend the conception of the NFP beyond a "yuppie" social base.

On Taxes

Neil Hartigan

- Neil Hartigan has already pledged to return $340 million into the pockets of taxpayers from the Edgar income tax surcharge.

- Neil Hartigan opposes creation of a local income tax.

- Neil Hartigan has opposed and stopped the 1989 legislative pay raise.

- Neil Hartigan opposes the increase of any tax without performance and results.

Jim Edgar

- Jim Edgar supports the $750 million permanent income tax increase. The first in Illinois' history.

- Jim Edgar supported creation of a local income tax, without a cap on increases.

- Jim Edgar voted himself a 33% legislative pay increase after only one term in the General Assembly.

- Jim Edgar supports increases in your property taxes by over $400 million a year, *forever*, without voter approval.

On Performance

Neil Hartigan

- Fought to protect seniors from nursing home abuse.

- Prosecuted toxic waste dumpers and polluters.

- Successfully fought against utility rate hikes.

- Kept convicted murderers behind bars in critical appeals cases.

- Cut his budget four times in the last 6 years.

Jim Edgar

- State Librarian

- Distributes license plates

- Sells drivers licenses

- Keeper of the State Seal

- Groundskeeper for Capitol Complex

FIGURE 8.2 Neil Hartigan Campaign Literature

(continues)

178

To the Taxpayers of Illinois,

You don't need a governor who says higher taxes are the only way to run Illinois—you need a governor who will manage the taxes you pay today.

I've introduced a plan that does just that, and I've called it "Giving Taxpayers their Money's Worth—for a Change"—a change Illinois desperately needs. In eight points, I've shown where we can cut $573 million in government waste and inefficiency while still maintaining critical human services.

Jim Edgar announced only nineteen days after the *temporary* tax increase was passed that it should be made permanent. I said we should wait to see if it resulted in better performance. **I said no results—no performance—no new taxes!**

Jim Edgar's only significant piece of legislation as a one term legislator was to introduce a bill to create a local income tax on top of existing property taxes. His most significant vote was to vote himself a 33% raise after one term in office. **That's the difference between Jim Edgar and myself. His first response is to tax you more, while I know I can manage Illinois better with the money we spend today.**

The difference is clear. You can vote for more of the same old tax and spend policies of the past 14 years, or **you can vote for real change in Illinois**—a change we desperately need. *The choice is yours!*

Neil Hartigan
Candidate for Governor

FIGURE 8.2 (*continued*)

Populist Millionaire Al Hofeld

In late 1991, veteran political pundits snickered at the candidacies of Cook County Recorder of Deeds Carol Moseley-Braun and a political neophyte named Albert Hofeld. No one could beat U.S. Senator Alan J. Dixon in a Democratic primary. Dixon was a popular incumbent with bipartisan support. He had never lost an election in his long and distinguished career. Besides, "Al the Pal" had a campaign war chest that could scare off any strong challenge from within or without his party.

Dixon had voted against authorizing the use of force in the Persian Gulf—as a member of the Senate Democratic leadership he couldn't vote for it—although that was unpopular with the general public and especially with his more conservative supporters. He voted, however, for the confirmation of Judge Clarence Thomas to the Supreme Court—a position which the majority of his constituents, especially the conservatives, supported. Nonetheless, opposition to this latter vote was the publicly stated reason why both quixotic liberals challenged Dixon in the primary. Moseley-Braun might draw some die-hard white liberal and African-American votes. However, Dixon's projected margin downstate and in the white ethnic wards should more than compensate for any defections to Moseley-Braun. As for Al Hofeld, he had no base, no name recognition, and no experience.

Then, the TV commercials began.

Albert Hofeld might have been a neophyte, but he wasn't stupid. He knew enough to hire Axelrod to help him put together a media campaign. Unlike Richard Phelan, Hofeld had little time to organize a traditional street-level campaign and had as much name recognition as the ambassador from Mali. Hofeld's campaign, however, was not the least bit traditional.

Hofeld ran on an NFP platform. His main appeal was to individual voters, not to "blocs" of votes delivered by ward bosses. His campaign centered on "taking on the special interests" and career politicians. Hofeld tried to make his weaknesses (inexperience, low name recognition, wealth) into strengths and Dixon's strengths (incumbency, middle-of-the-road non-ideology, high name recognition) into weaknesses. This political judo had a profound effect.

Hofeld ran a campaign unparalleled in Illinois history. He poured millions of his own dollars into a made-for-TV campaign. He ran commercial after commercial to define himself and the election for the voters of Illinois. In his commercials the veteran trial lawyer would look directly into the camera and deliver carefully crafted sound bites. He attacked Dixon as a political insider who was out of touch with the voters and as the willing agent of "special interests." Still, pre-election reports were skeptical:

Television is . . . making Hofeld a player, but not likely a winner . . . Hofeld's campaign marks the first time in Illinois a candidacy has been spawned and developed almost entirely through paid TV spots. Unlike Dixon or [Moseley-] Braun, who have established political bases, Hofeld came into the race without a constituency. He has had to carve out a niche for himself and is heavily dependent on television to do the job (*Chicago Sun-Times*, March 9, 1992).

Hofeld based his platform on his "outsider" image. His millions paid for "slick" red, white, and blue campaign literature. His issues were "tax fairness for the middle class," affordable health care, expanded access to college, new jobs, and "fair trade"—all extremely popular. (See Figure 8.3.)

Hofeld's platform was certainly New Fiscal Populist. Tax fairness and reduced spending on the military are traditional liberal positions but still fiscally conservative. His pro-choice, pro-gun control themes were typical liberal/NFP social positions. His focus, however, was on reforming the political system. This was the basis of his "populist" appeal and what truly makes him an NFP candidate.

The Chicago media quickly framed the race as Dixon the incumbent political insider vs. Hofeld the rich Johnny-come-lately. Almost every print article about Hofeld focused on his spending millions of his own dollars to finance his campaign. He claimed that he was staying free of special-interest PAC contributions; Dixon and the establishment press alleged he was trying to "buy a Senate seat" for himself.

Dixon and Hofeld fell into an all-out mud brawl over the airwaves. Attack and counterattack commercials flooded the media. A popular joke in the inexpensive downstate media markets was "We now interrupt this Al Hofeld commercial to bring you your regularly scheduled programming . . ."

Dixon, for the first time in his career, declined to accept an endorsement from a slate-making session. The acknowledged favorite of most politicians, he did not want to appear any more of an insider than necessary. To bolster his sagging image, Dixon called on his friend and fellow senator Paul Simon to make a commercial endorsement for him. A staunch liberal with a reputation as an independent thinker, and the most popular officeholder in the state, Simon perhaps could help Dixon with white liberals and African-Americans. In fact, Simon's endorsement seemed to hurt Simon more than it helped Dixon.

Meanwhile Carol Moseley-Braun, without the money to join the fray, kept a low profile. She ran a "grassroots" campaign that focused on her core liberal and African-American support. She displayed her ignorance of statewide geography when in responding to a reporter's question she indicated that she would work very hard to win the Lincoln County vote and would be in touch with the Democratic chair of the county. Unfortunately, there is no Lincoln County in Illinois. Moseley-Braun was seen as a hopelessly liberal, parochial Chicago politician. Trying not to offend potential voters, both Dixon and Hofeld kept a fairly "hands-off" approach to the darling of liberal elites.

A *Chicago Sun-Times* poll taken March 3-5, two short weeks before the primary

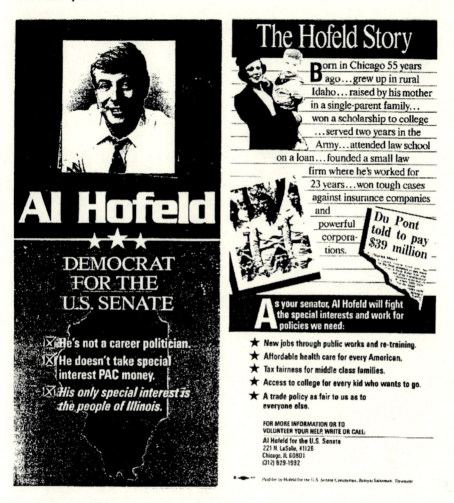

FIGURE 8.3   Al Hofeld Campaign Literature

election, showed Dixon leading with 44% to Hofeld's 23% and Moseley-Braun's 22%. "Dixon Pulls away in Senate contest" proclaimed the headline. Then the one and only Senate primary debate came along. Allegations, counter-allegations, and more mudslinging were the order of the day in the televised debate. Senator Dixon asked Carol Moseley-Braun to explain the importance of party unity to Hofeld (who had refused to commit to endorse Dixon should he be renominated). "Senator Dixon, I think he's clueless about how government works, and that's the problem," she said. "He's a product of his media handlers." Hofeld responded to the double-team by the officeholders, emphasizing his outsider (i.e., NFP) status: "They should team up. There is no difference between her and Alan Dixon; they are two peas in a pod and birds of a feather. I am too independent for them." He "hammered his rivals as 'career politicians.' He questioned Moseley-Braun's record as a state representative, accusing her of voting for 13 tax increases." Senator Dixon avoided a direct attack on Carol Moseley-Braun. Instead, he lashed out at the veteran trial lawyer saying, ". . . Al Hofeld fights insurance companies and other companies for one-third of what he can get" (*Chicago Tribune* and *Chicago Sun-Times*, March 9, 1992).

In the final days of the campaign, statewide polls of likely Democratic primary voters were inconclusive. Moseley-Braun and Hofeld surged and declined. Dixon, who had led decisively until this point, kept declining.

Despite a last-minute upswing in the opinion polls, Al Hofeld lost to Carol Moseley-Braun, who narrowly edged out Dixon. A strong showing for Hofeld in the suburban "collar counties" and a sizable second place in downstate returns ate into Dixon's conservative and moderate base. Moseley-Braun's strong showing in Chicago, the collar counties, and downstate college towns outdistanced Dixon's diminished showing.

Although immediate media reaction proclaimed an upset ("Senate Stunner" proclaimed the *Chicago Tribune*), later analysts indicated that Hofeld had, in essence, bought the election for Moseley-Braun: ". . . if Hofeld had not been in the race using expensive and extensive TV campaigning, most of his downstate voters would have supported Dixon" (Green 1992: 12). Some speculated on the amount of support the Daley machine gave Dixon; if Moseley-Braun had lost, she would have been well positioned to challenge Mayor Richard M. Daley in 1995.[3]

Did the NFP candidate (Hofeld) draw mainly on NFP voters? Since he armed himself with only a message (lacking a base vote or grassroots machine) it is reasonable to assume that operationally NFP voters (people who not only support NFP in principle but vote for NFP candidates based on their policy preferences) made up a sizable portion of Hofeld's 27% statewide vote. Some NFP voters might have trickled over to Moseley-Braun as a protest (or out of a belief that Hofeld wasn't really an outsider). Like other NFP candidates, Hofeld's support was stronger in the suburbs, and in white ethnic wards. He did not, however, win a single Chicago ward. His best performances were in the "suburban-like" 41st (35.9%) and 38th (35.5%) wards. Still, his greatest strength was in northern Illinois' midsized cities (recall that Elazar [1970] classified northern Illinois politics as "New England" in style).

Al Hofeld represented the new NFP candidate. Before the 1992 Senate primary, he did not have the political network and contacts that the other candidates developed over a career. Presidential-hopeful Senator Paul Tsongas received a political death blow in that Illinois primary; however, his framing of his own race as "the message versus the machine" could just as easily have applied to Al Hofeld's Senate bid. Unlike Dan Walker, Hofeld had the money to get his message out over the airwaves. However, also unlike Walker, Hofeld lacked a grassroots network of supporters to work the polls on election day. He did not build his campaign with a patronage army. He built it on a popular message aimed at the great mass of Illinois voters—not a coalition of different groups (whether class, race, or geography based). He targeted the new median voter in Illinois.

Analysis of Case Studies

However the political future of Chicago may sort itself out, demography dictates that, to survive, the Cook County Democratic organization will have to adapt itself to the changes that are taking place in its natural habitat.

—Melvin Kahn, *The Winning Ticket*, 1984

"Chicago ain't ready for reform."

—Alderman Mathias "Paddy" Bauler, circa 1955

The case studies above provide four examples of NFP in action. The quasi-journalistic stories of each candidate, however, say nothing systematic about NFP. To impose a system, the candidates have been compared to a listing of characteristics of an ideal NFP candidate. The listing was generated by expanding the Clark and Ferguson (1983) NFP candidate traits—using more specific positions and styles—and integrating ideas from the introduction to this paper. The result is Table 8.1.

Candidate Characteristics

By more than doubling the number of characteristics from the original five, and by increasing distinctions within each general category, the variations between candidates are sharpened. For instance, Dan Walker is closest to the prototypical NFP candidate using the revised categories. However, in the original Clark and Ferguson description, this is difficult to discern since Richard Phelan scores the same as Dan Walker. Under the revised system, Phelan's emphasis on political reform and public involvement differentiate him from Walker or Hofeld.

The degree of populism and fiscal conservatism varies especially across candidates. His status as a political "insider" for over twenty years undercut Neil Hartigan's populist appeal. By contrast, Al Hofeld's populist appeal was strong, but his fiscal conservative credentials were weak. Consequently, while Hofeld hammered away on his credentials as a populist outsider, all of the other NFP candidates studied made their fiscal views central. Dan Walker was going to "hold the line" on taxes and spending. Neil Hartigan promised to let the income tax surcharge expire and find government savings to make up the revenues.

TABLE 8.1 Characteristics of NFP Candidates

Candidate	Walker	Walker	Phelan	Hartigan	Hofeld
Election	1972 Primary	1972 General	1990 Primary	1990 General	1992 Primary
Populism					
Political Outsider	+	+	+	-	+
General welfare, not patronage	+	+	+	+	+
Reform political system	+	+	x	x	+
Increase public involvement	+	+	x	x	+
Appeal to individual citizens	+	+	+	x	+
Use of mass media	x	+	+	+	+
Fiscal Conservatism					
Government efficiency	+	+	+	+	x
Austerity in government	+	+	+	+	-
Reject "tax and spend"	+	+	+	+	x
Social Liberalism					
Tolerance of "nontraditional" lifestyles	+	+	+	+	+
Progressive on social issues	+	+	+	+	+
New Policies					
Non-ideological	+	+	+	+	x
Government as problem solver	+	+	x	+	+
Clark/Ferguson NFP					
Fiscal Conservatism	+	+	+	+	x
Social Liberalism	+	+	+	+	+
Populism	+	+	+	+	+
New	+	+	+	-	+
Democratic	+	+	+	+	+
New Policies	+	+	+	x	x

(+) Fits description
(-) Does not fit description
(x) Mixed fit with description

TABLE 8.2   Social Bases of NFP Support

Candidate	Walker	Walker	Phelan	Hartigan	Hofeld
Election	1972 *Primary*	1972 *General*	1990 *Primary*	1990 *General*	1992 *Primary*
Group					
African-Americans	-	+	-	+	-
White ethnic machine	-	x	x	+	-
White ethnic non-machine	x	x	+	+	-
Independent liberals	+	x	x	x	-
Latinos	?	?	?	+	-
Suburban	+	+	+	x	x
Counties with midsized cities	+	+	na	+	+
"Downstate" counties	+	+	na	+	x
Counties with college towns	+	+	na	x	x

(+) Solid Support
(-) Weak support
(x) Mixed support
(?) Unknown

Richard Phelan promised to make county government more efficient. In office, he was not able to keep his pledge to keep property taxes down and instituted the first county-wide sales tax—but he did, nonetheless, cut government payrolls significantly. Phelan went much farther as a fiscal conservative than as a champion of populist causes.

Electoral Support

Table 8.2 indicates support for the candidates by various groups. Support was distinguished using only voting results and media accounts, which are less sensitive than voter surveys. Even with these sometimes crude results, however, a pattern emerges.

The first five categories in Table 8.2 are limited to the city of Chicago. Non-machine white ethnics are "Reagan-Democrats" and tend to vote for Republicans for higher offices and for ethnic Democrats locally. Independent liberals are the non-poor, well-educated "yuppies," loathe to vote for a straight party ticket. Counties with midsized cities include: Winnebago (Rockford), Rock Island (Quad Cities), Peoria, Macon (Decatur) McLean (Bloomington-Normal) and Madison/St. Clair (East St. Louis, Alton, and Bellville). "College" counties are Champaign (University of Illinois), DeKalb (Northern Illinois University), and Jackson (Southern Illinois University). "Downstate" includes every county outside the six-county Chicago metropolitan area. Figure 8.1 indicates the location within Illinois of each of these political regions.

African-Americans support Democratic candidates in general elections, but
not NFP Democrats in primary elections. One should explore specific political
culture, poverty, and race effects in the future. Machine Democrats, likewise,
avoid NFP Democrats if given a choice. Phelan received moderate support
from machine Democrats, but the reasons for this support are unclear and may
include back-room deals. Non-machine ethnics are more supportive than machine backers, although not enthusiastic about NFP candidates. Their "Reagan-
Democrat" status implies that the anti-tax, anti-insider message is preferable to
the alternatives—but they might vote Republican anyway. Traditional liberals
are unenthusiastic about NFP. Walker felt that they opposed the machine by
voting for him in the 1972 primary, but voted for Ogilvie in the general for the
same reason. In both 1990 races, liberals divided their votes. In 1992 they supported the come-from-behind candidacy of Carol Moseley-Braun. It is difficult
to detect Latino response to NFP. Only in the last decade did the Latino community become a force in local politics—and its loyalties divided between liberal
reformers like Harold Washington and the Daley machine.

Following the conventional wisdom, suburban Democrats have supported
NFP candidates. The bulk of suburban Cook County townships and the collar
counties still vote Republican in general elections. However, since Dan Walker's
revolution, the Democratic party has made inroads into the suburbs. Will County
(with the Democratic city of Joliet) has become increasingly Democratic—in
the 1992 general elections, local Democrats took all but one of the county-wide
offices. In the suburbs, NFP Democrats like Neil Hartigan do far better than
their traditional New Deal liberal counterparts.

The most sustained support for NFP, however, has come from "downstate"
Illinois. The true "cities of the prairie" and a good number of rural counties have
turned out more Democratic votes for NFP candidates. The "moralists" and
"individualists" who represent the major types of Elazar's political cultures
have been mobilized by the populist rhetoric and style of NFP candidates.[4]

The Big Picture: Illinois Gubernatorial Elections, 1956-1990

The Democratic statewide coalition has shifted since the 1950s. The last ten
gubernatorial elections demonstrate this. Democratic candidates have increasingly relied on "downstate" and suburban voters. To be more competitive in
gubernatorial and other statewide elections, more Democratic candidates have
adopted NFP themes.

Figure 8.4 presents the historical model used to explain the emergence of
NFP. Changes in the characteristics of the Downsian "median" voter comprise
the centerpiece of the model. As geographic and demographic shifts in the population lead the median voter's concerns and priorities to change, the political
system adapts by focusing on new political issues and styles. NFP is thus a
response by certain political elites to changes in the political marketplace. This

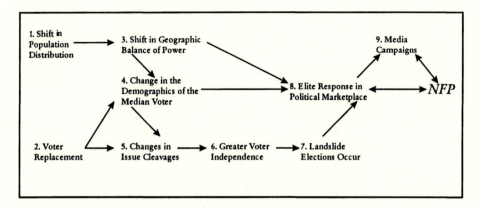

FIGURE 8.4 Historical Model of the Emergence of NFP

Note: Explanation of Model Components:

A. When a shift in a political unit's internal population distribution occurs (point 1), the geographic balance of power shifts (point 3); that is, more voters moving to a particular region increase the political power of that region.

B. Existing voters are replaced as the young people come of age and older voters die off (point 2).

C. As voter replacement and population changes occur, the demographic characteristics of the median voter in the system change (point 4): e.g., if more people move to the suburbs and a higher percentage of voters are first-time voters, the demographics of the median voter will be different from past elections.

D. As voters are replaced and the "center" of the political debate changes (because the median voter has changed), new issues divide a changed electorate in a changed system (point 5).

E. Changes in issue cleavages lead to greater voter independence (point 6); that is, the old partisan structures will tend not to reflect the new cleavages, so voters are forced to look beyond party lines for guidance in voting.

F. Greater voter independence increases the chance of "landslide" elections (point 7)—the increase in "floating voters" (voters who will not automatically vote for candidates of one particular political party) makes "landslides" possible.

G. Political elites ignore shifts in the balance of power at their own peril; after a few landslide elections, elites must respond or face political oblivion (point 8).

H. Media campaigns are a modern response to voter independence (point 9).

I. Analysis in this chapter (accompanying Figures 8.5 and 8.6) indicates that changing demographics, issues, and elite responses in Illinois since the early 1970s have generated a rise of New Fiscal Populism (NFP).

does not mean that NFP candidates are insincere. The response may come as elites who stand for new ideas replace older elites. The model is not Illinois-specific. Other political systems may operate on these same "Downsian" principles (cf. esp. Hoffmann-Martinot, forthcoming).

While NFP Democrats effectively adapt to the shift in the Illinois median voter, traditional Democrats find themselves at an increasing political disadvantage. Figures 8.5 and 8.6 demonstrate this. Figure 8.5 shows that from 1956 to 1990, Democratic gubernatorial candidates have fared increasingly well within Chicago, done about the same in suburban Cook County, and declined in their ability to garner votes from the suburban "collar" counties and from "downstate." These results seem at odds with the results in Figure 8.6, which show that over the same time period, the total proportion of gubernatorial votes for Democrats that originate in Chicago has declined, while the proportions of Democratic votes coming from all three of the other three regions have *risen*. To understand these results, the key lies in Illinois's changing population distribution, and hence its changing geographic balance of power. Since the Illinois voting population has shifted away from Chicago, even though Chicagoans increasingly vote Democratic, their votes are no longer sufficient to provide Democrats with a decisive proportion of their overall, statewide vote totals. The evidence in Figures 8.5 and 8.6 thus combines to reveal that Democrats are faring better within just the Illinois political regions where the voting population is dwindling, while Democrats are faring worse where the population is growing and hence where there are many more votes to be won. However, these patterns do *not* apply equally to traditional and NFP Democrats. Results in the highlighted years in Figure 8.5 show that the *NFP* gubernatorial candidates running in 1972 and 1990 (Walker and Hardigan) did better than traditional Democrats in the three regions lying outside of Chicago, while those NFP candidates did just as well within Chicago. Results in the highlighted years in Figure 8.6 reveal a consequent pattern of NFP candidates garnering a higher proportion of their overall, statewide vote totals than traditional Democrats from outside of Chicago: that is, from the increasingly pivotal regions where the voting population is growing.

To summarize, Figures 8.5 and 8.6 demonstrate that: (1) due to geographic shifts in the population, all Democratic candidates must rely increasingly on winning votes from outside of Chicago (and hence from outside the remnants of the Democratic machine), and (2) NFP candidates are more successful in obtaining suburban and "downstate" votes than traditional Democrats. This suggests that winning Democratic candidates will increasingly be NFP ones. By appealing more to voters outside of Chicago, NFP candidates adapt to the changing political marketplace. Dan Walker was ahead of his time in drawing non-Chicago support to the Democratic party. Neil Hartigan followed Walker's lead by focusing his efforts primarily on winning downstate and suburban voters.

The decline in the Chicago machine—a result of greater voter independence

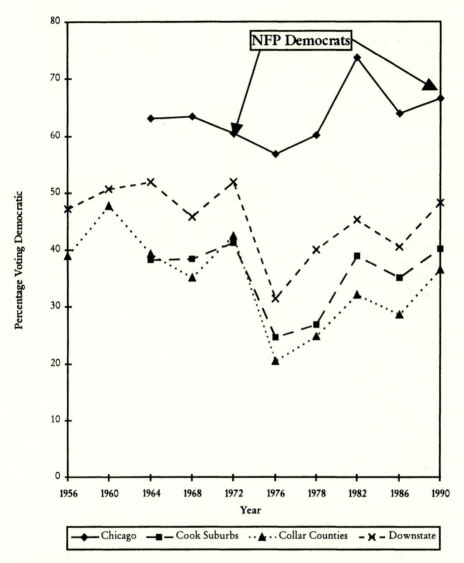

FIGURE 8.5 NFP Democrats Fare Better Than Traditional Democrats Outside of Chicago; Traditional Democrats Have Done Increasingly Well in Chicago but Less Well in the Other Political Regions, 1956-1990.

Note: This figure shows the proportions of votes that Democratic candidates won, respectively, for each of Illinois's four political regions, in gubernatorial elections from 1956 to 1990. Since NFP Democrats (Walker and Hartigan) ran for governor in 1972 and 1990, the election results for those two years indicate how NFP Democrats performed in comparison with traditional Democrats.

Source: Secretary of State (and State Board of Elections), *Reports on General Elections for Governor, 1956-1990.*

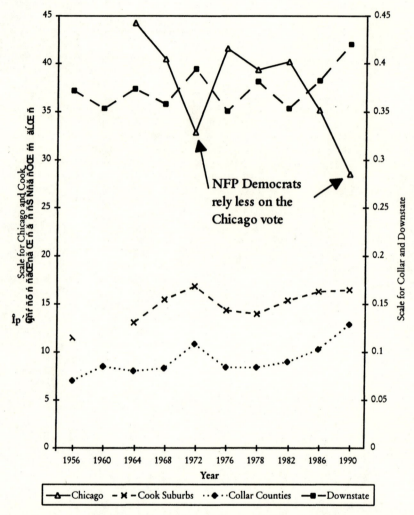

FIGURE 8.6. Population Shifts Mean That Declining Proportions of Democratic Voters Live in Chicago; NFP Democrats Adapt by Relying Less Than Traditional Democrats on the Chicago Vote, 1956-1990.

Note: This figure shows the proportions of total statewide votes for Democrats in Gubernatorial elections from 1956 to 1990 that come from each of Illinois's four political regions (the four regional percentages should thus total 100%). The left scale ranges from 0 to 45%, the right scale from 0 to .45%. Since NFP Democrats (Walker and Hartigan) ran for governor in 1972 and 1990, the election results for those two years indicate the relative regional vote proportions obtained by NFP Democrats versus traditional Democrats.

Source: Secretary of State (and State Board of Elections), *Reports on General Elections for Governor, 1956-1990.*

and a shift in the geographic balance of voting power in the state—forces Democratic candidates to appeal to voters beyond the original New Deal coalition. Candidates increasingly stress the concerns of suburban and small town voters: for instance, concerns like low taxes and a clean environment, which are more important to suburban voters than labor laws or patronage, concerns that remain central to ethnic union members in Chicago.

There is a dearth of research on voter choice for Illinois state offices, but some surveys are available. A 1990 survey by the Center for Governmental Studies at Northern Illinois University asked 794 Illinois residents, "What was/will be the most important factor or issue in your choice of who to vote for [in the election for governor]?" Of those who could give an answer, "personality" was most significant, cited by 17.1%, followed by 9.3% for "taxes." Only 8.8% answered political party. Still, as 22.4% were undecided, the responses should be interpreted cautiously. Interestingly, there was no significant correlation between preference for governor and views on extending the infamous income tax surcharge or belief that "taxes and spending" were the most important problem facing the state. For instance, the correlation between opposition to extension of the tax surcharge and preference for governor (among those who had a choice) was only 0.0422. Seven-part party identification (PID), on the other hand, had a correlation of 0.5043 (a=0.001) with candidate preference. This indicates that party ID is not dead. Instead, it might be more important than some issue positions. These results, however, omit the growing impact over time of personality and populism: of the NFP *style*.

If personality and taxes have grown more important to voters, it makes Downsian sense for Neil Hartigan or others to switch to an NFP platform. Machine politicians who raise taxes are less popular with the median voter than reformers who visibly oppose "tax-and-spend" policies.

What Does This Mean?

The traditional Daley era is over in Illinois. Major Democratic candidates need support beyond urban machines and party elites. The past twenty years have seen the rise of candidate-centered elections, increasing partisan dealignment, and continuing changes in both media technology and electoral demographics. These processes have interacted with the traditional New Deal Democratic coalition and its leaders to generate New Fiscal Populism (NFP) in Illinois politics. Charismatic nonprofessionals are more frequent and successful as major Democratic candidates. The lack of strong party structure increasingly loosens candidates for major offices from the hierarchical control of traditional party leaders.

Yet this is not necessarily true for "lesser" candidates. For example, Illinois House Democrats still use considerable party discipline. Their leader, Michael Madigan, can use campaign money and resources to enforce the party line. The large number of "marginal" districts coupled with the spiraling cost of competitive legislative races has increased Madigan's leverage. The decline of the machine has thus "freed" major candidates from the party but simultaneously reinforced party ties for candidates without the personal resources to finance their campaigns. Some junior state legislators are publicly critical of party leadership, its control of information on pending bills and policy staff, and an unwillingness to include them in major policy decisions. Still, change continues: Madigan's public pronouncements grew increasingly NFP in the 1980s and early 1990s—he tried to seize the issue of taxes from the Republicans, while remaining a "let's make a deal" ethnic Democrat with strong ties to organized labor.

Despite the effort to move towards NFP policies, every marginal Democratic incumbent in the Illinois General Assembly was defeated in 1994. The current electoral map was drawn by Republicans to elect a Republican legislature. NFP Democrats were able to forestall the Republican takeover of the Illinois House for only one election cycle; in most cases, marginally Republican districts elected an NFP Democrat in 1992 but then a Republican in 1994. Conventional wisdom points towards two conflicting causes of the electoral switch. Some activists claim that the NFP Democrats did not energize the traditional Democratic base—leading to a lower turnout and electoral disaster. Other party regulars believe that gubernatorial candidate Dawn Clark Netsch's perceived status as a "tax and spend" liberal undercut the NFP Democrats' message and alienated key "swing" voters in the highly competitive districts.

This dichotomy symbolizes the transition that the Illinois Democratic party is undergoing. Party regulars ("hacks" in the vernacular) and liberal activists skirmish in primaries and campaign strategy sessions. Fights between the "new" Democrats and their more liberal counterparts are not likely to dissipate anytime in the foreseeable future.

Conclusions

1. NFP candidates' populist component is more politically salient than their social or fiscal agendas. NFP candidates pay increased attention to individual citizens. Successful NFP candidates focus on *populism*. Traditional partisan candidates focus on traditional social and fiscal issues. (See analysis of the 1990 Vote for Governor above.)

2. The NFP "base" consists of non-poor, non-urban, well-educated, "young" voters; NFP candidates, however, garner support from voters of many different backgrounds. Election returns at the ward and county levels indicate that NFP candidates depend more on suburban and rural votes than do traditional Democratic candidates. Regressions of election returns indicate growing dependence of winning Democrats on suburban votes.

3. The electoral strength and makeup of NFP depend a great deal on its specific, current context; NFP is not a static ideology, but a flexible set of politi-

cal norms and values. In 1972 Dan Walker won. In 1992 Al Hofeld lost. Each challenged a prominent Democrat in a statewide primary contest. Walker opposed a machine-slated candidate with a fiscally liberal record; hence anti-machine independents and "downstate" and suburban voters formed Walker's political base. Personal wealth and opposition to "special interests" were all Hofeld brought to his campaign. A vicious three-way primary obscured his NFP message, and without a clear political base, Hofeld fell short.

4. NFP candidates campaign and govern by going "to the people" instead of focusing on political elites. Governor Walker faced a partisan Republican legislature and a hostile Democratic caucus; he appealed to the people whenever possible. Likewise, not back-room deals but television made Al Hofeld a player and enabled him to bypass political and media elites.

5. NFP has increased as a style of campaigning or governing over the past twenty years; with the breakdown of the urban machine and bloc voting, major Democratic candidates are turning to NFP to fill the void left in the aftermath of the New Deal coalition. For good reasons Neil Hartigan abandoned his New Deal roots. A different statewide appeal was necessary. Three out of the five preceding traditional Democrats had been crushed. Even established partisan elites can be swayed by such devastating electoral evidence.

Epilogue: NFP and the Future of Political Culture

In 1970, Dan Walker won in part because he recognized that the suburbs and downstate Illinois had political cultures antagonistic to the Chicago Democratic machine. In 1992, Al Hofeld chose by contrast not to concentrate on appealing to the alleged distinct political cultures of Illinois's mid-sized cities; instead, he ran identical television commercials across the state—and received a positive response from a range of different political cultures. Does this change over twenty years among like-minded NFP candidates signal that political cultural differences have grown less important? Perhaps the population shifts to the suburbs, the increasing migration of the population, and the expanding prevalence of inexpensive media have weakened or diluted traditional political cultures.

I do not argue that political culture has become obsolete. Nor do I assert that it is not important in certain geographic areas and communities. My assertion is rather that exogenous factors are weakening the old political order. The NFP "mishmash" of more traditional political cultures appears to appeal to an increasingly diverse and diffuse constituency. Since NFP can appeal so broadly, it has been and will be adopted as the style of many future political leaders in Illinois. It is no accident that Neil Hartigan and Jim Edgar sounded so much alike in 1990. Nor is it an accident that most of the Illinois gubernatorial candidates in 1994 sounded like Dan Walker over twenty years ago.[5] NFP is becoming a major political culture in Illinois.[6]

Every state begins with a unique political culture or distribution of political cultures. Some prove more fertile for NFP than others. Former presidential candidates Paul Tsongas and Gary Hart, and Bill Clinton demonstrate growing NFP strength as a national political force. Political elites increasingly ignore NFP at their peril.

Notes

1. For an exploration of Illinois as a microcosm and bellwether see David H. Everson, "Illinois as a bellwether: So what?" *Illinois Issues*, February 1990, pp. 9-10.

2. Walker's background, views, and campaign are discussed at length in *Dan Walker Memoir*. Springfield, IL: Sangamon State University, 1984.

3. This interpretation follows from the machine's consistent valuing of local offices over national and state offices; after all, how many patronage jobs does a U.S. senator control when compared to the mayor of Chicago?

4. *Cities of the Prairie* (1970) discusses the political cultures of Illinois, from which he built his national theories in later works.

5. Three major Democrats ran in the 1994 primaries against Governor Edgar: Roland Burris, an African-American Dan Walker protégé; Richard Phelan, again sounding NFP themes; and Comptroller Dawn Clark Netsch, known for her fiscal prudence and "lake shore liberal" status. She won the primary but lost the general election to Edgar in a landslide. Meanwhile, Al Hofeld ran a more competitive race for attorney general, defeating a machine-backed former Chicago City Council member with a liberal reputation in the primary, but losing to his Republican opponent in the general election. Pat Quinn, another Walker protégé, and the incumbent state treasurer, defeated a "regular" Democratic candidate in the primary and lost in the general election.

6. Daniel Elazar's (1970) classic on political culture in Illinois has been updated by him and coworkers three times. In a 1994 round of meetings where they monitored changes with local civic and political leaders in many Illinois towns, a dominant theme was the rise of the media. It was seriously criticized by many as undermining democracy, voter turnout, and the civic role of voluntary associations. It was directly attacked by many local officials, to the extent of legally terminating the license for controversial talk shows. The meeting in Decatur concluded: ". . . when reporters do not behave responsibly or appropriately, they should be banished or reported to the FCC." *The Federalism Report* (1995: 12).

9

Contemporary Ideological Cleavages in the United States

Michael Rempel

Introduction

Political analysts have long relied on the classic "left-right" cleavage to define opposing sides of major political issues. Recently, though, doubt has arisen about whether that one cleavage is sufficient. Some analysts now see two cleavages: one on *economic* issues, like jobs, welfare policy, and labor relations, and another on *social* issues, like the environment, civil rights, and the threat of crime. Some even see two cleavages within the economic realm: one on questions of *redistribution,* or the transfer of resources from some citizens to others, and another on spending programs which extend benefits to a wider segment of the population. Further, cleavages on "new social movement" issues—like civil rights, free speech, and the environment, which became objects of New Left activism during the 1960s—may differ from "law and order" issues like violent crime and drug abuse. Finally, some analysts maintain that politics is no longer reducible to any overarching cleavages, but consists mainly of conflicts on unconnected "single issues." I assess these alternatives, drawing on evidence from

AUTHOR'S NOTE: I would like to express my appreciation to Terry Clark, who commented on two previous versions of this chapter and to Howard Runyon, for his helpful editorial feedback. Also, I would like to thank Jurek Bartkowski and Ed Vytlacil, who kindly advised me on statistical methods. This paper reports many simple correlation coefficients (Pearson r's) rather than b statistics to facilitate communication and since the variance across subgroups compared is comparable enough not to generate the sorts of methodological problems that Achen (1978) and others have discussed.

the General Social Survey (GSS), a public opinion survey of United States citizens administered repeatedly since 1972.

Five Conceptions of Ideological Cleavages

The Classic "Left-Right" Model

This model remains central for many journalists and academics. Lipset and Rokkan (1967) trace it to the 19th-century Industrial Revolution, when class conflict spread through most industrializing countries, leading to the formation of political parties along a class-based "left-right" divide. The left represented a working-class interest in instituting a large welfare state to ensure economic growth and foster equality; the right represented employers' interests in preserving free-market competition and using government to promote continuing profits for business. In some countries the right also supported a strong centralized state in the name of national economic progress, but typically it stood against the local autonomy of ordinary citizens.

Distinguishing Economic from Social Issues

Some authors propose that the classic left-right model should be replaced by one positing separate cleavages on economic and social issues (e.g., Clark and Lipset 1991; Clark, Lipset, and Rempel 1993; Dalton, Flanagan, and Beck 1984; Flanagan 1987; Inglehart 1990; Lipset 1981; Rempel 1996). Many credit the widespread political activism of the 1960s with forming "new social movements" around issues like global peace, the environment, African-American civil rights, women's rights, gay rights, and abortion (e.g., Bowles and Gintis 1987; Clark et al. 1993; Dalton and Kuechler 1990). Others link the rise of these movements to longer-term socioeconomic and demographic trends, like rising economic growth or educational expansion.

Even if social issues have gained salience, might they connect with economic views under a modified left-right division? Hout, Brooks, and Manza (1993) suggest that some citizens may continue to think in terms of just one cleavage, preferring to be able to invoke a simple "psychological heuristic" when selecting views on multiple specific issues (see derivation of this analysis in Sniderman, Brody, and Tetlock 1990). In this case, the rise of social issues may not so much undermine the singular left-right cleavage as transform it from a cleavage based mainly on class conflict into one subsuming social concerns too.

Distinguishing Redistributive from Non-Redistributive Economic Issues

Redistributive issues concern the transfer of socioeconomic resources from economically privileged to more marginalized subgroups—for example, rich to poor, employers to workers, or, in the United States, whites to African-Americans. *Non-redistributive* or "middle-class" issues concern spending programs perceived to benefit not just select subgroups but most of the citizenry. Classic examples are police and fire protection, public health programs, and environmental protection. Brint, Cunningham, and Li (this volume) report that across five industrialized countries, blue-collar workers are the most pro-spending subgroup on redistributive issues (e.g., unemployment benefits, old-age pensions, and reduction of income disparities), whereas middle-income professionals are the most pro-spending subgroup on "middle-class" issues (e.g., the arts, environment, and education).

Distinguishing "New Social Movement" from "Law and Order" Issues

In the United States, liberal views rose from 1972 to 1989 on race, gender equality, and free speech, but declined on crime and religion (Davis 1992). Rempel and Clark (this volume) generalize that social liberalism is rising on new social movement issues but declining on law and order ones (although more specific country and period effects remain).

Single-Issue Politics

Some authors contend that all ideological cleavages have become mere conceptual constructs. Political organizations are now more single-issue-oriented, and citizens more prone to evaluate issues piecemeal, without reference to *any* overarching ideologies. Turner (1988) theorizes that, on economic issues, numerous single-issue *status blocs* have arisen, each demanding more government support for a specific program benefitting a select constituency. (See Rempel and Clark, this volume, on origins of single-issue politics.)

Results of the Analysis

I studied General Social Survey (GSS) questions on redistributive, non-redistributive, new social movement–based, and law and order issues. Appendix A gives the specific questions and classifications used.

Support for the Left Across Different Economic Issues

Table 9.1 shows mean citizen support for the pro-spending left on nine economic issues. Throughout the testing period, support for spending is lowest on the three redistribution items: (1) income redistribution from rich to poor, (2) spending on welfare, and (3) aid to African-Americans.

TABLE 9.1 Citizen Views on Economic Spending Issues
Citizens Support Redistribution Much Less Than Non-Redistributive Spending

	% Who Answer Govt Spends "Too Little" for All Years, 1973-1993	Overall Mean, (1-3 Scale) for All Years, 1973-1993	Mean in 1973	Mean in 1993	Change in the Mean, 1973 to 1993
Redistributive Issues:					
EQWLTH Income Redistribution	N/A	2.12[*,#]	2.11[*,#]	2.10[*]	−.01[*,#]
NATFARE Welfare	20.5%	1.70	1.67	1.61	−.06
NATRACE Helping African-Americans	33.5%	2.12	2.11	2.23	+.12
Non-Redistributive Spending Issues:					
NATENVIR Environment	60.0%	2.51	2.57	2.49	−.08
NATEDUC Education	58.5%	2.51	2.42	2.63	+.21
NATHEAL Health Care	63.5%	2.58	2.58	2.66	+.08
NATCITY Big Cities	51.3%	2.34	2.41	2.48	+.07
NATCRIME Crime	70.4%	2.65	2.64	2.69	+.05
NATDRUG Drug Addiction	63.7%	2.56	2.64	2.56	−.08

Note: The means of all variables are on 1-3 scales, with the higher value representing the more pro-left, pro-spending response: "3" = government currently spends "too little money"; "2" = government spending is "about the right amount"; and "1" = government currently spends "too much money."

Note: This and all subsequent tables were computed by the author from raw data.

[*] EQWLTH was originally coded on a 1-7 scale; the number in the table is based on a proportional translation of the original value to a 1-3 scale, with a higher value representing support for more income redistribution.

[#] The EQWLTH question was not asked until 1978; thus where 1973 means are reported for other questions, the 1978 mean is reported, or used to calculate changes over time, for EQWLTH.

Source: National Opinion Research Center: General Social Survey (GSS), 1972-1993.

Correlations Between Left-Right Views Across Multiple Issues

Table 9.2 gives simple correlations between citizen views on every possible pair of the GSS political issues analyzed. These show to what degree citizens hold political views consistently on either the left or the right across multiple issues.

Table 9.2A gives results for economic issues. All 36 correlations are positive and statistically significant at the .01 level. Citizens on the left on one economic issue *are* more likely to be on the left on any of the others. This holds across both redistributive and non-redistributive issues.

Table 9.2B gives similar results for social issues. All 21 correlations that do not include capital punishment or wiretapping are positive and statistically significant at the .01 level; 8 of 15 correlations that include at least one of those two law and order issues are negative or statistically insignificant. Apparently, many citizens see causes like African-American civil rights, women's rights, and freedom of expression—all championed by New Left activists during the 1960s—as sharing a common ideological dimension, but consider law and order issues separately. (However, the legalization of marijuana, another "law and order" concern, did correlate more like the new social movement issues.)

Table 9.2C presents results for correlations matching economic with social views. These correlations are positive and statistically significant in almost three-fourths of the table's 81 cells, but the numbers are much weaker than in Tables 9.2A and 9.2B. Of 81 correlations, only 5 exceed .15, whereas most corre-

TABLE 9.2 Correlations Between Citizen Views on Different Political Issues

A. Views on Economic Spending Issues
Citizens Exhibit Ideological Consistency Across Different Economic Issues

	EQWLTH	NATFARE	NATRACE	NATENVI	NATEDUC	NATHEAL	NATCITY	NATCRIME
Redistributive Issues:								
EQWLTH Income Redistribution								
NATFARE Welfare	.21							
NATRACE Economic Aid for African-Americans	.16	.33						
Non-Redistributive Spending Issues:								
NATENVIR Environment	.11	.12	.22					
NATEDUC Education	.10	.16	.28	.24				
NATHEAL Health Care	.17	.16	.21	.27	.25			
NATCITY Big Cities	.14	.20	.33	.25	.23	.26		
NATCRIME Crime	.07	.05	.14	.12	.16	.19	.25	
NATDRUG Drug Addiction	.10	.09	.19	.13	.19	.19	.21	.39

(continues)

TABLE 9.2 *(continued)*

B. Views on Different Social Issues
Citizens Exhibit Ideological Consistency Across Different New Social Movement Issues, But Not Across Law and Order Issues

New Social Movement Issues:	FEMINIS	CIVRIGH	SPEECH	ABANY	HOMOSEX	SEXEDUC	GRASS	CAPPUN
FEMINISM Women's Equality								
CIVRIGHT Equality of African-Americans	.35							
SPEECH Free Speech Rights	.35	.37						
ABANY Legality of Abortion	.21	.12	.25					
HOMOSEX Homosexual Rights	.35	.24	.31	.33				
SEXEDUC Sex Education in Schools	.32	.19	.26	.19	.19			
Law and Order Issues:								
GRASS Legalization of Marijuana	.16	.14	.24	.23	.33	.13		
CAPPUN Capital Punishment	xx	.08	.04	−.03	.09	xx	.06	
WIRTAP Wiretapping	xx	xx	−.05	xx	.03	xx	.04	.14

C. Views on Economic Correlated with Views on Social Issues
Citizens Do Not Exhibit Much Ideological Consistency Across their Economic and Social Views

Economic Issues	FEMINIS	CIVRIGH	SPEECH	ABANY	HOMOSEX	SEXEDUC	GRASS	CAPPUN	WIRTAP
Redistributive Issues:									
EQWLTH Income Redistribution	−.05	−.03	−.13	−.07	−.03	xx	xx	.11	.08
NATFARE Welfare	xx	.08	xx	.01	.04	.03	.05	.17	.09
NATRACE Economic Aid for African-Americans	.12	.29	.10	.03	.10	.11	.08	.20	.12
Non-Redistributive Spending Issues:									
NATENVIR Environment	.17	.14	.14	.05	.14	.14	.12	.08	.07
NATEDUC Education	.15	.12	.10	.05	.09	.16	.07	.06	.08
NATHEAL Health Care	.07	.06	.05	xx	.07	.09	.05	.07	.07
NATCITY Big Cities	.09	.12	.09	.05	.11	.10	.09	.11	.08
NATCRIME Crime	xx	xx	−.03	−.02	xx	.06	−.06	−.04	xx
NATDRUG Drug Addiction	xx	xx	−.05	−.07	−.06	.06	−.09	.03	xx

Note: All correlation coefficients (Pearson's r) are statistically significant at the .01 level, unless the coefficient is deleted and replaced by an "xx," in which case the coefficient was not significant at that level; in all instances where a correlation coefficient was not statistically significant, its value, r, was less than .03.

Source: National Opinion Research Center: General Social Survey (GSS), 1972-1993.

lations in Tables 9.2A and 9.2B exceed that level. Thus the evidence is that most citizens evaluate economic and social issues differently.

Effects of Social Background Characteristics on Political Views

One reason for separating economic from social issues is that different social background characteristics affect views on each type. Economic status links with the material interests affecting economic views, whereas education and age link with the more qualitative, lifestyle-oriented values affecting social views (e.g., Brint and Kelley 1993; Flanagan 1982).

Table 9.3 gives results of ordinary least-squares regressions testing the effects of different social background characteristics on citizens' political views on (1) the three redistribution questions, (2) a non-redistributive spending views index, (3) a new-social-movement views index, and (4) a law and order views index. (See Rempel 1995 for regressions on the 15 individual issues incorporated in the indices.)

As earlier research suggested, higher income makes citizens less inclined to support redistribution. But income has no discernible effect on non-redistributive spending views. This calls into question generalizations about the social bases of economic or "fiscal" policy views. It seems that the material interests of middle-income and upper-middle-income citizens lead them to oppose redistribution but not necessarily to oppose spending on less redistributive programs (see also Brint et al. this volume; Greenstein 1991; Skocpol 1991; Wilson 1987).

Years of education and vocabulary score are the GSS's two operational measures of what Inglehart (1990) calls "cognitive mobilization"—the possession and use of advanced intellectual capacities. The two measures exert the same directional effect in every Table 9.3 regression. Their effects are inconsistent for the four regressions on economic views, but in both regressions on social views, more cognitively mobilized citizens support the left (fifth and sixth columns). This effect is much stronger in the regression on new social movement than on law and order views.

Of all the background characteristics, older age has the strongest negative effect on support for the left on (1) non-redistributive and (2) new social movement issues. The greater liberalism of the young on those issues supports Inglehart's (1990) view that recently socialized young persons tend especially to favor new political tendencies. However, the greater liberalism of younger citizens is more marked when comparing the views of those aged 31–50 with those aged 51 and older than when comparing the views of the youngest generation, aged 18–30, with those aged 31–50. Perhaps this is because citizens in the middle 31–50 generation grew up during the relatively liberal 1960s, whereas today's youngest citizens did not likewise encounter that era's liberalizing impact. That may have led the youngest citizens surveyed not to reflect the otherwise strong generational trend towards greater liberalism.

The strong impact of race, though not directly germane to research issues discussed above, deserves mention. In all four of the regressions on economic issues, being African-American is the most influential background characteristic in eliciting pro-spending views. The effect is strongest on support for welfare and for aid to African-Americans. This strongly confirms research by Clark (1994) on the great impact of race on United States redistributive politics (see also Rempel 1996).

Intervening Social Background Effects on Ideological Consistency

Do "cognitively mobilized" citizens more often conjoin issues under a single left-right framework? These citizens possess greater political knowledge and skills than others. They may therefore have greater exposure to dominant binaries of the political culture, like the classic left-right cleavage. Cognitively mobilized citizens may use such binaries as heuristics for organizing their views on the myriad specific issues that confront them. To test this, I compared the strength of each correlation in Table 9.2 (which was for *all* respondents) with the same correlations for "cognitively mobilized" citizens. The results show that the cognitively mobilized fall more consistently on either the left or the right across multiple issues (see Table 9.4). Left-right correlations are higher for the cognitively mobilized on different pairs of economic issues (26 of 36 correlations are higher) and on different pairs of social issues (20 of 36 correlations are higher). The weaker effects on the social issues may stem from their lacking a past history of incorporation under a singular, largely class-based left-right divide. Finally, comparing left-right correlations *between* economic and social views, 51 of 81 are higher for the cognitively mobilized, and 19 are lower.

Table 9.5 further focuses on the impact of social background on ideological consistency. The correlations between views on redistributive and social issues rise for citizens who (1) attended college, (2) correctly answered at least six GSS vocabulary questions, or (3) belong to any political club. Further, among respondents who are both cognitively *and* politically mobilized—who possess all three of these characteristics—the correlations rise even more. Other tests not shown found neither income nor age to have such consistent, significant effects on these correlations.

Discussion and Conclusion

Most citizens in the United States evaluate economic and social issues differently. Correlations between views on each type are generally negligible. Also, income and race most affect economic views, while cognitive training and age most affect social views.

However, the simple categories "economic" and "social" appear too broad. Among social issues, correlations are much higher between views on new social

TABLE 9.3 Regressions of Social Background Characteristics on Political Views

	EQWLTH Rich-Poor Income Redistr.	NATFARE Spending on Welfare	NATRACE Spending on African-Ams	NONRED6X Non-Redistrib. Spending	NSMX Social Leftism (NSM Issues)	LAWORDX Social Leftism (Law and Order Issues)
Adjusted R Square	.09	.12	.19	.08	.29	.09
Background Variables:	Beta	Beta	Beta	Beta	Beta	Beta
Economic Status Measures:						
INCOME (Income)	−.09**	−.17**	−.04**	−.01	.05**	−.08**
PRESTIGE (Occupational Prestige)	−.02	−.03*	−.01	−.01	.05**	−.01
Cognitive Mobilization Measures:						
EDUC (Years of Education)	−.07**	.02	.08**	.02	.15**	.03*
WORDSUM (Vocabulary Test Score)	−.12**	.00	.05**	.02	.20**	.07**
Age/Time Measures:						
AGE (Age of Respondent)	−.03*	−.03**	−.05**	−.15**	−.22**	−.08**
YEAR (Year of Survey)	.03	.13**	.08**	.12**	−.03**	−.12**
Other Background Characteristics:						
AFRAM (African-American vs. Other)	.13**	.23**	.39**	.13**	.03**	.19**
CATHOLIC (Catholic vs. Other)	.04*	.01	.02	.00	.01	.03**
MARITAL (Marital Status 3 = married)	−.03*	−.03*	−.03**	.00	−.04	−.05**
NEAST (Northeast vs. Other)	.00	−.01	.01	.05**	.05**	−.01
NORELIG (No Religious Affiliation vs. Other)	.03	.02	.03*	−.02	.12**	.09**
PAC (Pacific Coast vs. Other)	−.03*	.01	−.01	−.02	.06**	.01
SEX (Female vs. Male)	.06**	.00	.04**	.07**	.01	.05**
SOUTH (South vs. Other)	−.10**	.00	−.05**	.01	−.08**	−.01
XNORCSIZ (Locality Size)	.00	.05**	.03**	.09**	.09**	.01

(*continues*)

204

TABLE 9.3 *(continued)*

	EQWLTH Rich-Poor Income Redistr.	NATFARE Spending on Welfare	NATRACE Spending on African-Ams	NONRED6X Non-Redistrib. Spending	NSMX Social Leftism (NSM Issues)	LAWORDX Social Leftism (Law and Order Issues)
Alternative Model #1: Impact of young and old (versus middle) age groupings (versus using the continuous "age" variable)						
AGE1830 (ages 18-30)	.03	.02	.04**	.04**	.07**	.04**
AGE51UP (ages 51 and older)	-.01	-.02	-.02	-.12**	-.16**	-.06**

Note #1: For all six political variables—EQWLTH, NATFARE, NATRACE, NONRED6X, NSMX, and LAWORDX—a higher value represents a more pro-left response (pro-spending on economic issues, and pro-rights on social issues). Therefore, positive beta values mean that possessing a higher level of the given social background characteristic leads citizens to be more likely to be on the left politically. Redistributive views are in EQWLTH, NATFARE, and NATRACE; non-redistributive views are in NONRED6X; new social movement views are in NSMX; and (4) law and order views are in LAWORDX.

Note #2: In the basic regression model, I used a standard battery of social background characteristic variables: age, education, income, occupational prestige, race, marital status, sex, size of locality, region (separate variables for Pacific Coast versus elsewhere, Northeast versus elsewhere, and South versus elsewhere), and religion (separate variables for Catholic versus other, and no religion versus other). I also included the year of survey as a variable to assess changes from 1972 to 1993. The social background variables used here are virtually identical to those used by Butts (this volume) in his cross-national study of the social origins of feminist views. See Butts for further discussion of predicted effects of these variables, especially on social views.

Note #3: For alternative model #1, beta values are reported only for age variables. However, that regression model included all of the same background characteristic variables included in the primary model, when using "AGE" as a continuous variable.

* Significant at the .05 level (2-tailed).
** Significant at the .01 level (2-tailed).
Source: National Opinion Research Center: General Social Survey (GSS), 1972-1993.

TABLE 9.4   The Impact of Cognitive Mobilization on Correlations of Views Across Different Political Issues
Cognitively Mobilized Citizens Exhibit Greater Ideological Consistency Than the General Population

	Correlations of Views on Different Economic Issues	Correlations of Views on Different Social Issues	Correlations of Economic with Social Views
Reference Correlations (r's) in Table 9.2	see Table 9.2A	see Table 9.2B	see Table 9.2C
r is Higher for the Cognitively Mobilized:	26 cells	20 cells	51 cells
r is Higher for the General Population:	8 cells	14 cells	19 cells
r is Virtually Identical:	2 cells	2 cells	11 cells
Total # Correlations (r's) in the table:	36 cells	36 cells	81 cells

Note #1: The summary statistics reported in this table are based on a cell-by-cell comparison of the results displayed in Table 9.2 for correlations when considering all citizens and the equivalent results (not displayed) just for citizens who are "cognitively mobilized": who both attended at least some college *and* who correctly answered at least six of the GSS's ten vocabulary questions. Pearson's r values defined as "virtually identical" are within .01 of each other; where one value is defined as "higher" than the other, the difference in r values exceeds .01. The precise Pearson's r values for cognitively mobilized citizens are available in Rempel (1995) or from the author upon request.
Note #2: Many of the differences which this table recognizes between particular sets of correlations are not nearly statistically significant (although there are many which *are* significant as well). The summary statistics hence should not be interpreted as yielding definitive, precise counts but more as indicating the general direction of the differences: that consistently in more instances than not, the correlations for the same pairs of variables are higher for cognitively mobilized citizens than for the general population.
Source: National Opinion Research Center: General Social Survey (GSS), 1972-1993.

TABLE 9.5 The Impact of Social Background Characteristics on Correlations Between Economic and Social View *Cognitively and Politically Mobilized Citizens Exhibit Greater Ideological Consistency Than Others Across Economic and Social Issues*

All correlations are with SOCLEFTX (index of all GSS social views)

	1 Overall Correlations	2 Impact of Education		3 Impact of Vocabulary		4 Impact of Political Activism		5 Impact of Both Cognitive and Political Mobilization
	For Entire Sample Population	Did Not Attend College	Did Attend College	Knew >5 of 10 Words	Knew <6 of 10 Words	Not Political Club Member	Political Club Member	Did Attend College, Knew 5 of 10 Words, & Political Club Member
Redistributive Issues:								
EQWLTH Income Redistribution	.00	.00	.15°	.01	.06°	.00	.14*	.27°
NATFARE Welfare	.12	.10	.24°	.14	.19*	.11	.32*	.60°
NATRACE Economic Aid for Afr-Ams.	.23	.22	.26°	.27	.27°	.21	.32*	.35

Note #1: This table compares correlations (Pearson's r) between the redistributive and social views of five different sets of sub-populations (see each of the five columns): (1) all GSS respondents; (2) those who attended at least some college versus those who never attended college; (3) those who correctly answered at least six of the GSS's ten vocabulary questions versus those who correctly answered fewer than six; (4) those who are not versus those who are members of a "political club"; and (5) those who combine both high cognitive and high political mobilization (i.e., attended some college, correctly answered at least six vocabulary questions, *and* are in a political club). All correlations are between the respective redistributive issues variables noted at the left and SOCLEFTX: an index of views on all nine of the GSS social issues tested in the present study (see Appendix A).

Note #2: The procedure used to test for whether there is a statistically significant difference between two correlation coefficients is in Blalock (1979: 415-425).
° There is a statistically significant increase, with at least a 95% probability, in the given correlation, as compared with the "overall" correlation: the correlation given in column #1 of the table (same row).
* There is a statistically significant increase, with at least a 95% probability, in the given correlation, as compared with the correlation for the alternative sub-population: the correlation given immediately to the left in the table, under the same column.

Source: National Opinion Research Center: General Social Survey (GSS), 1972-1993.

movement issues than when one of any two correlated social issues concerns law and order. Among economic issues, public support is markedly lower for redistribution than non-redistributive or middle class spending. The implications of the low support for *redistribution* are especially poignant. Since 1973 the economies of advanced industrial societies have grown less stable, leaving many citizens less secure economically (see Wilson 1987). One might have expected this change to foster support for redistributive programs, but it has not done so— perhaps because today there is a larger "middle-class" population whose members still do too well to qualify for benefits. This is especially true in countries like the United States and the United Kingdom, where most welfare programs only target persons at the bottom of the economic ladder. The regression results confirm that middle to upper income subgroups tend to oppose redistribution but are *not* more likely than others to oppose programs generally perceived as non-redistributive. So there may be a growing discrepancy between a continuing need for redistribution to certain economically marginalized subgroups and declining overall public support for it. Separately analyzing redistributive and non-redistributive issues, instead of analyzing opinion trends on all economic issues at once, importantly improves our ability to identify economic and political dynamics that might underlie such a discrepancy.

An important qualification of many findings is that although the classic left-right cleavage may not greatly illuminate the political thinking of *most* citizens, overall ideological consistency is higher among those who are well educated, possess strong cognitive skills, or belong to a political club.

Even for the general population, politics is not yet reducible to the play of unconnected single issues. Rather, views on many social and economic issues remain significantly intercorrelated. Whereas only some citizens rely on one encompassing left-right divide, many report ideologically consistent views across narrower bands of issues. Framing politics in terms of *several* overarching cleavages thus remains a useful way for social scientists to tap the political thinking of many citizens.

Appendix: General Social Survey (GSS) Political Questions

Redistributive Issues

1. EQWLTH: "Some people think that the government in Washington ought to reduce the income differences between the rich and the poor, perhaps by raising the taxes of wealthy families or by giving income assistance to the poor. Others think that the government should not concern itself with reducing this income difference between the rich and the poor. Here is a card with a scale from 1 to 7. Think of a score of 1 as meaning that the government ought to reduce the income differences between rich and poor, and a score of 7 meaning that the government should not concern itself with reducing income differences. What score between 1 and 7 comes closest to the way you feel?"

2. NATFARE: "We are faced with many problems in this country, none of which can be solved easily or inexpensively. I'm going to name some of these problems, and for each one I'd like you to tell me whether you think we're spending too much money on it, too little money, or about the right amount ... Welfare." [After recoding, 1 = too much, 2 = about right, 3 = too little.]

3. NATRACE (same introduction as NATFARE): "Improving the conditions of Blacks."

Non-Redistributive Spending Issues

(All questions follow the same introduction as NATFARE above.)
1. NATENVIR: "Improving and protesting the environment."
2. NATEDUC: "Improving the nation's education system."
3. NATHEAL: "Improving and protecting the nation's health."
4. NATCITY: "Solving the problems of big cities."
5. NATCRIME: "Halting the rising crime rate."
6. NATDRUG: "Dealing with drug addiction."

NONRED6X: Mean score on NATENVIR, NATEDUC, NATHEAL, NATCITY, NATCRIME, and NATDRUG.

Social Issues

Appendix A of Rempel and Clark (this volume) gives complete question wording for all social issues used in the present chapter. The variables in this chapter considered to concern "new social movement" issues are the FEMINISM index (on civil rights for women), the CIVRIGHT index (civil rights for African-Americans), the SPEECH index (free speech), ABANY (abortion), HOMOSEX (civil rights for homosexuals), and SEXEDUC (conducting sex education in public schools). Also, NSMX is an index constructed from the mean scores on each of those five variables. The variables considered to concern "law and order" issues are GRASS (legalization of marijuana), CAPPUN (capital punishment), and WIRTAP (use of wiretapping). In constructing each of the following three indices, the variables were first recoded onto compatible 1-3 scales (3 = most pro-left response). For the HOMOSEX variable, this recoding also necessitated combining the two most pro-rights responses into one category.

NSMX: an index constructed from the mean scores on each of the six new social movement issue variables.

LAWORDX: an index constructed from the mean scores on each of the three law and order issue variables.

SOCLEFTX: an index constructed from the mean scores on all nine of the social issue variables.

10

The Social Origins of Feminism and Political Activism: Findings from Fourteen Countries

Paul Butts

The past two decades have spawned an expanding literature on feminism in the United States and Western Europe. However, the literature contains a predominant focus on feminist *organizations*, at the expense of research on feminist *views* among individual citizens. Also, most of the research on feminist views is not cross-national; yet, cross-national study could illuminate the important mediating influence of national political culture. Accordingly, in this chapter, I analyze the social origins of feminist views in 14 advanced industrial countries: the United States, Canada, Japan, and 11 Western European countries. I also analyze whether a relationship exists between holding feminist views and becoming politically active on either feminist or other political issues. These questions join with ones raised in the introduction to this volume, since feminism constitutes one of the major "new social movement" themes that Rempel and Clark claim have risen to the fore in the politics of "post-industrial" societies.

AUTHOR'S NOTE: I would like to thank Terry N. Clark for help in acquiring the data for this analysis, extensive advice on methods of analysis most appropriate to this study, comments on earlier versions of this paper and generally encouraging me along in this endeavor. I also thank Ronald Inglehart for making the World Value Survey data available; Vincent Hoffman-Martinot, Rowan Miranda and Art Michener for further assistance in acquiring the data; Carlen Rader for help in constructing several of the key results tables; and Julie Brines and Kara Joyner for pointing me to a number of helpful sources that I might otherwise have missed. However, I alone bear responsibility for any errors in the analyses and interpretations presented here.

Cross-National Variation in "Objective" Gender Equality

One possible mediating influence on the strength of feminist views is a country's degree of "objective gender equality." Table 10.1 displays three cross-national measures of such equality: the percentages of women versus men who are, respectively, in school at the university level, working in the labor force, and holding political office in the national legislature. Virtually all of the table's percentages are under 50%, indicating some degree of *inequality* everywhere, but clear cross-national differences do exist. While the Scandinavian countries tend to rank highest in equality, the United States, Canada and West Germany each score well on at least one but not on all three of the equality measures; finally, Japan, Britain, Ireland and Belgium possess the least equality of the 14 countries.

Wilcox (1991) theorizes that more "objective" equality raises the social acceptability of feminist views. However, others theorize that more "objective" equality may rob the feminist movement of its driving rationale, impeding the

TABLE 10.1 Gender Equality in 14 Countries

	Education[a]	Labor Force[b]	Legislature[c]
Belgium	38	34	7.5
Britain	37	40	4.3
Canada	51	45.9[#]	9.6
Denmark	50	44	24
France	49*	34.5	5.5
Italy	44*	32	8
Ireland	40	28	8
Japan	33	--	1.4
The Netherlands	41	30	19
Norway	49	42	35
Spain	45	--	5
Sweden	46	45	28
United States	51*	42	5
West Germany	42	38	10

[a] Education statistic: percentage of university and third-level students who are women, 1981; source: Norris 1987; except: * = UNESCO Statistical Yearbook 1987, data for 1982.
[b] Labor force statistic: percentage of women in labor force, 1981; source: Lovenduski 1986; except # = Hartman 1981, data for 1977.
[c] Legislature statistic: percentage of women in lower house of parliament, 1984-87; Spain figure from 1982; source: Randall 1982.

continued dissemination of feminist views and hence the achievement of more objective gains in the future (Katzenstein 1987; Wilcox 1991). Davis and Robinson (1991) suggest that the relevant political dynamics may vary from country to country, depending on how rapidly labor market opportunities for women expand. Davis and Robinson (and Gerson 1987) explain that where labor market opportunities for women expand rapidly, as in the United States, non-employed women may oppose efforts to increase equality further, viewing such efforts as devaluing their status as "homemakers" and possibly eroding their husbands' earnings. By contrast, where labor market opportunities expand more gradually, homemakers may be less likely to perceive employed women as a sudden and serious threat; in that case, non-employed women may then be less likely to oppose the continued proliferation of feminist attitudes.

Possible Social Origins of Feminism and Political Activism

Recently, a cross-national literature has begun to surface on the social origins of feminist views. (See especially Davis and Robinson 1991; Klein 1987; Plutzer and Banaszak 1991; and Wilcox 1991.) I draw many of my hypotheses from these studies. The hypotheses specify linkages of social background characteristics with (1) feminism and (2) political activism, as shown in Figure 10.1 below.

Sex

Since women have more to gain from equality, they should be more likely to support it. Yet, existing "gender gap" research fails to show that women are either consistently to the "left" or to the "right" of men on issues like the Equal Rights Amendment (ERA) in the United States, or abortion or divorce more globally. Some Western European studies even conclude that where men and women differ, women are more conservative (Almond and Verba 1963; Dogan 1967; Durant 1969; Duverger 1955; Randall 1982; Rose and Waldahl 1982; see also Terry 1984 on the gender gap in Canada). In interpreting this, some argue that when controlling for age, much of this sex-based difference arises merely because women outlive men, and older citizens of either sex tend to be more conservative on all social issues (Charlot 1981; Dogan 1967; Hills 1981; Rose & Waldahl 1982). Others propose that the stronger religiosity of women is responsible for their greater conservatism (Lipset 1960; Devaud 1968; Dogan 1967). Time-series data confirms that there is greater female than male conservatism but that this difference has declined in recent years (Randall 1982).

Compared with the attitudinal literature, political activism research presents a clearer portrait of sex-based differences. This research shows that women tend to consider themselves less "political" than men and to participate in politics less often in ways besides voting (Almond and Verba 1963; Baxter and Lansing 1983; Nie, Verba and Petrocik 1976; Verba, Nie and Kim 1978).

Education

Much research ties education to greater support for women's rights and to the rights of minority groups (Almond and Verba 1963; Lipset 1960; Smith 1985a; Weil 1985). Some researchers identify an advanced education as especially related to the dissemination of feminist ideals among *women* (Klein 1984; Plutzer and Banaszak 1991). In explaining education's impact, Davis and Robinson propose two contradictory hypotheses. The "enlightenment thesis" holds that education generates greater awareness of inequality, and that this awareness leads citizens to favor measures to redress inequality. The "reproduction thesis" agrees that education increases awareness but contends that this awareness does not generate protest but acceptance, based on recognition of the "Social Darwinian" principle of the inevitability and appropriateness of a biological meritocracy (1991: 73). This latter thesis challenges the more prevalent empirical assumption, which I adopt in my hypotheses (below), that more educated citizens are, on net, *more* likely to support gender equality.

Existing research clearly indicates that more educated persons are more often politically active, although the strength of this relationship appears to vary cross-nationally (Almond and Verba 1963; Nie, Verba and Kim 1978; Nie, Verba and Petrocik 1976).

Employment Status

Several theorists suggest that the expansion of women's labor force participation increases support for feminism among both women and men (Banaszak and Plutzer 1991; Chafetz and Dworkin 1986; Dahlerup 1986; Gerson 1987; Klein 1984, 1987; Norris 1985). Klein (1984) offers several reasons for this effect. First, with more women working in the labor force, it becomes apparent that women can perform traditional male jobs quite effectively; that serves to undermine previously existing gender stereotypes (1984: 36). Second, the increased financial independence which working women obtain from their work may allow them to feel freer to reject traditional gender roles (1984: 69). Third, work experiences are likely to expose women to types of discrimination normally hidden from "homemakers"; this exposure may increase working women's interest in feminist political concerns (1984: 92). In sum, Klein implies a disproportionate effect on working *women* versus men; yet, she also posits that rising women's labor force participation should produce somewhat more egalitarian attitudes throughout all social subgroups. By contrast, as noted above, Gerson (1985, 1987; see also Duverger 1955) holds that rising women's labor force participation may cause "homemakers," in particular, to become more conservative than before, due to the perceived threat to the security of their traditional role which working women pose. However, from her in-depth interviews with 63 women, Gerson suggests that the relationship between employment status and feminism is highly complex and that employment status may be a poor overall predictor. In synthesizing these arguments, I hypothesize that although employment status will significantly predict whether respondents hold feminist views in places like the United States and Scandinavia, where female employment levels are high and where non-employed homemakers may thus feel especially threatened, employment status should be a weak predictor of feminist views in most other countries.

As for the political activism connection, previous research establishes employment as a significant determinant, especially among women (Anderson 1975; Constantini 1990; Nie, Verba and Petrocik 1976; Klein 1984; Welch 1977). This is because employment brings citizens into more frequent contact with unions, government agencies and other politically relevant organizations. This "routine" contact may then create a heightened interest in becoming more intentionally and proactively involved in political activities. For women in particular, the experiences provided by daily institutional contacts may create greater confidence in their potential for achieving political efficacy. Welch theorizes: "The woman who goes to work outside the household may be a more adventurous, self-confident person than one who stays home, and this self-confidence could carry over into the political arena; or, conversely, the work experience itself may produce confidence which transmits itself into increased political efficacy" (1977: 724).

Religiosity and Religious Affiliation

Previous research identifies religiosity and Catholicism as significant predictors of political conservatism. Due to the Catholic Church's explicit proscriptions against abortion and divorce, I expect Catholicism to be an especially influential determinant of conservatism on those issues. By contrast, the political influence of Protestantism seems less clear. The Scandinavian countries exhibiting the greatest degree of gender equality in Table 10.1 are also the most Protestant (Sweden at 95%, Norway at 90% and Denmark at 91%) (World Values Survey 1981-82). However, given the extreme conservatism of some Protestant sects, from Puritanism to Fundamentalism, I would not expect adherence to Protestantism to predict support for liberal, feminist views consistently. In fact, existing evidence suggests that, although perhaps to varying degrees by sect, *all* Western religions and religious institutions promote and reinforce traditional gender norms (Himmelstein 1986; Mayer and Smith 1985). Thus in spite of the significant allowance of individual choice in many Protestant sects, it seems likely that less religiosity in *any* faith will be a better predictor of feminism than a positive identification with certain particular faiths. This means, for instance, that the average views of residents in a primarily Catholic but *non-religious* country like France may be more liberal than the views prevalent in a *religiously* Catholic country like Ireland or Italy. Inglehart (1977) supports this position in finding religiosity to distinguish postmaterialists from materialists and to produce variation in other attitudes as well. Also, in their introduction to this volume, Rempel and Clark identify religious citizens as among the least likely to incorporate aspects of the newly arising political culture of "post-industrial politics."

The effect of religion on political behavior has long been a subject of sociological inquiry, from Max Weber to more recent studies. Weber (1958) held that Protestantism fosters a unique sense of obligation to the community. American Puritanism illustrates this, with its promulgation of the "moralistic" view that political involvement is an obligatory responsibility (Elazar 1975). Protestantism may thus increase the relative degree of political activism among its adherents.

Socioeconomic Status

Three possible effects of socioeconomic status (SES) can be derived respectively from the "solidarity," the "threat," and the "postmaterialist" theses. The solidarity thesis predicts that citizens with a low SES are more likely to empathize with the position of other disadvantaged groups, in this case women (Davis and Robinson 1991; Robinson 1983). The threat thesis proposes, by contrast, that citizens with a low SES may fear the increased job competition coming from women who are newly moving into the work force; hence citizens at the lower end may be more likely to side not with but against women (Davis and Robinson 1991; Husbands 1979). The postmaterialist thesis also concludes that citizens with a lower SES are *less* likely to support women's equality, but its reasoning differs from the threat thesis; here, the postmaterialist argument is that lower SES citizens can less afford to concern themselves with liberal, "postmaterialist" issues, like feminism, due to the need to address more immediately pressing material needs (Inglehart 1977, 1990). Putting a damper on all three theses is that few existing studies find income or occupational status to be important predictors of feminist views in *any* direction (see Davis and Robinson 1991; Plutzer and Banaszak 1991; Wilcox 1991).

Most American studies do uncover a strong correlation between SES and political participation. Verba and colleagues theorize that a primary reason why SES affects activism has to do with the possession, among higher SES citizens, of more competitive material and other resources; the possession of these resources may not, per se, lead higher SES citizens to seek out political causes, but it may lead political causes to seek *them* out for financial support (Almond and Verba 1963; Nie, Verba, and Petrocik 1976; Verba, Nie, and Kim 1978; see also Wolfinger and Rosenstone 1980).

Family Status

Marital status and size of household are the most frequently cited family status variables. Many propose that having employed spouses may lead men to develop more awareness and acceptance of women's rights (Gerson 1987; Klein 1984; Davis and Robinson 1991; Smith 1985b). However, actual results to date show that having an employed wife does *not* have much of an impact on men's attitudes. Davis and Robinson propose as a counter-hypothesis that men with working spouses possess an interest in *preventing* their advancement as a means of protecting their male power, which they derive from having a higher-paying job (1991: 80).

As for the influence of marital status on women, some posit that single or divorced women may be more likely to favor gender equality than married women with employed husbands (Gerson 1987; Davis and Robinson 1991). This is the case as unmarried women are more likely than married ones to require opportunities to work for a living themselves and also, unlike their married counterparts, unmarried women would not have to worry about competition from other women for their husbands' jobs. Contradicting this prediction, some American studies find that nonetheless, married women are *more* pro-feminist than single or divorced ones (Huber and Spitze 1983; Plutzer 1988). Davis and Robinson take a conditional view, holding that marital status only has a significant effect when separating out marriages with an employed spouse versus an unemployed spouse. As my data set does not provide information on spouses' employment, I cannot precisely replicate their analysis.

Some researchers assume that a larger household size indicates a family with more traditional outlooks (Plutzer 1988). However, merely using household size may mask what could be two types of effects. In the first, "Yuppie"-type parents of households with only one child may have distinctly different attitudes than the parents of large, traditional families. In the second, all parents, independent of their number of children, may have distinct attitudes from non-parents. I test these two types of potential effects statistically by including a measure of net household size and a dummy variable measuring simply whether respondents have any children at all or not.

Youth

In their introduction to this volume, Rempel and Clark identify youth as an important factor driving the rise of a "post-industrial politics." Lipset and Ladd (1971) explain that the social context when citizens come of age politically specifically tends to affect their attitudes toward inequality. Citizens reaching their twenties when the feminist movement had already become strong ought to be more pro-feminist than citizens from older generations. While second-wave feminism swept through the United States, Canada and most of Western Europe in the 1960s and early 1970s, Lovenduski (1986) reports that first-wave feminism never gained momentum, from the beginning, in Catholic Italy and Belgium. Since older generations might be less aware of feminist arguments in these latter countries, this may cause youth to be a more significant predictor of feminism. On the opposite extreme, highly successful first-wave feminist groups arose in Scandinavia in the late 1800s and early 1900s and have not since disbanded (Wilcox 1991). Consequently, this is where youth ought to have the smallest effect in predicting feminism. The available literature generally confirms these expectations (Davis and Robinson 1991; Plutzer 1988; Plutzer and Banaszak 1991).

Apart from having a greater probability of holding feminist views, consistent evidence shows that younger citizens are also more politically active (Verba, Nie and Kim 1978; Inglehart 1977, 1990).

Size of Home Town

Value changes are often more apparent in urban areas, where there is less attachment to the traditional life and culture of small communities. Wilcox (1991) confirms that on women's issues, urban respondents are more often aware of feminist concerns. However, in an unexpected contrast, Plutzer and Banaszak (1991) find that citizens from medium-size towns are more pro-feminist than city dwellers. Both of these studies use fewer controls than do I. In addition, Wilcox only uses data for women, and Plutzer and Banaszak do not run separate analyses by country.

Regarding political activism, cross-national research finds that women tend to be more active in politics when they live in urban rather than rural settings (Baxter and Lansing 1993: 46). Comparable data for men are not previously available.

Union Membership

Membership in labor unions has been important in political activism research but has seldom entered into analyses of feminist political views. Hence, I primarily include a union membership variable to measure its effect on activism. Still, I do not rule out the possibility that unions stimulate the dissemination of feminist views as well, for example by providing an institutional setting for the discussion of gender discrimination on-the-job.

Hypotheses

My hypotheses fall into three basic categories: (1) effects of social background characteristics on feminism, (2) effects of social background characteristics on political activism, and (3) the relationship between feminism and political activism. Figure 10.1 models these linkages.

Social background indicators are not likely to change, due to variation in a citizen's degree of feminism or political activism. Thus I represent the direction

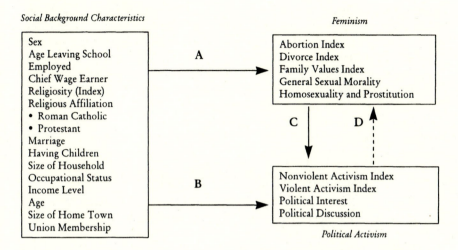

FIGURE 10.1   Path Diagram of Linkages Between Social Background, Feminism, and Political Activism

of causation in paths A and B as from left to right. However, the direction of causation between feminism and political activism is less clear. It is conceivable that increased political activism provokes citizens to re-assess some of their political views or to form new ones. Still, with Verba, Nie, and Kim (1987), I assume that the effect of political views on activism is likely to be stronger than the reverse. This would seem especially to hold for the views on which I focus; matters such as sexual morality, family values and views on marital roles are, after all, closely tied to a citizen's more original, fundamental beliefs. Nonetheless, I recognize that path D (above) could operate and indicate this with a dotted arrow. In accord with the findings and arguments reported in the literature review, I offer the following hypotheses:

Effect of Social Background Characteristics on Feminism (Path A)

Hypothesis 1.1. Women are more likely to hold feminist views than men.

Hypothesis 1.2. More educated citizens are more likely to hold feminist views.

Hypothesis 1.3. Employed women are more likely to hold feminist views than unemployed women.

Hypothesis 1.4. Religion relates to feminism as follows: (a) religious citizens of any faith are less likely than others to hold feminist views; (b) neither Catholicism nor Protestantism promotes feminism, although a Catholic religious affiliation should have an especially significant negative effect.

Hypothesis 1.5. Family life relates to feminism as follows: (a) married women are less likely than unmarried women to hold feminist views; (b) married men are less likely than married women to hold feminist views; and (c) women with children, and especially those with several children, are less likely than other women to hold feminist views.

Hypothesis 1.6. Citizens with a higher income and occupational status, especially women, are more likely to hold feminist views.

Hypothesis 1.7. Younger citizens are more likely to hold feminist views.

Hypothesis 1.8. Citizens from larger home towns are more likely to hold feminist views.

Effect of Demographics on Political Activism and Interest (Path B)

Hypothesis 2.1. Men are more likely than women to be politically active.

Hypothesis 2.2. More educated citizens are more likely to be politically active.

Hypothesis 2.3. Employment status affects the political behavior of women as follows: (a) employed women are more likely than unemployed women to be politically active; (b) this is especially true in countries where a high proportion of women are in the work force; and (c) employment status has a greater effect on the political behavior of women than of men.

Hypothesis 2.4. Citizens with a higher income and occupational status are more likely to be politically active.

Hypothesis 2.5. Younger citizens are more likely to be politically active.

Hypothesis 2.6. Members of unions are more likely to be politically active.

Hypothesis 2.7. Citizens living in larger towns are more likely to be politically active.

Effect of Feminism on Political Activism and Interest (Path C)

Hypothesis 3.1. Citizens holding feminist views are more likely than others to become politically active.

Hypothesis 3.2. The relationship between feminism and political activism varies with sex, such that holding feminist views will be especially likely to produce increased activism among women.

Data and Methods

I use data from the 1981-82 World Values Survey (WVS) of approximately 1,000 adults in each of 21 countries. I selected fourteen countries for analysis: Belgium, Britain, Canada, Denmark, France, Ireland, Italy, Japan, the Netherlands, Norway, Spain, Sweden, the United States and West Germany. All are relatively far along in industrialization, and all except Japan are located in the West.

TABLE 10.2   Legal Grounds for Granting Abortion in 1984

Mother's Life at Risk (1)	Mother's Health at Risk (2)	Rape or Incest (3)	Baby's Health at Risk (4)	Economic Strain (5)	On Demand (6)
Ireland*	Belgium			Britain	Denmark
Spain	Canada			Japan	France
				West Germany	Holland
					Italy**
					Norway
					Sweden
					U.S.A.***

* Not only is abortion illegal in Ireland in every case but this one, there is also a law restricting further reform now built into the constitution.
** Italian doctors are allowed to refuse on the grounds of "conscientious objection," making legal abortion nearly impossible in Italy's traditional South.
*** The precise law varies considerably by state.
Source: Norris 1987: 93-97.

Most of my independent social indicator variables are simply coded and contain responses to a single question. A few required a degree of recoding from original survey variables, but I leave a discussion of those instances to the Appendix. I explain each dependent variable here, since their derivations are more complicated and important to the substantive interpretations of results. In general, I coded all of them so that a higher score indicates either stronger feminist views or greater political activism.

The Feminism Indices

Abortion Index. Both popular views about abortion and the specifics of abortion laws vary greatly. At one pole are attitudes and laws supporting "abortion on demand." At the other is opposition to abortion in all circumstances, or making an exception only where the mother's life is in danger. In Table 10.2, I classify the laws of the 14 countries surveyed. For the measurement of popular attitudes, I use a scale built from responses to two questions. One asks whether abortion is always justified, never justified or somewhere in between on a 10-point scale. The second offers four circumstances and asks if respondents approve or disapprove of abortion under each; from this item, I constructed a variable with values ranging from 0 for those approving of abortion in no circumstances to four for those approving in all. I then re-scaled both questions from 0-10 and created the abortion index from the mean.

Divorce Index. Civil divorce has become available in most countries, although a woman's right to ask for it has only recently become legal in some. Currently under debate by some legislatures are "no-fault" divorce laws; these treat both partners as having equal rights in the outcome, regardless of the reason for the divorce. Weitzman (1985) demonstrates that divorce tends to hurt women and to help men economically; nonetheless, feminists tend to view the availability of a divorce option for women as an indicator of freedom from rigid patriarchal norms. Similar in construction to the abortion index, I build my divorce measure from two questions. The first asks whether divorce is always justified, never justified or somewhere in between, coded on a 10-point scale. The second offers ten circumstances, asks if respondents approve or disapprove of divorce under each, and codes answers on a 10-point scale, based on the number of circumstances meeting approval. My divorce index takes the mean of responses on these two variables.

Family Values Index. An important goal of the women's movement has been to challenge traditional notions about women's roles as homemakers. In many countries, there have consequently emerged new familial role structures and household arrangements which feminists tend to support. To assess approval of these arrangements, I combined responses to six items into an index of liberalism on *family values.* The first three items are whether (1) respondents believe marriage is an outdated institution, (2) respondents approve or disapprove of a woman choosing to have a child without having a steady partner, and (3) respondents believe that a child needs to have both parents in the home to grow up happy. A fourth item addresses respondents' acceptance of the traditional view that a woman's primary purpose is mothering by asking whether respondents think that women need to have children to "feel fulfilled." Also included in the family values index are two items on the relationship between children and parents. One asks whether respondents feel that children must always love and respect their parents or whether parents must earn their child's respect. The other asks whether it is the duty of parents to do the best for their children or whether their own well-being should come before "sacrifice . . . for the sake of their children." These last two questions address traditional notions of filial piety and parental responsibility.

General Sexual Morality Index. Although not always explicit, many theorists consider strong feelings about sexual conventions to underlie many conflicts between feminists and their opponents (see Luker 1984; Petchesky 1984). To measure these feelings, I created an index of general sexual values. Two of the items going into it address general rules of sexuality. One asks, "If someone said that individuals should have the chance to enjoy complete sexual freedom without being restricted, would you tend to agree or disagree?" and the second asks, "If someone says that sex cannot be entirely left to individual choice, there have to be moral rules to which everyone adheres, would you tend to agree or disagree?" The other items address sexual encounters which society traditionally views as shocking social crimes or "sins." They are whether having an affair while married can always be justified, never be justified or something in between (on a 10-point scale), and whether respondents think that sex under the legal age of consent can always be justified, never be justified or something in between.

Homosexuality and Prostitution Index. I composed a second index from just two sexual values items, asking respectively for "justification" ratings, from never to always, on (1) homosexuality and (2) prostitution. I composed a separate index for these two questions in light of the results of a factor analysis that included all of the sexual morality questions (these two, plus those used in constructing the preceding index). The homosexuality and prostitution items both had particularly strong correlations and were placed together by the factor analysis.[1]

The Political Activism Indices

Nonviolent Activism Index. This index measures some of the most important forms of political activism beyond voting. It is composed of questions on whether respondents say they either have participated or would potentially participate in each of the following political activities: (1) signing a petition, (2) joining a boycott, (3) attending a lawful demonstration, (4) joining an unofficial strike, or (5) occupying a building or factory. The highest possible score on this index would be for a respondent who has done every one of those activities at some time. The lowest possible score would be for someone who "would never do" any of them.

Violent Activism Index. The same question asked for the four categories of nonviolent political action was also asked for two forms of more demonstrative action: (1) damaging things, like breaking windows, removing road signs, etc., or (2) using personal violence, like fighting with other demonstrators or the police. Citizens willing to engage in these activities may not be identical to those willing to participate in less demonstrative forms of activism. In fact, from conducting a factor analysis with all the activism and interest variables (maximum-likelihood extraction), I obtained precisely the groupings represented here by my four indices.

Political Interest. I derived this item from the response to a single question. It asks respondents to rate their interest in politics by identifying with one of four statements ranging from "I take an active interest in politics" to "I'm not interested in politics at all." This self-assessment may show some bias if respondents on average claim more interest than is true, out of a feeling of social obligation or embarrassment over an actual lack of concern. Nonetheless, results for this measure may help to supplement those for the first two, which focus on more explicit and direct forms of activism.

Discuss Politics Index. I composed this index from two survey items, asking about the frequency with which respondents (1) discuss political matters with friends, or (2) find themselves persuading friends, relatives or coworkers to share their views when they hold a strong opinion. Again, while the index may reveal some interesting patterns of its own, I primarily included it as a supplement to the first two direct activism indices.

Regression Models

Since many hypotheses include different expectations for women and for men, I ran all of the regressions separately for each sex, and then ran a third regression model for all respondents, regardless of sex. I used this last model to test for the effect of sex itself on the feminism and political activism variables.

I performed three sets of regressions and discuss the results for each in separate subsections below. First, I regressed each feminism index on the social background variables. Second, I regressed each political activism indicator on those same social background variables. Third, with the political activism indicators again as the dependent variables, I ran a set of regressions that included both the social background and the feminism indicators as independent. These regressions tested the path C hypothesis (see Figure 10.1 above) on the relation between holding feminist views and having a propensity to be politically active. For purposes of simplification, the tables for these last regressions show statistically significant beta coefficients only for the feminism indices, not for the social background variables; this is because the impacts of the latter on activism are already displayed for the prior set of (path B) regressions. The last set of tables also displays the R^2 values from the path B analysis right above the R^2 values for the present (path C) computations, as a way of revealing the degree to which adding the feminism indices improves the net explanatory power of a citizen's propensity to be politically active.[2]

Results

Support for Feminism by Country

Before analyzing cross-national social origins, I first present the mean feminism levels, for each country surveyed, on each of the five feminism indices. (See Figure 10.2.) A cursory comparison between the results obtained here and those presented in Table 10.1 reveals that where more "objective" gender equality exists, more *support* for equality also exists. The three Scandinavian countries, Denmark, Norway and Sweden, display high scores on *both* the objective equality measures in Table 10.1 and on the attitudinal measures in Figure 10.2. Also, Belgium and Ireland have low scores on both sets of measures. Many other countries, however, still have significant variation (1) among the three objective equality measures, (2) among the five attitudinal indices, and (3) between the two sets of measures. For instance, while Japan and Britain both score low on the objective measures, they average somewhere in the middle of the pack on the attitudinal measures.

Effect of Social Background Characteristics on Feminism (Path A)

My first hypothesis (1.1) was that women are more likely to hold feminist views than men. It is generally confirmed. (See entries on the last lines of Tables 10.3A-E.) This is especially so on the indices most related to prominent feminist movement goals: the abortion, divorce, and family values indices. On the latter two, sex is a highly consistent predictor. Women are significantly more accepting of divorce in every country except in Belgium, Ireland and Canada, and women are significantly more liberal on family values everywhere except in Ireland and Japan. On the abortion index, every statistically significant effect also shows women to be more pro-feminist, but such effects appear only for the United States, France, Italy, the Netherlands, Denmark and Canada. In these countries, abortion was a "hot" political issue when the WVS was carried out; so sex-based differences may have surfaced there in connection with the production of a heightened political awareness of the issue and its gender-specific implications.[3]

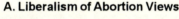

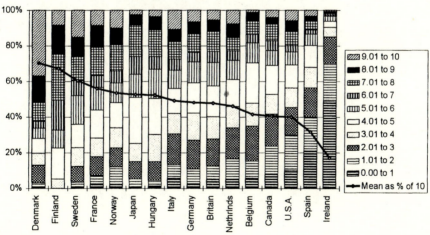

A. Liberalism of Abortion Views

FIGURE 10.2 Cross-National Support for Feminism

(continues)

224

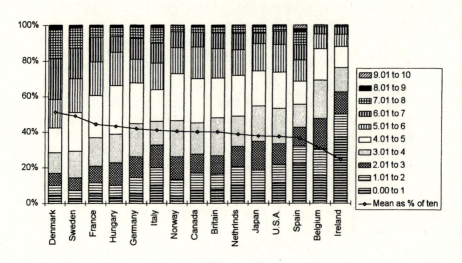

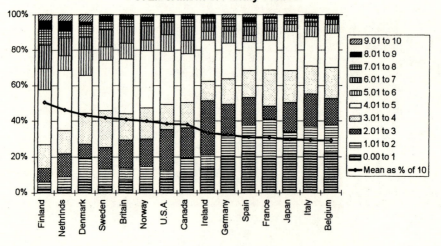

FIGURE 10.2 *(continued)*

D. General Sexual Liberalism Index

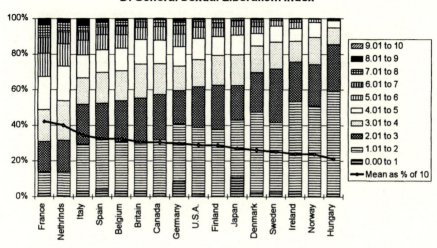

E. Liberalism of Views Towards Homosexuality and Prostitution

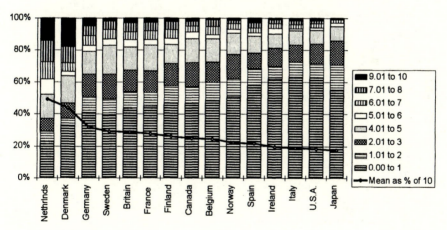

FIGURE 10.2 *(continued)*
Source: World Values Survey (WVS), 1981-82.

TABLE 10.3 The Impact of Social Background Characteristics on Feminism

A.

Abortion Index by Sex	U.S.A.		France		Britain		W. Germany		Italy		Netherlands	
	F	M	F	M	F	M	F	M	F	M	F	M
n	986	790	568	511	554	511	643	572	639	613	575	407
R2	0.27	0.25	0.23	0.29	0.24	0.16	0.31	0.26	0.27	0.27	0.32	0.31
Religiosity (relig)	-0.34	-0.41	-0.38	-0.35	-0.33	-0.24	-0.37	-0.39	-0.45	-0.43	-0.45	-0.42
Age finished school (v319)	0.10			0.12	0.17		0.11				0.20	0.16
Age (v345)				-0.19			-0.19		-0.11		-0.13	
Family income level (v339)	0.08					0.16	0.09					
Size of household (v320)	-0.14					-0.22	-0.09					
Size of town (v337)			0.11				0.08					
Fam. occup. status (ses2)	0.10	0.12									0.14	
Have children?											0.14	
Married?	-0.12										0.11	
Employed? (v328)					0.11						0.09	
Chief wage earner? (cwearn)											0.11	
Roman Catholic? (romcath)						-0.11	-0.16	-0.16				-0.11
Protestant? (prot)	-0.16	-0.10							na	na		
Belong to union? (v334)	0.08									0.11		
Sex (1 = female; 0 = male)	0.06		0.11						0.07		0.12	

B.

Divorce Index by Sex	U.S.A.		France		Britain		W. Germany		Italy		Netherlands	
	F	M	F	M	F	M	F	M	F	M	F	M
n	1248	1024	610	568	629	573	690	608	664	641	671	480
R2	0.10	0.12	0.22	0.22	0.15	0.12	0.28	0.19	0.21	0.20	0.28	0.24
Religiosity (relig)	-0.18	-0.24	-0.29	-0.26	-0.22	-0.20	-0.27	-0.30	-0.33	-0.36	-0.27	-0.35
Age (v345)	-0.10			-0.19	-0.14		-0.25	-0.14	-0.12		-0.23	-0.17
Age finished school (v319)	0.09		0.13	0.12		0.11	0.15		0.10		0.24	0.18
Size of town (v337)			0.13						0.08	0.09	0.09	
Married?	-0.09	-0.15					-0.12					
Family income level (v339)						0.10						
Size of household (v320)	-0.07					-0.19	-0.09					
Have children?	0.07											
Employed (328)	0.08											
Fam. occupational status (ses)										0.08	0.13	
Chief wage earner? (cwearn)											0.10	
Roman Catholic? (romcath)												
Protestant? (prot)		-0.12			0.12				na	na		
Belong to union? (v334)										0.13		
Sex (1 = female; 0 = male)	0.08		0.15		0.08		0.14		0.07		0.12	

Denmark		Belgium		Spain		Ireland		Canada		Japan		Norway		Sweden	
F	M	F	M	F	M	F	M	F	M	F	M	F	M	F	M
534	508	504	454	1096	1048	606	456	456	468	206	249	446	513	336	377
0.20	0.20	0.18	0.18	0.43	0.34	0.26	0.33	0.24	0.21	0.13	0.07	0.26	0.23	0.13	0.14
-0.36	-0.31	-0.30	-0.32	-0.52	-0.41	-0.40	-0.51	-0.41	-0.40			-0.36	-0.43	-0.22	-0.26
0.14	0.11					-0.09			0.16	0.20					0.12
		-0.13	-0.20	-0.14	-0.15	-0.17	-0.18								
			0.11	-0.07									0.12		
					-0.06										
na	na			0.08								0.15	0.09		
								0.10				0.13		na	na
												na	na	na	na
		0.15													
0.14															-0.13
	-0.12			-0.07	-0.11			na	na	na	-0.13				0.11
0.13								na	na						
0.09								0.13							

Denmark		Belgium		Spain		Ireland		Canada		Japan		Norway		Sweden	
F	M	F	M	F	M	F	M	F	M	F	M	F	M	F	M
593	575	556	492	1138	1082	656	512	618	611	517	519	563	643	438	477
0.15	0.19	0.13	0.14	0.38	0.3	0.26	0.30	0.18	0.18	0.16	0.07	0.21	0.12	0.18	0.10
-0.29	-0.26	-0.23	-0.23	-0.36	-0.34	-0.27	-0.34	-0.32	-0.33			-0.27	-0.21	-0.18	-0.22
	-0.16		-0.18	-0.27	-0.19	-0.29	-0.30	-0.12	-0.13	-0.12	-0.18	-0.24			
0.12	0.10				0.10			0.15	0.11	0.18				0.19	0.11
na	na		0.09	0.09	0.06	0.09		0.10	0.09				0.09	0.12	
			-0.19						-0.11	-0.10		na	na	na	na
		0.11									0.14			0.10	
										-0.16				-0.15	
								0.17	0.13						
													-0.12		
														na	na
		-0.11	0.15									0.13			
	-0.15							na	na	Budd=					
								na	na	-0.10				0.12	
					0.08										
0.08				0.07				0.13		0.10		0.07		0.09	

(continues)

228

TABLE 10.3 *(continued)*

C. Family Values Index by Sex

	U.S.A F	U.S.A M	France F	France M	Britain F	Britain M	W. Germany F	W. Germany M	Italy F	Italy M	Netherlands F	Netherlands M
n	1074	837	505	450	533	466	322	237	570	548	505	370
R2	0.19	0.12	0.26	0.29	0.14	0.19	0.37	0.35	0.19	0.22	0.30	0.33
Religiosity (relig)	-0.20	-0.22	-0.33	-0.27	-0.22	-0.25	-0.24	-0.37	-0.32	-0.31	-0.27	-0.29
Age (v345)	-0.10			-0.20	-0.15	-0.29	-0.26				-0.33	-0.22
Age finished school (v319)	0.16	0.09	0.14	0.13	0.10		0.13		0.09		0.12	0.15
Size of household (v320)							-0.13			-0.14	-0.14	
Have children?								-0.23				
Married?	-0.11			-0.19			-0.15					
Size of town (v337)			0.11				-0.10		0.09			
Family income level (v339)				0.11			0.16					
Fam. occupational status (ses2)											0.09	
Employed? (v328)	0.14											
Belong to union? (v334)												
Roman Catholic? (romcath)		-0.11					-0.39					
Protestant? (prot)		-0.13					-0.32		na	na		
Chief wage earner? (cwearn)			0.23	0.13								
Sex (1 = female; 0 = male)	0.16		0.16		0.17		0.16		0.13		0.14	

D. General Sexual Liberalism by Sex

	U.S.A F	U.S.A M	France F	France M	Britain F	Britain M	W. Germany F	W. Germany M	Italy F	Italy M	Netherlands F	Netherlands M
n	1057	876	471	447	525	507	579	495	578	595	549	394
R2	0.23	0.20	0.22	0.31	0.23	0.26	0.31	0.29	0.27	0.27	0.26	0.27
Religiosity (relig)	-0.29	-0.22	-0.24	-0.16	-0.19	-0.24	-0.33	-0.26	-0.33	-0.32	-0.32	-0.34
Age (v345)	-0.23	-0.21	-0.19	-0.31	-0.26	-0.28	-0.31	-0.22	-0.16	-0.16	-0.26	-0.17
Age finished school (v319)						-0.10	0.10			0.09	0.13	
Married?	-0.14	-0.11		-0.17	-0.17	-0.19	-0.15					
Family income level (v339)	-0.09	-0.11	0.11									-0.10
Size of household (v320)			-0.11	-0.14			-0.10					
Have children?												
Size of town (v337)	0.10	0.07			0.09							0.10
Chief wage earner? (cwearn)												
Fam. occup. status (ses2)							-0.10			0.09		
Roman Catholic? (romcath)				-0.15					-0.10			
Protestant? (prot)								na	na			
Belong to union? (v334)									-0.08	0.08		
Employed? (v328)							-0.11					
Sex (1 = female; 0 = male)	-0.07						-0.10					

Denmark		Belgium		Spain		Ireland		Canada		Japan		Norway		Sweden	
F	M	F	M	F	M	F	M	F	M	F	M	F	M	F	M
348	305	377	326	958	848	527	352	528	502	274	299	457	497	340.00	358
0.31	0.21	0.19	0.26	0.41	0.35	0.20	0.18	0.14	0.22	0.13	0.04	0.22	0.15	0.14	0.21
-0.36	-0.11	-0.19	-0.36	-0.46	-0.34	-0.25	-0.32	-0.30	-0.35	-0.15		-0.31	-0.22	-0.22	-0.24
	-0.28				-0.13	-0.19			-0.21			-0.18	-0.17		-0.31
0.11	0.19		0.20		0.08			0.18	0.10			0.11			
	-0.25			0.06					-0.12					-0.19	
-0.15		-0.17		-0.10	-0.14				0.12						
			-0.16									na	na	na	na
na	na												0.10		na
				-0.06										na	
				0.07											
					0.09										
				-0.09	-0.16			na	na	Budd=					
								na	na	-0.16					
										0.17					
0.18		0.09		0.08				0.11				0.19		0.17	

Denmark		Belgium		Spain		Ireland		Canada		Japan		Norway		Sweden	
F	M	F	M	F	M	F	M	F	M	F	M	F	M	F	M
497	470	390	365	939	946	526	399	550	568	323	409	489	599	358	421
0.20	0.16	0.17	0.21	0.33	0.31	0.28	0.28	0.14	0.22	0.15	0.18	0.16	0.15	0.17	0.15
-0.13	-0.16	-0.23	-0.29	-0.35	-0.27	-0.40	-0.40	-0.19	-0.28			-0.28	-0.23		-0.17
-0.21	-0.23				-0.19	-0.24	-0.18	-0.20	-0.21	-0.25	-0.20			-0.28	-0.27
0.17														0.18	
			0.17		-0.14				-0.23			na	na	na	na
						-0.15						0.13		-0.14	
-0.15				-0.13							-0.16				
na	na							0.09				0.13			
0.09		-0.16												na	na
				-0.15	-0.12			na	na					0.16	
								na	na						
		-0.14			0.10					-0.15					
														0.13	-0.70
				-0.05				-0.09		-0.13					

(continues)

TABLE 10.3   *(continued)*

E. Homosex/Prostitution by Sex	U.S.A. F	U.S.A. M	France F	France M	Britain F	Britain M	W. Germany F	W. Germany M	Italy F	Italy M	Netherlands F	Netherlands M
n	1217	1002	589	549	597	563	686	607	653	638	639	456
R2	0.19	0.13	0.24	0.29	0.23	0.18	0.26	0.14	0.18	0.15	0.30	0.23
Age (v345)	-0.12		-0.20	-0.37	-0.24	-0.25	-0.31	-0.18	-0.19		-0.33	-0.32
Religiosity (relig)	-0.27	-0.28	-0.16	-0.14	-0.22	-0.15	-0.21	-0.22	-0.19	-0.22	-0.31	-0.27
Age finished school (v319)	0.13	0.09	0.23	0.11	0.15	0.10	0.17				0.17	0.20
Fam. Occupatl. Status (ses2)	0.11			0.12		0.16			0.08	0.09	0.13	
Size of town (v337)												0.10
Size of Household (v320)	-0.07						-0.16					-0.13
Chief wage earner? (cwern)			0.18	0.23								
Married?		-0.08		-0.12							0.14	
Family Income level (v339)							0.16					
Belong to union? (v334)			0.08									
Have children?							0.12					0.15
Roman Catholic? (romcath)	-0.14								-0.09			
Protestant? (prot)									na	na	0.09	
Employed? (v328)				-0.13								
Sex (1 = female; 0 = male)			0.11		0.12						0.10	

Note 1: All beta coefficients shown have p-values below .05. Co-efficients with p-values below .005 are shaded.

Note 2: The beta coefficients for sex (see last row of each table) are from a separate regression model. This model included both women and men, and then added a dummy variable for sex. Beta coefficents generated by that model for the impact of the other social background characteristics are not displayed.

Source: World Values Survey (WVS), 1981-82.

Women are also more liberal than men on the prostitution and homosexuality index in six of the countries, although Japanese women are more conservative than Japanese men.

On the general sexual liberalism index, in a reversal of the pattern on the others, in the five countries where sex produces significant variation, men rather than women are more liberal. While this may seem incongruent, the finding is consistent with Gerson's (1978) argument that women, more often dependent on the opposite sex financially, are more likely than men to feel threatened by relaxed sexual morals or extramarital sexual affairs. Also, women may have insight, which men lack, on the threat of having sex at younger ages to the future economic and emotional lives of young women, who risk more than young men from engaging in under-age sexual encounters.

Contrary to the findings of Davis and Robinson (1991) but consistent with my hypothesis 1.2, and with most other research, education is a fairly significant predictor of feminist views among members of both sexes. More educated

Denmark		Belgium		Spain		Ireland		Canada		Japan		Norway		Sweden	
F	M	F	M	F	M	F	M	F	M	F	M	F	M	F	M
585	573	541	489	1089	1053	591	473	604	603	498	514	536	624	393	436
0.26	0.17	0.09	0.08	0.25	0.27	0.24	0.27	0.18	0.15	0.12	0.08	0.20	0.11	0.17	0.10
-0.22	-0.18		-0.14		-0.17	-0.25	-0.18	-0.23	-0.13	-0.16	-0.17	-0.15		-0.23	
-0.26	-0.18			-0.30	-0.29	-0.25	-0.26	-0.26	-0.23			-0.28	-0.16	-0.13	-0.12
0.18	0.09							0.12	0.17				0.13	0.16	0.21
0.08			-0.11		0.07		0.12					0.09		na	na
na	na	-0.12				0.15	0.19					0.11			
-0.12														-0.16	
0.12					0.12										
					-0.12				-0.12	-0.10		na	na	na	na
0.12	0.19														0.17
					0.06								0.09		
0.11				-0.09	-0.09			na	na						
	-0.10			-0.11	-0.12			na	na						
						0.11							-0.10		
0.14								0.07		-0.16				0.13	

women are significantly more likely to approve of abortion in six countries, of divorce in eight, of non-traditional family values in nine and of homosexuality and prostitution in eight. Education less frequently affects women's general sexual liberalism, but does do so in a positive direction in four countries. Education has an especially marked impact in the Netherlands and Denmark, where it significantly increases liberalism on all five indices. Also, in West Germany and the United States, education increases women's liberalism on four of the five feminism indices.

A closer inspection of the few countries where education does not have a significant impact indicates the potential for a mediating *religious* influence. In the predominantly Catholic countries of Ireland, Italy, Spain and Belgium, years of education less often increase feminism among women. This may be because a Catholic education is more prevalent in those countries, and such an education may discourage citizens from forming feminist views. Indeed, in heavily Catholic Ireland, increased years of schooling actually has a *conservative* effect on women's views on abortion. The difference between Catholic and non-Catholic countries in education's effect is more pronounced among women than men; but this is consistent with my proposed explanation, since according to Margaret Inglehart (1981), men in Catholic countries receive a religious education less frequently than women.

Evidence for my hypothesis (1.3) that employed women are more likely to be pro-feminist than unemployed women is inconclusive. When employment status is significant, it is more likely to predict liberalism than conservatism among women; but most of the time, employment is not statistically significant in any direction for women. By contrast, employed men are more *anti-feminist* than their unemployed counterparts. Perhaps employed men see liberated women as a threat to their jobs and familial authority, while unemployed men are more sensitive to the trials of finding employment or to the importance of their wives' having an income.

As hypothesized (1.4a), religiosity predicts conservatism on all of the feminism indices. Nearly everywhere except in Japan, religiosity is the strongest predictor (highest beta values) of all the social background variables. As I based my religiosity measure on Western religious views, it is unsurprising that the Japanese results do not conform with the others. Indeed, in this volume, Umemori reports that in Japan, a distinctly individualistic form of religiosity, conducive more to socially liberal than to conservative views, is currently on the rise.

The results verified the expectation (1.4b) that Catholicism would be a stronger predictor of conservatism than Protestantism. Catholicism more often exerts a significant effect and is consistently influential in a conservative direction. The only instances where Catholicism predicts greater liberalism were among Norwegian and Swedish men, for whom the number of Catholic respondents was only 2 and 4 respectively, which make those findings substantively meaningless. By contrast, the impact of Protestantism is less clear. While Protestants are more conservative than non-Protestants in the United States, West Germany and Norway, they are more liberal in Ireland, Denmark and the Netherlands. These patterns on the impact of religion in the survey's various countries suggest an alternative hypothesis to my own on religion's impact. It is that rather than the *denomination* of one's religion, what truly matters is whether a given religion is the dominant or minority one in the country. The reasoning here is that membership in a socially dominant religion provokes greater social and political complacency and conservatism, while membership in a minority religion provokes liberalism, whether on feminist or other issues.

Marital status only exerts a significant effect in a few countries on any of the indices. The general trend is that married respondents are more conservative than non-married ones. This is consistent with hypothesis 1.5a.

I wrongly predicted that the effect of marriage on men's attitudes would be *less* often significant than on women's (1.5b). Even though marital status nowhere has a significant influence on men's acceptance of abortion, marriage does have a significant conservative effect nearly twice as often for men as for women on the four other feminism indices.

The effect of having children is somewhat ambiguous. The results on the household size indicator are consistent with hypothesis 1.5c that citizens in larger families will be less pro-feminist. However, the variable separating parents from all others is significant less often than the household size variable.

Also, in five countries where the "parental status" variable *is* significant, it predicts greater *liberalism*, while in the same regressions, having a larger net family size predicts greater *conservatism*. One interpretation of these seemingly disparate results follows from Inglehart's (1990) description of many socially liberal "postmaterialists" as dual-career "yuppie" parents with few children. Their small number of children results from the time constraints involved in both parents' decisions to pursue careers. As the theory goes, such parents would certainly be more socially liberal than parents in more traditional, large families but the former parents might also be more socially liberal than citizens who are not parents at all.

Contrary to hypothesis 1.6, the results indicate that neither income nor occupational status is a major determinant of feminist views. Where those variables are significant, consistent with expectations, they tend to evoke more liberal views; but this slight tendency reverses itself among Spanish and Belgian women, where income and occupation are weak but significant predictors of conservatism.

As hypothesized (1.7), youth is a highly significant predictor of feminist views. In many countries, a younger age has an especially strong liberalizing effect on the homosexuality and prostitution index; this may be because the gay right's movement and efforts to legalize prostitution are fairly recent, such that young citizens may be distinctly unlikely to have formed predispositions that might dampen the probability of their developing supportive views.

On the abortion index, consistent with Davis and Robinson (1991), I find that youth is more often influential in Catholic countries. There, early, first-wave feminist movements never gained popularity. This means that the more recent movements embody values altogether alien to those held by the older residents; so again, on the abortion issue, newly socialized young persons may lack conservative predispositions that older citizens possess.

My final hypothesis (1.8) in this series is that persons from larger towns are more likely than others to have feminist views. Although the results support this hypothesis in almost every instance where size of home town exerts a significant effect, this adds up to under half of the regressions using that variable. Also, as with many other social background variables, the predominant trend has several exceptions that weaken generalizability.

Effect of Social Background Characteristics on Political Activism (Path B)

I expected to find that men are more politically active than women (hypothesis 2.1). This is so on each of the four activism indices for 9 of the 14 countries. (See entries on the last lines of Tables 10.4A-D.) In the remaining instances, the sex variable does not exert a significant effect in any direction.

Consistent with my next hypothesis (2.2), and with findings from previous works, the most cross-nationally significant predictor of political activism on

TABLE 10.4 The Impact of Social Background Characteristics on Political Activism

A. Non Violent Activism

by Sex	U.S.A.		France		Britain		W. Germany		Italy		Netherlands	
	F	M	F	M	F	M	F	M	F	M	F	M
n	1050	889	545	494	575	548	545	483	505	512	598	435
R2	0.23	0.18	0.29	0.36	0.27	0.17	0.20	0.22	0.32	0.19	0.27	0.28
Age finished school (v319)	0.28	0.20	0.25	0.25	0.28	0.16	0.20	0.20	0.22	0.13	0.23	0.27
Age (v345)	-0.16	-0.18	-0.22	-0.30	-0.15	-0.15	-0.26	-0.30	-0.14	-0.15	-0.23	
Belong to union? (v334)	0.09	0.15	0.12	0.24	0.14	0.24	0.09		0.08	0.20	0.10	0.15
Religiosity (relig)		-0.07	-0.11		-0.11				-0.25	-0.17	-0.13	-0.20
Size of town (v337)			0.08		0.12	0.09					0.08	0.13
Family income level (v339)		0.10								0.14		-0.12
Fam. occup. status (ses2)	0.15								0.08		0.09	
Chief wage earner? (cwearn)			0.13	0.13								
Married?	-0.08	-0.11										
Have children?	0.07								-0.16			
Size of household (v320)	-0.08											
Roman Catholic? (romcath)		-0.14	-0.10	-0.10			-0.20	-0.17				
Protestant? (prot)		-0.12		-0.09			-0.17		na	na		
Employed? (v328)												
Sex (1 = female; 0 = male)	-0.07		-0.07		-0.15		-0.12					

B. Violent Activism

by Sex	U.S.A.		France		Britain		W. Germany		Italy		Netherlands	
	F	M	F	M	F	M	F	M	F	M	F	M
n	1236	1010	608	545	638	569	661	571	654	618	681	482
R2	0.03	0.05	0.10	0.16	0.04	0.12	0.02	0.07	0.05	0.08	0.06	0.07
Religiosity (relig)			-0.10						-0.08	-0.17	-0.10	-0.14
Age (v345)		-0.09	-0.13	-0.20	-0.12	-0.15						
Married?									-0.14			
Belong to union? (v334)		0.12										
Chief wage earner? (cwearn)			0.13	0.18							0.13	
Age finished school (v319)						-0.12						
Have children?												
Size of household (v320)						0.16						
Fam. occup. status (ses2)												
Family income level (v339)								-0.10				-0.09
Employed? (v328)						-0.15						
Roman Catholic? (romcath)	-0.18	-0.11	-0.13	-0.15			-0.15	-0.18	-0.09			
Protestant? (prot)	-0.20	-0.10							na	na		
Size of town (v337)											0.08	
Sex (1 = female; 0 = male)	-0.08				-0.18				-0.08			

Denmark		Belgium		Spain		Ireland		Canada		Japan		Norway		Sweden	
F	M	F	M	F	M	F	M	F	M	F	M	F	M	F	M
441	450	461	409	854	879	567	441	554	561	317	352	510	600	380.00	442
0.38	0.32	0.20	0.11	0.36	0.23	0.23	0.30	0.22	0.23	0.14	0.10	0.29	0.13	0.20	0.16
0.16	0.10	0.27		0.21	0.14	0.14		0.28	0.18			0.17	0.09	0.17	
-0.35	-0.49	-0.23	-0.18	-0.10	-0.15	-0.19	-0.28	-0.14	-0.26			-0.26	-0.26	-0.28	-0.34
				0.13	0.23		0.19		0.16	0.12	0.14			0.11	0.16
-0.11	-0.10		-0.15	-0.27	-0.18	-0.24	-0.27	-0.13	-0.15	-0.15		-0.12			
na	na			0.08		0.17	0.20		0.15						
			0.12												
	-0.10									0.18				na	na
				-0.08							0.18				
			-0.16									na	na	na	na
-0.12	0.12										0.12				
							-0.10								
	-0.09	-0.15		-0.11	-0.16			na	na						
	-0.09							na	na	0.14	0.15	-0.18	-0.14	-0.11	
0.11												0.12			
		-0.13		-0.16		-0.16				-0.14				-0.08	

Denmark		Belgium		Spain		Ireland		Canada		Japan		Norway		Sweden	
F	M	F	M	F	M	F	M	F	M	F	M	F	M	F	M
583	555	547	482	1039	986	661	512	619	607	515	501	574	652	447	493
0.06	0.08	0.02	0.03	0.06	0.09	0.04	0.13	0.06	0.07	0.03	0.07	0.02	0.08	0.12	0.04
	-0.11			-0.12	-0.09	-0.16	-0.30	-0.11	-0.10						
					-0.11		-0.15		-0.18		-0.14				
									-0.16		-0.09	na	na	na	na
					0.09										
	-0.17												-0.14	na	na
									0.15						
	-0.12			0.11										0.12	
			-0.16		-0.11					0.11					
0.10					-0.10			na	na	Budd=				0.30	
	-0.12							na	na		-0.09	-0.10	-0.23		
na	na														
-0.13		-0.12		-0.09		-0.09		-0.08		-0.18		-0.12		-0.09	

(continues)

TABLE 10.4 *(continued)*

C.

Political Interest by Sex	U.S.A. F	U.S.A. M	France F	France M	Britain F	Britain M	W. Germany F	W. Germany M	Italy F	Italy M	Netherlands F	Netherlands M
n	1242	1034	620	577	649	580	681	606	683	665	697	506
R2	0.14	0.11	0.07	0.13	0.12	0.13	0.12	0.11	0.14	0.14	0.12	0.15
Age finished school (v319)	0.25	0.16	0.19		0.15	0.18	0.25	0.12	0.11	0.17	0.27	0.20
Fam. occup. status (ses2)		0.08			0.17	0.19		0.14		0.10	0.12	0.23
Age (v345)	0.14	0.08		0.18	0.22	0.16				0.14		
Family income level (v339)		0.14	0.10	0.11			0.10		0.09	0.16		
Belong to union? (v334)	0.09		0.11	0.26		0.12	0.10		0.14	0.20		0.15
Religiosity (relig)	0.09	0.11					0.13		-0.18	-0.09	0.10	
Married?									-0.11		0.12	
Chief wage earner? (cwearn)				0.15					-0.12		0.11	
Size of town (v337)								0.10		-0.14		
Size of household (v320)	-0.07	-0.10										
Have children?												
Roman Catholic? (romcath)		-0.11					-0.21				-0.10	
Protestant? (prot)	-0.10	-0.17							na	na		
Employed? (v328)				-0.13								
Sex (1 = female; 0 = male)	-0.08				-0.16		-0.21		-0.19		-0.11	

D.

Discuss Politics by Sex	U.S.A. F	U.S.A. M	France F	France M	Britain F	Britain M	W. Germany F	W. Germany M	Italy F	Italy M	Netherlands F	Netherlands M
n	1255	1039	608	569	642	578	643	581	660	654	679	493
R2	0.11	0.10	0.21	0.18	0.13	0.11	0.15	0.10	0.16	0.10	0.21	0.09
Age finished school (v319)	0.21	0.16	0.37	0.29	0.23	0.16	0.24	0.13	0.11	0.14	0.34	0.18
Fam. occup. status (ses2)				0.08		0.10		0.16	0.10	0.08	0.14	0.17
Belong to union? (v334)	0.06	0.07	0.14		0.14					0.14		
Family income level (v339)	0.08	0.15	0.16				0.10			0.15		
Chief wage earner? (cwearn)	-0.09			0.13	0.11			0.13	-0.11		0.16	
Size of town (v337)		-0.08										
Religiosity (relig)	0.07		0.10			0.11		0.11		-0.16	0.12	
Age (v345)		-0.10						-0.12				-0.10
Have children?				0.08						-0.13		
Employed? (v328)									0.18			
Married?	-0.10											
Roman Catholic? (romcath)		-0.10			-0.11	-0.10	-0.22	-0.21				
Protestant? (prot)	-0.13	-0.15			-0.13			-0.21	na	na		
Size of household (v320)	-0.09											
Sex (1 = female; 0 = male)	-0.15		-0.10		-0.22		-0.10		-0.20			

Note 1: All beta coefficients shown have p-values below .05. Co-efficients with p-values below .005 are shaded.

Note 1: All beta coefficients shown have p-values below .05. Co-efficients with p-values below .005 are shaded.

Note 2: The beta coefficients for sex (see last row of each table) are from a separate regression model. This model included both women and men, and then added a dummy variable for sex. Beta coefficients generated by that model for the impact of the other social background characteristics are not displayed.

Source: World Values Survey (WVS), 1981-82.

Denmark		Belgium		Spain		Ireland		Canada		Japan		Norway		Sweden	
F	M	F	M	F	M	F	M	F	M	F	M	F	M	F	M
598	582	594	531	1171	1110	679	531	629	619	641	581	580	664	455	499
0.08	0.09	0.10	0.08	0.24	0.18	0.09	0.10	0.09	0.09	0.10	0.09	0.10	0.06	0.04	0.04
0.21	0.10	0.21	0.14	0.28	0.33	0.17	0.25	0.15	0.10	0.10		0.18	0.17	0.11	0.15
		0.14	0.14		0.08	0.17		0.11				0.11		na	na
0.21		0.16				0.18		0.30			0.20	0.17	0.16	0.16	0.22
0.13			0.13	0.08						0.19					
				0.05	0.18										
	0.14			-0.20	-0.11				0.11			-0.10			
					0.11				0.15			na	na	na	na
	0.16	0.10	0.17				0.12								
na	na			0.10			-0.12		0.13						
										-0.10					
										0.24					
	-0.10							na	na						
	-0.13							na	na		0.11	-0.13	-0.09		
-0.15		-0.09		-0.06		-0.18		-0.08		-0.22		-0.12		-0.12	

Denmark		Belgium		Spain		Ireland		Canada		Japan		Norway		Sweden	
F	M	F	M	F	M	F	M	F	M	F	M	F	M	F	M
560	550	564	505	1106	1079	664	524	620	611	523	527	572	655	449	495
0.17	0.09	0.16	0.13	0.19	0.12	0.14	0.09	0.09	0.11	0.07	0.10	0.17	0.11	0.09	0.09
0.21	0.18	0.23	0.11	0.24	0.23	0.16	0.12	0.20	0.09			0.17	0.15	0.19	0.17
0.10		0.16	0.17	0.06	0.13			0.10	0.12			0.09	0.12	na	na
	-0.11			0.07	0.14								0.10		
0.13									0.12	0.15					
na	na		0.13	0.12			0.10		0.14				0.10		0.13
-0.10				-0.07	-0.11	-0.16									
				-0.10						0.13		-0.17			
									0.13		0.21				
										0.11					
				0.11								na	na	na	na
								na	na	Budd=					
								na	na	-0.10		-0.08		-0.14	
		0.10	0.10												
		-0.11		-0.14		-0.15				-0.19		-0.18			

TABLE 10.5   The Impact of Holding Feminist Views on Political Activism

A.

NonViolent Activism by Sex	U.S.A. F	M	France F	M	Britain F	M	W. Germany F	M	Italy F	M	Netherlands F	M
Model 1	1050	889	545	494	575	548	545	483	505	512	598	435
R2	0.23	0.18	0.29	0.36	0.27	0.17	0.2	0.22	0.32	0.19	0.27	0.28
Model 2	665	563	356	322	351	376	254	174	376	382	341	241
R2	0.28	0.23	0.31	0.35	0.37	0.23	0.32	0.40	0.36	0.27	0.46	0.49
Family Values Index	0.13				0.18		0.24		0.13		0.24	0.33
General Sexual Index							0.24					0.27
Homosex./Prostitution Index	0.13	0.23				0.17		0.28	0.18	0.19		0.21
Abortion Index	0.14			0.18	0.20						0.17	
Divorce Index		0.11	0.15			0.14						

B.

Violent Activism by Sex	U.S.A. F	M	France F	M	Britain F	M	W. Germany F	M	Italy F	M	Netherlands F	M
Model 1	1236	1010	608	545	638	569	661	571	654	618	681	482
R2	0.03	0.05	0.1	0.16	0.04	0.12	0.02	0.07	0.05	0.08	0.06	0.07
Model 2	742	604	374	331	370	378	257	197	460	447	365	258
R2	0.05	0.08	0.19	0.22	0.15	0.16	0.07	0.15	0.10	0.13	0.12	0.16
Family Values Index			0.18		0.11				0.13			
General Sexual Index					0.30		0.19				0.16	0.17
Homosex./Prostitution Index									0.13			
Abortion Index					0.15							
Divorce Index												

C.

Political Interest by Sex	U.S.A. F	M	France F	M	Britain F	M	W. Germany F	M	Italy F	M	Netherlands F	M
Model 1	1242	1034	620	577	649	580	681	606	683	665	697	506
R2	0.14	0.11	0.07	0.13	0.12	0.13	0.12	0.11	0.14	0.14	0.12	0.15
Model 2	742	607	380	340	373	381	259	202	476	478	369	264
R2	0.14	0.14	0.08	0.14	0.13	0.15	0.16	0.15	0.18	0.15	0.15	0.14
Family Values Index												
General Sexual Index						-0.14						
Homosex./Prostitution Index												
Abortion Index												
Divorce Index			0.15	0.18	0.16				0.14			

D.

Discuss Politics by Sex	U.S.A. F	M	France F	M	Britain F	M	W. Germany F	M	Italy F	M	Netherlands F	M
Model 1	1255	1039	608	569	642	578	643	581	660	654	679	493
R2	0.11	0.1	0.21	0.18	0.13	0.11	0.15	0.1	0.16	0.1	0.21	0.09
Model 2	750	614	375	340	372	380	254	198	468	475	364	261
R2	0.12	0.11	0.17	0.22	0.18	0.12	0.24	0.20	0.15	0.10	0.26	0.14
Family Values Index											0.13	
General Sexual Index												
Homosex./Prostitution Index					0.18				0.12			
Abortion Index												
Divorce Index							0.25					

Note 1: All Beta co-efficients shown have p-values below .05. Co-efficients with p-values below .005 are shaded.

Denmark		Belgium		Spain		Ireland		Canada		Japan		Norway		Sweden	
F	M	F	M	F	M	F	M	F	M	F	M	F	M	F	M
441	450	461	409	854	879	567	441	554	561	317	352	510	600	380	442
0.38	0.32	0.2	0.11	0.36	0.24	0.23	0.3	0.22	0.23	0.14	0.1	0.29	0	0.2	0
216	203	244	208	581	613	355	251	336	356	64	121	301	364	190	235
0.45	0.31	0.32	0.20	0.45	0.27	0.27	0.35	0.33	0.29	0.38	0.30	0.37	0.18	0.32	0.16
0.23				0.17				0.16				0.17			
0.18				0.16								0.14			
	0.20	0.14				0.17	0.14	0.17	0.13						
		0.16	-0.26	0.19	0.18				0.15	0.34					
			0.21			0.14	0.21		0.12						

Denmark		Belgium		Spain		Ireland		Canada		Japan		Norway		Sweden	
F	M	F	M	F	M	F	M	F	M	F	M	F	M	F	M
583	555	547	482	1039	986	661	512	619	607	515	501	574	652	447	493
0.06	0.08	0.02	0.03	0.06	0.09	0.04	0.13	0.06	0.07	0.03	0.07	0.02	0	0.12	0
266	244	265	229	691	655	393	280	352	370	93	142	324	378	207	242
0.16	0.14	0.21	0.11	0.13	0.16	0.10	0.22	0.10	0.11	0.26	0.25	0.05	0.16	0.09	0.09
												0.16			
0.24		0.12		0.13		0.19					0.35	0.14	0.18		
		0.21			0.11										0.18
		0.21		0.11	0.21		0.17			0.27					
		-0.23			-0.13										

Denmark		Belgium		Spain		Ireland		Canada		Japan		Norway		Sweden	
F	M	F	M	F	M	F	M	F	M	F	M	F	M	F	M
598	582	594	531	1171	1110	679	531	629	619	614	581	580	664	455	499
0.08	0.09	0.1	0.08	0.24	0.18	0.09	0.1	0.09	0.09	0.1	0.09	0.1	0	0.04	0
270	248	270	238	749	724	396	281	356	372	104	145	325	381	209	245
0.14	0.16	0.17	0.21	0.27	0.20	0.10	0.16	0.15	0.09	0.42	0.30	0.12	0.10	0.09	0.10
				0.15	0.10										
			0.16		-0.14			0.20							
														0.18	
										0.24					
		0.16	0.16	0.10											

Denmark		Belgium		Spain		Ireland		Canada		Japan		Norway		Sweden	
F	M	F	M	F	M	F	M	F	M	F	M	F	M	F	M
560	550	564	505	1106	1079	664	524	620	611	523	527	572	655	449	495
0.17	0.09	0.16	0.13	0.19	0.12	0.14	0.09	0.09	0.11	0.07	0.1	0.17	0	0.09	0
260	239	267	234	737	717	393	281	353	368	102	141	323	379	209	243
0.19	0.19	0.18	0.14	0.20	0.14	0.17	0.13	0.14	0.16	0.30	0.14	0.18	0.15	0.15	0.18
				0.10									0.12		
								0.12							
				0.11		0.13									
					0.13										
									0.15						

Note 2: Model 1 is the regression equation using the social background variables in Table 10.4. Model 2 includes the social background variables (not shown), and adds the 5 feminism indices as additional independent variables.
Source: World Values Survey (WVS), 1981-82.

three of my four indices is education. For both the nonviolent activism and the political discussion indices, education is significant everywhere except in Japan. Also, on the political interest measure, education is significant everywhere, except among women in Japan and France, and education is the strongest social background predictor of any in almost half of the regressions.

When turning to the violent activism index, I find that education only exerts a significant effect among women in Britain and for both sexes in France; and the coefficients there are *negative*, indicating that citizens with more education there are *less* likely than others to participate in violent activism. Education's opposite effects on violent and nonviolent forms of political activism reinforce the decision to create separate indices.

Employment status rarely exerts a significant effect on activism in either direction, casting doubt on all three sub-hypotheses under 2.3. Still, when it is significant, employment among women consistently predicts *more* activism, as in 2.3a.

Higher income and occupational prestige consistently lead respondents to discuss politics more and to be more interested in politics. This confirms hypothesis 2.4. Of the income and occupational prestige measures, at least one of the beta coefficients is significant for both sexes in almost every country studied. However, results are much weaker for the two direct activism indices.

In seeming accord with hypothesis 2.5, younger citizens are consistently more likely than their elders to engage in nonviolent forms of activism, everywhere except in Japan and among Dutch men. Yet, younger citizens of *both* sexes claim on average to be *less interested in politics* than their elders in the United States, Britain, Norway and Sweden; also, younger citizens claim less interest in seven other countries. In no country do younger citizens of either sex claim *more* political interest than their elders. Does the preceding contradictory evidence on youth activism (high) versus youth political interests (low) mean that today's youth are more likely to attend demonstrations, sign petitions or engage in other forms of overt activism, in spite of lacking strong political concerns (perhaps done simply for entertainment or as a social activity)? Or could it be that the young are more active on issues of genuine concern to them, but because there are a limited number of such issues, they do not deem it appropriate to rate themselves as in the general sense "interested in politics"? Or could it be that fewer young than old citizens are interested in politics, but among those young citizens who *are* interested, a disproportionate number become politically active? Specifying this transcends our data but comprises an important area for future research, as the tendencies of the young will naturally bear heavily on the overall future of political involvement in industrialized societies.

Regarding the final two hypotheses for this series, as predicted by 2.6, union membership is a good predictor of nonviolent activism, significant in every country except Belgium, Denmark, and Norway. Also, as predicted by 2.7, coming from a larger home town more often than not predicts having a greater propensity for political activism.

Although I did not offer any hypothesis on the effects of religion or religiosity on political activism, I did obtain some noteworthy results; on the nonviolent and violent activism measures, whenever significant, religiosity *reduces* political activity. In fact, on the nonviolent activism index, religiosity has a significant depoliticizing effect for at least one sex in every country except Sweden and West Germany and for both sexes in six countries. Also, on the violent activism index, religiosity has a significant depoliticizing effect for at least one sex in half of the countries surveyed.

Regarding the effect of Catholicism and Protestantism, while their beta coefficients are significant in only about one-third of the regressions with the four activism measures, in those instances, the direction is nearly always to deter interest or activism.

The combined evidence from the religiosity, Catholicism and Protestantism variables strongly suggests that regardless of religious faith, any form of positive religious attachment usually *dampens* activism and practically never fosters it. This contradicts theories which hold that religiosity in some traditions, such as early American Puritanism, may promote activism (Elazar 1975).

Effect of Feminism on Political Activism (Path C)

I find strong support for both of my path C hypotheses. As Table 10.5 indicates, the R^2 values are nearly always greater for model 2 (which includes both social background and feminism indicators) than for model 1 (just including the social background indicators). This demonstrates that adding the feminism indicators improves the explanation of political activism over that of using only social background indicators.

The beta coefficients for individual feminism indicators are generally positive, confirming hypothesis 3.1 that holding feminist views *increases* political activity. The sole exceptions are Spanish men and Belgian women who are more likely to engage in violent activism if they hold anti-abortion views. Every other statistically significant result indicates that holding more liberal, pro-feminist views generates more political activity or interest.

I also hypothesized (3.2) that holding feminist views would increase political activism among women more often than among men. This too holds up, as at least one of the five feminism indices has a significant positive effect on activism in more countries in the regressions for women than for men. For nonviolent activism, significant coefficients exist for women in 13 countries, and 11 for men. However, the difference increases on the other three activism indices, in roughly twice as many countries as for men.

Conclusions

The Social Origins of Feminism

In explaining variation in feminist views, the most consistent cross-national predictors are respondents' sex, religiosity, education and age. Women are more liberal than men in their views toward divorce, non-traditional family values, prostitution, and homosexuality, and more conservative on sexual morality; finally, women tend to be stronger supporters of abortion in countries where political and media attention make abortion salient. These findings strongly contradict past research, which contends that substantial differences between men and women in their support for feminist causes do not exist (Cherlin and Walters 1981; Davis and Robinson 1990; Ferree 1974; Roper Organization 1980).

I also find that religiosity greatly reduces the probability of holding feminist views. Regardless of a nation's religion, religiosity was the single most significant cross-national predictor of *conservatism* across all five feminism indices. Similarly, education has a less liberalizing impact in the highly Catholic countries, where the Catholic Church presumably exerts more conservatively directed control over educational institutions. This strong evidence of religion's influence on political views calls into question studies which fail to control for religiosity, or which use only a simple measure of church attendance.

Although Davis and Robinson (1991) cast doubt on the effect of education on feminist views, I find that education exerts a fairly consistent liberal effect on all five feminism indices. There were 65 statistically significant findings concerning the impact of education on the various feminism indices, for men or for women, across the fourteen countries; more education *increased* pro-feminist responses for all but 2 of the 65. Perhaps Davis and Robinson did not uncover as many statistically significant findings on education's impact due to their smaller sample sizes. In any case, it does appear that education creates some form of awareness or exposure conducive to support for equality between the sexes.

Feminism also obtains greater support from the young, especially young women.

The Social Origins of Political Activism

Education increases political activism. However, comparison of nonviolent and violent activism indices reveals that while education is a strong predictor of *nonviolent* activism, it is a poor predictor of activism involving personal violence or property damage.

By contrast with education, sex is not nearly as significant a predictor of political activism as past research indicates. Although men in many countries are significantly more likely than women to claim an "active interest" in politics, in most countries, men are not significantly more likely to participate in actual, nonviolent forms of political activism. Could past research on the gender gap in political participation be flawed? More probable is that the gender gap is narrowing.

Religiosity is intriguing. It has little impact on political interest and discussion, but is an extremely strong predictor of both violent and nonviolent political activism. Either more religiosity, or religious affiliation with Catholicism or Protestantism, strongly *discourages* activism in nearly every country surveyed.

The Relationship Between Feminism and Political Activism

Empirical studies which analyze both feminist views and political activism are rare; therefore, with this study, I was able to assess hypotheses which other studies have by necessity left virtually unexplored. In particular, I could analyze whether feminist views contribute to citizen activity on feminist or other political issues.

My results confirm that citizens who hold feminist views are more politically active. This relationship is especially strong among women, and for both sexes concerning participation in *nonviolent* political activism. In every country except Sweden, at least one of the five feminism indices is a statistically significant predictor of nonviolent political activism. Additionally, two or more feminism indices are significant predictors of such activism in all but three countries.

Since pro-feminist citizens are more politically active, pro-feminist citizens are more likely to be active on issues relevant to feminist causes. This bodes well for the feminist movement, in its capacity to influence policy-making and to spread its views with the general public.

Notes

1. Of all the variables contributing to my five feminism indices, these two questions were the most strongly correlated ($r = .63$, $< .01$ significance). Also, a maximum-likelihood factor analysis (oblimin) of the same set of variables resulted in five factors, the first of which contained only these two items.

2. Social background characteristic variables for a few countries were unavailable. I indicate where this was the case in the regression tables with an "na" for "not applicable." Also, in Japan, I added a dummy variable for whether the respondent's religion is Buddhism.

3. As the WVS was administered, an unpopular pro-abortion law had just passed in Italy; the American women's movement was keeping the abortion issue alive in conjunction with their efforts to ratify the ERA; Danish women were riding a wave of feminist-sponsored laws passed in the 1970s including the legalization of abortion in 1973; and Dutch women were preparing for an imminent vote on the repeal of an anti-abortion law.

Appendix: Demographic Variables

Of the independent demographic variables, I measured age, number of citizens in the household and age finishing school by the raw numbers. I measured size of home town according to the respondents' own estimation on a 3-point scale from rural (1) to large town (3). Family income included 10 possibilities, calculated to be approximately equivalent in each country. I then created dummy variables to measure the following categorical distinctions: whether respondent is married, has children, belongs to a union, is Roman Catholic, Protestant, and is the family's chief wage earner. In Japan, I included an additional dummy variable for Buddhist, since Catholics and Protestants represent a small proportion of the Japanese population.

The measure of occupational prestige (SES2) which I use in every country except the United States and Sweden is derived from a list of 14 job categories. I recoded these into the four groupings below (with original categories indicated by letters a-l):

1. Unskilled to semi-skilled manual worker: (a) agricultural worker, (b) unskilled worker, and (c) semi-skilled worker.

2. Skilled manual worker: (d) skilled manual worker, (e) foreperson and supervisor (manual), (f) member of armed forces, and (g) farmer (employer, manager or own account).

3. Sales, clerical & other non-manual: (h) middle level non-manual (office worker, etc.) and (i) junior level non-manual (office worker, etc.).

4. Professional/managerial: (j) professional (e.g., lawyer, accountant, teacher), (k) employer and manager, small establishment, and (l) employer and manager, large establishment.

For the United States, the original 14-category variable was not available, so I had to use another occupational variable called V341. That variable is theoretically the same as my recoded index, except that the interviewers directly coded responses into the four categories. I chose not to use V341 for the other countries for two reasons. First, it did not exist for all the other countries. Second, it seemed to be coded with some inconsistency, leading me to be reluctant to trust it. For example, in France, V341 correlates almost perfectly with SES2 (+.92). Yet, there is a negative correlation between the two in Norway. Nonetheless, I did decide to use it in the United States rather than to relinquish the use of any occupational prestige measure in this obviously important country. No occupational prestige measure was available in Sweden.

To measure religiosity, I heeded Inglehart's (1977: 184) warning that church attendance is inadequate. Instead, I created a more robust index from six items: (1) church attendance apart from funerals, weddings and baptisms; (2) self-classification as religious "independent of whether you go to church or not"; (3) believes in God; (4) believes in a soul; (5) the importance of God in the respondent's life (on 10-point scale); and (6) does respondent "get comfort and strength from religion?" Each question received equal weight in the 0-10 scale, high indicating more religiosity. I recognize that this measure is somewhat inappropriate in Japan, since the predominant Japanese religions do not involve a monotheistic "God." Nonetheless, I use this measure in Japan as well as the other countries surveyed. The WVS offered few questions that might have been more appropriate, and my primary emphasis was on feminism in Western industrialized countries. I thus leave it to others to develop a better measure of religiosity in Japan and other non-Western countries.

Bibliography

Abo-Zena, Mona. 1993. Fieldwork reports for B.A. paper. University of Chicago.

Abramson, Paul, and Ronald Inglehart. 1995. *Value Change in Global Perspective*. Ann Arbor: University of Michigan Press.

Achen, Christopher H. 1977. "Measuring Representation: Perils of the Correlation Coefficient." *American Journal of Political Science* 21 (November): 805-815.

Aglietta, Michel. 1987. *A Theory of Capitalist Regulation: The U.S. Experience*. New York: Verso.

Almond, Gabriel, and Sidney Verba. 1963. *The Civic Culture: Political Attitudes and Democracy in Five Nations*. Princeton: Princeton University Press.

Anderson, Dewey, and Percey E. Davidson. 1943. *Ballots and Democratic Class Struggle*. Stanford, CA: Stanford University Press.

Anderson, Kristi. 1975. "Working Women and Political Participation, 1952-1972." *American Journal of Political Science* 19: 439-453.

Anon. 1976. "Walker carries 85 counties but loses: Daley's candidate, Howlett, wins primary." *Illinois Issues*. Vol. II, No. 5 (May): 24.

Apple, Michael. 1990. *Ideology and Curriculum*. New York: Routledge.

Arbach, Philip G. 1974. *Student Politics in America*. New York: McGraw-Hill.

Aronson, Robert. 1991. *Self-Employment: A Labor Market Perspective*. Ithaca, NY: ILR Press.

Astin, Alexander W. 1985. "The Changing American College Student." In *Prospectus for Change: American Private Higher Education*, ed. Elizabeth H. Locke, pp. 27-46. Charlotte, NC: Duke Endowment.

Astin, Alexander W. 1988. *Four Critical Years*. London: Jossey-Bass.

Astin, Alexander W., Kenneth C. Green, and William S. Korn. 1987. *The American Freshman: Twenty Year Trends, 1966-1985*. Los Angeles: University of California, Los Angeles, Higher Education Research Program.

Astin, Alexander W., William S. Korn, and Ellyne R. Berz. 1990. *The American Freshman: National Norms for Fall, 1990*. Los Angeles: University of California, Los Angeles, Higher Education Research Institute.

Bachman, Jerald G. 1983. "Premature Affluence: Do High School Students Earn Too Much?" *Economic Outlook USA* 10: 64-67.

Bachman, Jerald G. 1987. "An Eye on the Future." *Psychology Today* 21: 6-8.

Bachman, Jerald G., and Lloyd D. Johnston. 1979a. "Fewer Rebels, Fewer Causes: A Profile of Today's College Freshmen," Monitoring the Future Occasional Paper, no. 4. Ann Arbor, MI: Institute for Social Research.

Bachman, Jerald G., and Lloyd D. Johnston. 1979b. "The Freshmen, 1979." *Psychology Today* 13: 79-87.

Bachman, Jerald G., Lloyd D. Johnston, and Patrick M. O'Malley. 1980a, 1980b, 1981, 1984, 1985. 1987. *Monitoring the Future: Questionnaire Responses from the Nation's High School Seniors* (vols. for even numbered years 1976 to 1986). Ann Arbor, MI: Survey Research Center, Institute for Social Research.

Bachman, Jerald G., Lloyd D. Johnston, and Patrick M. O'Malley. 1986. "Recent Findings from 'Monitoring the Future: A Continuing Study of the Lifestyles and Values of Youth.'" *Research on the Quality of Life*, ed. Frank M. Andrews, pp. 215-234. Ann Arbor, MI: University of Michigan, Institute for Social Research.

Baldersheim, Harald, Richard Balme, Terry Nichols Clark, Vincent Hoffman-Martinot, and Hakkan Magnusson, eds. 1989. *New Leaders, Parties, and Groups: Comparative Tendencies in Local Leadership*. Paris and Bordeaux: CERVEL.

Banaszak, Lee Ann, and Eric Plutzer. 1991. "The Social Bases of Feminism in the European Community." Presented at annual meeting of the Midwest Political Science Association, April, Chicago.

Baron, James N. 1984. "Organizational Perspectives on Stratification." *Annual Review of Sociology* 10: 37-69.

Barry, John M. 1989. *The Ambition and the Power (The Fall of Jim Wright: A True Story of Washington)*. New York: Viking Penguin.

Bartels, Larry M. 1993. "Messages Received: The Political Impact of Media Exposure." *American Political Science Review* 87:2 (June): 267-285.

Bauman, Kurt. 1987. "Characteristics of the Low-Income Self-Employed." *Proceedings of the Industrial Relations Research Association* 40: 339-351.

Bechhofer, F. and B. Elliot. 1985. "The Petite Bourgeoisie in Late Capitalism." *Annual Review of Sociology* 11: 181-207.

Beck, E. M., Patrick M. Horan, and Charles M. Tolbert II. 1978. "Stratification in a Dual Economy: A Sectoral Model of Earnings Differentiation." *American Sociological Review* 43: 704-720.

Beer, Samuel H. 1965. *British Politics in the Collectivist Age*. New York: Alfred Knopf.

Bell, Daniel. 1973. *The Coming of Post-Industrial Society*. New York: Basic Books.

Bell, Daniel. 1976. *The Cultural Contradictions of Capitalism*. New York: Basic Books.

Bellah, Robert N., Richard Madsen, William M. Sullivan, Ann Swidler, and Steven M. Tipton. 1985. *Habits of the Heart*. Berkeley and Los Angeles: University of California Press.

Berger, Peter L. 1985. *The Capitalist Revolution: Fifty Propositions About Prosperity, Equality, and Liberty*. New York: Basic Books.

Berger, Suzanne. 1981. *Organizing Interests in Western Europe: Pluralism, Corporatism and the Transformation of Politics*. New York: Cambridge University Press.

Blalock, Hubert M., Jr. 1979. *Social Statistics*. Rev 2nd Ed. New York: McGraw-Hill.

B'ltken, Ferdinand, and Wolfgang Jagodzinski. 1985. "In an Environment of Insecurity: Postmaterialism in the European Community, 1970 to 1980." *Comparative Political Studies* 17: 453-484.

Blumenthal, Sidney. 1980. *The Permanent Campaign: Inside the World of Elite Political Operatives.* Boston, MA: Beacon Press.

Bourdieu, Pierre. 1984 [1979]. *Distinction.* Cambridge, MA: Harvard University Press.

Bowles, Samuel, and Herbert Gintis. 1976. *Schooling in Capitalist America: Educational Reform and the Contradictions of Economic Life.* New York: Basic Books.

Bowles, Samuel, and Herbert Gintis. 1987. *Democracy and Capitalism.* New York: Basic Books.

Brint, Steven. 1984. "'New Class' and Cumulative Trend Explanations of the Liberal Political Attitudes of Professionals." *American Journal of Sociology* 90: 30-70.

Brint, Steven. 1985. "The Political Attitudes of Professionals." *Annual Review of Sociology* 11: 389-414.

Brint, Steven, and Susan Kelley. 1993. "The Social Bases of Political Beliefs in the United States." *Research in Political Sociology* 6: 277-317.

Brint, Steven. 1994. *In an Age of Experts: The Changing Role of Professionals in Politics and Public Life.* Princeton, NJ: Princeton University Press.

Brody, Richard A. 1991. *Assessing the President: The Media, Elite Opinion, and Public Support.* Stanford, CA: Stanford University Press.

Brooks, Clem, and Jeff Manza. 1996. "Class Politics and Political Change in the United States Since the 1950s." Paper presented at the Annual Meeting of the American Sociological Association, New York, August 16-20.

Brooks, Clem, and Jeff Manza. 1997. "The Social and Ideological Bases of Middle Class Political Realignment in the United States, 1972-1992." *American Sociological Review* 62: in press.

Brown, William. 1990. "Class and Industrial Relations: Sociological Bricks Without Institutional Straw." In *John Goldthorpe: Consensus and Controversy,* eds. Jon Clark, Celia Modgil, and Sohan Modgil. New York: Falmer Press.

Bruce-Biggs, B., ed. 1979. *The New Class?* New Brunswick, N.J.: Transaction Press.

Burris, Val. 1986. "The Discovery of the Middle Class." *Theory and Society* 15.

Campbell, Angus, Gerald Gurin, and Warren E. Miller. 1954. *The Voter Decides.* Evanston, IL: Row, Peterson and Co.

Campbell, Angus, Philip E. Converse, Warren E. Miller, and Donald E. Stokes. 1960. *The American Voter.* Chicago: University of Chicago Press.

Center for Governmental Studies. "1990 Illinois Policy Survey." Northern Illinois University. DeKalb, IL: Unpublished.

Chafetz, Janet S., and Anthony Gary Dworkin. 1986. Female Revolt: *Women's Movements in World and Historical Perspective.* Totowa, NJ: Rowman and Allanheld.

Charlot, M. 1981. "Women and Elections." In *Britain at the Polls 1979,* ed. H.R. Penniman. London: AEI Studies in Political and Social Processes.

Cherlin, Andrew, and Pamela Barnhouse Walters. 1981. "Trends in U.S. Men's and Women's Sex Role Attitudes: 1972 to 1978." *American Sociological Review* 46: 453-460.

Chicago Sun-Times. Various editions (see citations in chapter 8).

Chicago Tribune. Various editions (see citations in chapter 8).

Clark, Terry Nichols, and Lorna Crowley Ferguson. 1983. *City Money.* New York: Columbia University Press.

Clark, Terry Nichols, and Ronald Inglehart. 1989, 1990. "The New Political Culture: Changing Dynamics of Support for Welfare State Policies in Post-Industrial Societies." Prepared for session of the Fiscal Austerity and Urban Innovation Project, annual meeting of the American Political Science Association, Atlanta, Georgia, August 31-September 3, 1989. Revised version presented to RC 03 sessions, International Sociological Association, Madrid, Spain, July 1990.

Clark, Terry Nichols, and Seymour Martin Lipset. 1991. "Are Social Classes Dying?" *International Sociology* 6 (December): 397-410.

Clark, Terry Nichols. 1993. "Local Democracy and Innovation in Eastern Europe." *Government and Policy* 11: 171-198.

Clark, Terry Nichols, Seymour Martin Lipset, and Michael Rempel. 1993. "The Declining Political Significance of Social Class." *International Sociology* 8:3 (December): 293-316.

Clark, Terry Nichols, and Vincent Hoffmann-Martinot, eds. 1997. *The New Political Culture.* Boulder: Westview.

Clark, Terry Nichols, ed. 1994. *Urban Innovation.* Thousand Oaks, CA: Sage.

Clarke, Harold D., and Nitish Dutt. 1991. "Measuring Value Change in Western Industrialized Societies: The Impact of Unemployment." *American Political Science Review* 85: 905-920.

Clogg, Clifford C., and Scott R. Eliason. 1986. "On Regression Standardization for Moments." *Sociological Methods & Research* 14: 423-446.

Coleman, James S. 1961. *The Adolescent Society.* New York: Free Press.

Collins, Randall. 1979. *The Credential Society.* New York: Academic Press.

Collins, Randall. 1988. *Theoretical Sociology.* New York: Norton.

Constantini, Edmond. 1990. "Political Women and Political Ambition: Closing the Gender Gap." *American Journal of Political Science* 34:741-770.

Converse, Philip E. 1964. "The Nature of Belief Systems in Mass Publics." In *Ideology and Discontent,* ed. David Apter. New York: Free Press.

Converse, Philip E. 1975. "Public Opinion and Voting Behavior." In *Handbook of Political Science,* ed. Fred I. Greenstein and Nelson W. Polsby: Volume 4, pp. 75-170. Reading, MA: Addison-Wesley.

Converse, Philip. 1992. "Comment on Davis's 'Changeable Weather in a Cooling Climate Atop the Liberal Plateau.'" *Public Opinion Quarterly* 56:3 (Fall): 307-310.

Corey, Lewis. 1935. *The Crisis of the Middle Class.* New York: Corvici-Friede Publishers.

Crimmins, Eileen M., Richard A. Easterlin, and Yasuhiko Saito. 1991. "Preference Changes Among American Youth: Family, Work and Goods Aspirations, 1976-86." *Population and Development Review* 17:1 (March): 115-133.

Dahlerup, Drude, ed. 1986. *The New Women's Movement: Feminism and Political Power in Europe and the U.S.A.* Beverly Hills: Sage.

Dale, Peter N. 1986. *The Myth of Japanese Uniqueness.* New York: St. Martin's Press.

Dalton, Russell. 1988. *Citizen Politics in Western Democracies: Public Opinion and Political Parties in the United States, Great Britain, West Germany and France.* Chatham, NJ: Chatham House.

Dalton, Russell J., Scott C. Flanagan, and Paul Allen Beck, eds. 1984. *Electoral Change in Advanced Industrial Democracies: Realignment or Dealignment?* Princeton, NJ: Princeton University Press.

Dalton, Russell, and Manfred Kuechler, eds. 1990. *Challenging the Political Order: New Social and Political Movements in Western Democracies.* New York: Oxford University Press.

Davis, James. 1992. "Changeable Weather in a Cooling Climate Atop the Liberal Plateau: Conversion and Replacement in Forty-two General Social Survey Items, 1972-1989." *Public Opinion Quarterly* 56:3 (Fall): 261-306.

Davis, James Allan and Tom W. Smith. *General Social Surveys, 1972-1993.* [machine-readable data file]. Principal Investigator, James A. Davis; Director and Co-Principal Investigator, Tom W. Smith. Chicago, IL: National Opinion Research Center, producer, 1993; Storrs, CT: the Roper Center for Public Opinion Research, University of Connecticut, distributor, 1 data file (29,388 logical records).

Davis, Nancy J., and Robert V. Robinson. 1991. "Men's and Women's Consciousness of Gender Inequality: Austria, West Germany, Great Britain and the United States." *American Sociological Review* 56:72-84.

Dawson, Richard E., Kenneth Prewitt, and Karen S. Dawson. 1977. *Political Socialization.* Boston, MA: Little, Brown.

Derber, Charles. 1983. *Project on Professionals: Report to Responding Organizations.* Boston, MA: Boston College (mimeo).

Derber, Charles, William Sullivan, and Yale Magrass. 1990. *Power in the Highest Degree.* New York: Oxford University Press.

Devaud, Marcelle Stanislas. 1968. "Political Participation of Western European Women." *Annals of American Academy of Political and Social Science* 375: 61-66.

Dogan, M. 1967. "Political Cleavage and Social Stratification in France and Italy." In *Party Systems and Voter Alignments,* ed. Seymour Martin Lipset and Stein Rokkan. New York: Free Press.

Downs, Anthony. 1957. *An Economic Theory of Democracy.* New York: Harper/Collins.

Durant, H. 1969. "Voting Behaviour in Britain, 1954-64." In *Studies in British Politics,* ed. R. Rose. London: Macmillan.

Durkheim, Emile. 1951 [1897]. *Suicide.* Glencoe, IL: Free Press.

Duverger, Maurice. 1955. *The Political Role of Women.* Paris: UNESCO.

Easterlin, Richard A., and Eileen M. Crimmins. 1991. "Private Materialism, Personal Self-Fulfillment, Family Life, and Public Interest: The Nature, Effects, and Causes of Recent Changes in the Values of American Youth." *Public Opinion Quarterly* 55:4 (Winter): 499-533.

Easterlin, Richard A. 1995. "Preferences and Prices in Choice of Career: The Switch to Business, 1972-87." *Journal of Economic Behavior and Organization* 27: 1-34.

Easterlin, Richard A. 1996. *Growth Triumphant: The Twenty-first Century in Historical Perspective.* Ann Arbor, MI: University of Michigan Press.

Edsall, Thomas. 1984. *The New Politics of Inequality.* New York: Norton.

Ehrenreich, John and Barbara Ehrenreich. 1979. "The Professional-Managerial Class." In *Between Labor and Capital,* ed. Ed. Pat Walker. Boston, MA: South End Press.

Elazar, Daniel J. 1970. *Cities of the Prairie: The Metropolitan Frontier and American Politics.* New York: Basic Books.

Elazar, Daniel J. 1975. "The American Cultural Matrix." In *The Ecology of American Political Culture,* ed. Daniel J. Elazar and J. Zikmund. New York: Cromwell.

Elazar, Daniel J. 1986. *Cities of the Prairie Revisited: The Closing of the Metropolitan Frontier.* Lincoln, NE: University of Nebraska Press.

Elazar, Daniel J., ed. 1995. "Improving Civic Community." *The Federalism Report*, Vol. 20, No. 2 (Winter): 8-13.

Esping-Andersen, Goesta. 1994. "Postindustrial Cleavage Structures: A Comparison of Evolving Patterns in Social Stratification in Germany, Sweden, and the United States." In *Social Stratificatiom*, ed. David B. Grusky. Boulder, CO: Westview Press.

Evans, David, and Linda Leighton. 1989. "Some Empirical Aspects of Entrepreneurship." *American Economic Review* 79: 519-529.

Evans, Geoff , ed. 1998. *The Future of Class Politics*. New York: Oxford University Press.

Fermin, Barbara, and William Grimshaw. 1992. "The Politics of Housing Policy." In *Research in Urban Policy IV*, ed. Kenneth Wong. JAI Press.

Ferree, Myra Marx. 1974. "A Woman for President?: Changing Responses, 1958-1972." *Public Opinion Quarterly* 38: 390-399.

Ferree, Myra Marx. 1987. *Analyzing Gender: A Handbook of Social Research*. Beverly Hills: Sage.

Firebaugh, Glenn. 1995. *Analyzing Repeated Surveys*. Thousand Oaks, CA: Sage.

Firebaugh, Glenn, and Kenneth E. Davis. 1988. "Trends in Antiblack Prejudice, 1972-1984: Region and Cohort Effects." *American Journal of Sociology* 94: 251-272.

Flanagan, Scott. 1982a. "Changing Values in Advanced Industrial Societies: Inglehart's Silent Revolution from the Perspective of Japanese Findings." *Comparative Political Studies* 14:4 (January): 403-444.

Flanagan, Scott. 1982b. "Measuring Value Change in Advanced Industrial Societies: A Rejoinder to Inglehart." *Comparative Political Studies* 15:1 (April): 99-128.

Flanagan, Scott. 1987. "Value Change in Industrial Societies." *American Political Science Review* 81:4 (December): 1298-1319.

Flora, Peter. 1986. *Growth to Limits: The Western European Welfare State Since World War II*. New York: Walter de Gruyter.

Form, William. 1985. *Divided We Stand: Working Class Stratification in America*. Urbana, IL: University of Illinois Press.

Franklin, Mark, Thomas T. Mackie, and Henry Valen et al. 1992. *Electoral Change: Responses to Evolving Social and Attitudinal Structures in Western Countries*. New York: Cambridge University Press.

Freidson, Eliot. 1986. *Professional Powers*. Chicago: University of Chicago Press.

Gekkan Yoron Chosa. October 1994. Tokyo: Sorifu Kohoshitsu.

Gergen, Kenneth J. 1991. *The Saturated Self: Dilemmas of Identity in Contemporary Life*. New York: Basic Books.

Gerson, Kathleen. 1985. *Hard Choices: How Women Decide About Work, Career, and Motherhood*. Berkeley, CA: University of California Press.

Gerson, Kathleen. 1987. "Emerging Social Divisions Among Women: Implications for the Welfare State." *Politics and Society* 15: 213-221.

Geser, Hans. 1994. Toward a One-Dimensional Ideological Culture? Evidence from Swiss Local Parties. Revised from a paper presented at Session 01 of Research Committee 03, "Transformations in Urban Leadership: The New Political Culture" at the XIII World Congress of Sociology, Bielefeld, July 18-23.

Gitlin, Todd. 1980. *The Whole World Is Watching*. Berkeley, CA: University of California Press.

Gitlin, Todd. 1987. *The Sixties: Years of Hope, Days of Rage*. New York: Bantam.

Goodman, Leo A. 1981. "Criteria for Determining Whether Certain Categories in a Cross-Classification Table Should Be Combined, with Special Reference to Occupational Categories in an Occupational Mobility Table." *American Journal of Sociology* 87: 612-650.

Goldthorpe, John H. 1982. "On the Service Class: Its Formation and Future." In *The New Working Class*, ed. Richard Hyman and Robert Price. London: Macmillan.

Goldthorpe, John H. 1995. "The Service Class Revisited." In *Social Change and the Middle Class*, ed. Tom Butler and Mike Savage. London: UCL Press.

Goldthorpe, John. 1996. "Class and Politics in Advanced Industrial Societies." In *Conflicts About Class*, ed. David J. Lee and Byron S. Turner.

Gouldner, Alvin W. 1979. *The Future of Intellectuals and the Rise of the New Class*. New York: Seabury Press.

Green, Kenneth C. 1989. "The Children of the Upheaval: A Look at Today's College Freshmen." Paper presented at the plenary session of the National Conference on the Freshman Year Experience, Columbia, SC.

Green, Kenneth C., and Alexander W. Astin. 1985. "The Mood on Campus: More Conservative or Just More Materialistic?" *Educational Record* 66: 45-48.

Green, Paul. 1992. "Analyzing the Illinois Primary Vote." *Illinois Issues*. Vol. XVIII, No. 6.

Greenstein, Robert. 1991. "Universal and Targeted Approaches to Relieving Poverty: An Alternative View." In *The Urban Underclass*, eds. Christopher Jencks and Paul E. Peterson. Washington, DC: The Brookings Institution.

Hamilton, Richard. 1975. *Restraining Myths: Critical Studies of U.S. Social Structure and Politics*. New York: Wiley.

Hammond, John L. 1986. "Yuppies." *Public Opinion Quarterly* 50: 487-501.

Hardiman, Niamh. 1990. "Capitalism and Corporatism: The Political Economy of Advanced Capitalist Societies." In *John Goldthorpe: Consensus and Controversy*, eds. John Clark, Celia Modgil, and Sohan Modgil. New York: Falmer Press.

Harding, Stephen, David Phillips, and Michael Fogarty. 1986. *Contrasting Values in Western Europe*. London: Macmillan.

Harrison, Bennett. 1994. *Lean and Mean*. New York: Basic Books.

Harrison, Bennett, and Barry Bluestone. 1988. *The Great U-Turn*. New York: Basic Books.

Hartmann, Heidi I. 1981. "The Family as the Locus of Gender, Class, and Political Struggle: the Example of Housework." *Signs* 6:366-94.

Hartz, Louis. 1955. *The Liberal Tradition in America*. Cambridge, MA: Harvard University Press.

Hashimoto, Shoji, and Takahashi, Koichi. 1994. "Nihonjin no Ishiki no Nijunen." *Hosokenkyu to Chosa*. Tokyo: NHK Hoso Bunka Kenkyujo.

Haskell, Thomas L. 1984. "Professionalism versus Capitalism." In *The Authority of Experts*, ed. Thomas Haskell. Bloomington, IN: Indiana University Press.

Hastings, Elizabeth, and Philip Hastings, eds. 1985-1989. *Index to International Public Opinion*. Westport, CT: Greenwood Press.

Heath, Anthony, Roger Jowell, and John Curtice. 1985. *How Britain Votes*. Oxford: Pergamon Press.

Heath, Anthony, Roger Jowell, and John Curtice. 1987. "Trendless Fluctuation: A Reply to Crewe." *Political Studies* 35: 356-377.

Heath, Anthony, Roger Jowell, John Curtice et al. 1991. *Understanding Political Change: The British Voter, 1964-1987.* Oxford: Pergamon Press.

Herzog, A. Regula, Jerald G. Bachman, and Lloyd D. Johnston. 1978. "Concern for Others and Its Relationship to Specific Attitudes on Race Relations, Sex Roles, Ecology, and Population Control." Monitoring the Future Occasional Paper, no. 2. Ann Arbor, MI: Institute for Social Research.

Higher Education Research Institute. 1990. *The American Freshman and Follow-up Survey.* Los Angeles: University of California, Los Angeles, Higher Education Research Institute.

Hills, Jill. 1981. "Candidates: The Impact of Gender." *Parliamentary Affairs* 34: 221-228.

Himmelstein, Jerome L. 1986. "The Social Basis of Antifeminism: Religious Networks and Culture." *Journal for the Scientific Study of Religion* 25: 1-15.

Hirschman, Albert O. 1982. *Shifting Involvements.* Princeton, NJ: Princeton University Press.

Hixson, William B. 1992. *Search for the American Right Wing.* Princeton, NJ: Princeton University Press.

Hoffman-Martinot, Vincent. "Local Political Parties and Cultural Transformations." Forthcoming in *The New Political Culture*, eds. Terry Nichols Clark and Vincent Hoffman-Martinot. Boulder, CO: Westview..

Hoge, Dean R., Cynthia L. Luna, and David K. Miller. 1981. "Trends in College Students' Values Between 1952 and 1979: A Return of the Fifties?" *Sociology of Education* 54: 263-274.

Horkheimer, Max, and Theodor W. Adorno. 1991 [1944]. *Dialectic of Enlightenment.* New York: Continuum.

Hout, Mike, Clem Brooks, and Jeff Manza. 1993. "The Persistence of Classes in Post-Industrial Societies." *International Sociology* 8:3 (September): 259-277.

Hout, Michael, Clem Brooks, and Jeff Manza. 1995. "The Democratic Class Struggle in the United States, 1948-1992." *American Sociological Review* 60: 6 (December): 805-828.

Howard, Robert P. 1988. *Mostly Good and Competent Men: Illinois Governors 1818-1988.* Springfield, IL: Sangamon State University.

Howe, Neil, and Bill Strauss. 1993. *13th Generation: Abort, Retry, Ignore, Fail?* New York: Vintage Books.

Huber, Joan, and Glenna Spitze. 1983. *Sex Stratification: Children, Housework and Jobs.* New York: Academic Press.

Husbands, Christopher T. 1979. "The 'Threat' Hypothesis and Racist Voting in England and the United States." In *Racism and Political Action in Britain*, ed. R. Miles and A. Phizacklea. London: Routledge & Kegan Paul.

Inglehart, Margaret. 1981. "Political Interest in West European Women: An Historical and Empirical Comparative Analysis." *Comparative Political Studies* 14: 3.

Inglehart, Ronald. 1971. "The Silent Revolution in Europe: Intergenerational Change in Post-Industrial Societies." *American Political Science Review* 65: 99-1017.

Inglehart, Ronald. 1977. *The Silent Revolution: Changing Values and Political Styles.* Princeton, NJ: Princeton University Press.

Inglehart, Ronald. 1981. "Post-Materialism in an Environment of Insecurity." *American Political Science Review* 75: 880-900.

Inglehart, Ronald. 1985. "New Perspectives on Value Change." *Comparative Political Studies* 17: 485-532.

Inglehart, Ronald. 1987. "Value Change in Industrial Societies." *American Political Science Review* 81:4 (December): 1289-1298.

Inglehart, Ronald. 1990. *Culture Shift in Advanced Industrial Society.* Princeton, NJ: Princeton University Press.

Inglehart, Ronald. 1994."Economic Security and Value Change." *American Political Science Review* 88: 2 (June): 336-354.

Ivy, Marilyn. 1989. "Critical Texts, Mass Artifacts: The Consumption of Knowledge in Post-modern Japan." In *Post-modernism and Japan*, eds. Masao Miyoshi and H. D. Harootunian. Durham, NC: Duke University Press.

Iyengar, Shanto. 1991. *Is Anyone Responsible? How Television Frames Political Issues.* Chicago, IL: University of Chicago Press.

Jackman, Mary R., and Michael Muha. 1984. "Education and Inter-Group Attitudes: Moral Enlightenment, Superficial Democratic Commitment, or Intellectual Refinement?" *American Sociological Review* 49: 751-769.

Jacobs, Lawrence R., Mark D. Watts, and Robert Y. Shapiro. 1995. "Media Coverage and Public Views on Social Security." *The Public Perspective* 6: 3 (April/May): 9-10, 48-49.

Jennings, M. Kent. 1992. "Ideological Thinking Among Mass Publics and Political Elites." *Public Opinion Quarterly* 56: 419-441.

Johnston, Lloyd D., Jerald G. Bachman, and Patrick M. O'Malley. 1980a, 1980b, 1980c, 1982, 1984, 1986. *Monitoring the Future: Questionnaire Responses from the Nation's High School Seniors* (vols. for odd numbered years 1975-87). Ann Arbor, MI: Survey Research Center, Institute for Social Research.

Kaase, Max, and Kenneth Newton, 1995. *Beliefs in Government.* Oxford: Oxford University Press.

Kahn, Melvin A., and Frances J. Majors. 1984. *The Winning Ticket.* New York: Praeger Publishers.

Kasarda, John D. 1988. "Jobs, Migration and Emerging Urban Mismatches." In *Urban Change and Poverty*, eds. Michael G. H. McGeary and Laurence E. Lynn, Jr. Washington, DC: National Academy Press.

Katzenstein, Mary Fainsod, and Carol McClurg Mueller. 1987. *The Women's Movements of the United States and Western Europe: Consciousness, Political Opportunities, and Public Policy.* Philadelphia: Temple University Press.

Kavanagh, Dennis. 1987. *Thatcherism and British Politics.* Oxford: Oxford University Press.

Kellner, Hansfried, and Frank Heuberger. *Hidden Technocrats.* New Brunswick, NJ: Rutgers University Press.

Keith, Bruce E., et al. 1992. *The Myth of the Independent Voter.* Berkeley: University of California Press.

Kitschelt, Herbert. 1990. "New Social Movements and the Decline of Party Organization." In *Challenging the Political Order: New Social and Political Movements in Western Democracies*, ed. Russell Dalton and Manfred Kuechler. New York: Oxford University Press.

Klein, Ethel. 1984. *Gender Politics.* Cambridge, MA: Harvard University Press.

Klein, Ethel. 1987. "The Diffusion of Consciousness in the U.S. and Western Europe." In *The Women's Movements of the United States and Western Europe*, ed. Mary Katzenstein and Carol Meuller. Philadelphia: Temple University Press.

Klingemann, Hans-Dieter, Richard I. Hofferbert, and Ian Budge. 1994. *Parties, Politics, and Democracy*. Boulder, CO: Westview Press.

Kohei, Shinsaku, Miyake, Ichiro, and Watanuki, Joji. 1991. "Issues and Voting Behavior." In *The Japanese Voter*, eds. Scott Flanagan et al. New Haven, CT: Yale University Press.

Kojima, Kazuhito. 1980. "Gendai Seinen no Seijiteki Mukansin no Keisei." In *Daini Nihonjin no Ishiki*. eds. NHK Seron Chosa Kenkyujo. Tokyo: Shiseido.

Kriesi, Hanspeter. 1989. "New Social Movements and the New Class in the Netherlands." *American Journal of Sociology* 94: 1078-1116.

Kristol, Irving. 1972. "About Equality." *Commentary* 54: 41-47.

Kristol, Irving. 1975. "Corporate Capitalism in America." *The Public Interest* 37: 124-143.

Kuttner, Robert. 1987. *The Life of the Party*. New York: Penguin.

La Palombara, Joseph. 1987. *Democracy: Italian Style*. New Haven, CT: Yale University Press.

Ladd, Everett Carll, Jr. 1979. "Pursuing the New Class: Social Theory and Survey Data." In *The New Class?* ed. B. Bruce-Briggs. New Brunswick, NJ: Transaction Books.

Lamont, Michele. 1993. *Men, Money and Morals: The Culture of the French and American Upper Middle Class*. Chicago: University of Chicago Press.

Landa, Martha Diaz de. 1995. "Tendencias en el liderazgo local y el Nuevo Populismo Fiscal." *Annuario del Centro de Investigaciones Juridicas y Sociales,* Universidad Nacaional de Cordoba.

Landa, Martha Diaz de. 1996. "Culturas politicas locales: Diversadad y emergencia de la Neuva Cultura o del Nuevo Populismo Fiscal." *Revista El Principe*, Vol. 4 (forthcoming).

Landa, Martha Diaz de. 1995. "Tendencias en el liderazgo local y el Nuevo Populismo Fiscal," *Annuario del Centro de Investigaciones Juridicas y Sociales,* Universidad Nacaional de Cordoba: 199-205.

Levine, Arthur. 1981. *When Dreams and Heroes Died*. San Francisco: Jossey-Bass.

Linder, Marc. 1989. *The Employment Relationship in Anglo-American Law*. Westport, CT: Greenwood.

Linder, Marc. 1994. *Farewell to the Self-Employed*. Westport, CT: Greenwood.

Linder, Marc, and John Houghton. 1990. "Self-Employment and the Petty Bourgeoisie: Comment on Steinmetz and Wright." *American Journal of Sociology* 96: 727-734.

Lipset, Seymour Martin. 1960. *Political Man: The Social Bases of Politics*. New York: Doubleday.

Lipset, Seymour M. 1963 [1955]. "The Sources of the Radical Right." In *The Radical Right*, ed. Daniel Bell, pp. 259-312. Garden City, NY: Doubleday & Company.

Lipset, Seymour Martin, and Stein Rokkan. 1967. "Cleavage Structures, Party Systems and Voter Alignments: An Introduction." In *Party Systems and Voter Alignments*, eds. Seymour Martin Lipset and Stein Rokkan. New York: Free Press.

Lipset, Seymour Martin, and Everett C. Ladd, Jr. 1971. "College Generations and Their Politics." *New Society* 16: 652-658.

Lipset, Seymour Martin. 1981. *Political Man: The Social Bases of Politics*. Baltimore, MD: Johns Hopkins University Press.

Lipset, Seymour Martin. 1991. "No Third Way: A Comparative Perspective on the Left." In *The Crisis of Leninism and the Decline of the Left*, ed. Daniel Chirot. Seattle/London: University of Washington Press.

Lovenduski, Joni. 1986. *Women and European Politics: Contemporary Feminism and Public Policy*. Amherst, MA: University of Massachusetts Press.

Luker, Kristen. 1984. *Abortion and the Politics of Motherhood*. Berkeley, CA: University of California Press.

MacLeod, Jay. 1995. *Ain't No Makin' It: Aspirations and Attainment in a Low-Income Neighborhood*. Boulder, CO: Westview.

Macy, Michael. 1988. "New-Class Dissent Among Social-Cultural Specialists." *Sociological Forum* 3: 325-356.

Mann, Michael. 1973. *Consciousness and Action Among the Western Working Class*. London: Macmillan.

Manza, Jeff, and Clem Brooks. 1996a. "Continuity and Change in the Social Bases of Political Alignments in the United States, 1960-1992." Paper presented at Conference on Social Class and Politics, Woodrow Wilson Center, Washington D.C., April 19-20.

Manza, Jeff, and Clem Brooks. 1996b. "Does Class Analysis Still Have Something to Contribute to the Study of Politics?" *Theory and Society* 26: in press.

Manza, Jeff, Michael Hout, and Clem Brooks. 1995. "Class Voting in Democratic Capitalist Societies Since World War II: Dealignment, Realignment, or Trendless Fluctuation?" *Annual Review of Sociology* 21: 137-163.

Marshall, Gordon, Howard Newby, David Rose, and Carolyn Vogler. 1988. *Social Class in Modern Britain*. London: Hutchison.

Martin, Bill. 1994. "Continuity and Discontinuity in the Politics of the Sixties Generation: A Reassessment." *Sociological Forum* 9: 403-430.

Maslow, A. H. 1954. *Motivation and Personality*. New York: Harper & Brothers.

Mayer, Lawrence, and Roland E. Smith. 1985. "Feminism and Religiosity: Female Behavior in Western Europe." *West European Politics* 8: 38-49.

Mayer, William G. 1993. "Trends in Media Usage." *Public Opinion Quarterly* 57:4 (Winter): 593-611.

McAdam, Doug. 1982. *Freedom Summer*. New York: Oxford University Press.

Miller, Alton, 1989. *Harold Washington*. Chicago: Bonus Books.

Mills, C. Wright. 1951. *White Collar*. New York: Oxford University Press.

Mita Munesuke. 1980. "Gendaiseinen no Ishiki no Henbo." In *Daini Nihonjin no Ishiki*, eds. NHK Seron Chosa Kenkyujo. Tokyo: Shiseido.

Miyake, Ichiro, et al., eds. 1985. *Nihon Seiji no Zahyo*. Tokyo: Yuikaku.

Miyake, Ichiro. 1989. *Tohyo Kodo*. Tokyo: Tokyo Daigaku Shyuppan Kai.

Miyoshi, Masao. 1989. "Against the Native Grain: The Japanese Novel and the 'Postmodern' West." In *Postmodernism and Japan*, eds. Masao Miyoshi and H. D. Harootunian. Durham, NC: Duke University Press.

Neuman, W. Russell. 1993. "The Threshold of Public Attention." *Public Opinion Quarterly* 54: 159-176.

New York Times. 1992. "Clinton, Savoring Victory, Starts Sizing Up Job Ahead" (November 5): A1, B4.

NHK Hoso Bunka Chosa Kenkyujo, eds. 1986. *NHK Seron Chosa Shiryoshu* 4. Tokyo: NHK Service Center.

NHK Hoso Bunka Chosa Kenkyujo, eds. 1989. *NHK Seron Chosa Shiryoshu* 5. Tokyo: NHK Service Center.

NHK Hoso Bunka Chosa Kenkyujo, unpublished materials.

NHK Seron Chosabu, eds. 1991. *Gendai Nihonjin no Ishiki Kozo.* Tokyo: Nihon Hoso Shuppan Kyokai.

Nie, Norman H., Sidney Verba, and J. Petrocik. 1976. *The Changing American Voter.* Cambridge, MA: Harvard University Press.

Norris, Pippa. 1985. "Women's Legislative Participation in Western Europe." *West European Politics* 8: 90-101.

Norris, Pippa. 1987. *Politics and Sexual Equality: The Comparative Position of Women in Western Democracies.* Boulder, CO: Rienner Press.

OECD. 1981. *Economic Outlook No. 29.*

OECD. 1986. *Economic Outlook No. 39.*

OECD. 1987. *Economic Outlook: Historical Statistics.*

Offe, Claus. 1987. "Challenging the Boundaries of Institutional Politics: Social Movements Since the 1960s." In *The Changing Boundaries of the Political,* ed. Charles S. Maier. New York: Cambridge University Press.

Ogburn, William F. 1961. "The Hypothesis of Cultural Lag." In *Theories of Society: Foundations of Modern Sociological Theory,* eds. Talcott Parsons et al. New York: Free Press.

Oyen, Else, ed. 1990. *Comparative Methodology.* Newbury Park, CA: Sage.

Page, Benjamin I., and Robert Y. Shapiro. 1992. *The Rational Public: Fifty Years of Trends in Americans' Policy Preferences.* Chicago, IL: University of Chicago Press.

Pakulski, Jan. 1993. "The Dying of Class or of Marxist Class Theory?" *International Sociology* 8:3 (September): 279-292.

Pakulski, Jan, and Malcolm Waters. 1996a. "The Reshaping and Dissolution of Social Class in Advanced Society." *Theory and Society* 26: in press.

Pakulski, Jan, and Malcolm Waters. 1996b. *The Death of Class.* Thousand Oaks, CA: Sage.

Pensoneau, Taylor, and Bob Ellis. 1993. *Dan Walker: The Glory and the Tragedy.* Evansville, IN: Smith-Collins.

Petchesky, Rosalind P. 1984. *Abortion and Woman's Choice: The State, Sexuality, and Reproductive Freedom.* New York: Longman.

Phillips, Kevin. 1991. *The Politics of Rich and Poor.* New York: Harper.

Plutzer, Eric. 1988. "Work Life, Family Life, and Women's Support of Feminism." *American Sociological Review* 53: 640-649.

Plutzer, Eric, and Lee Ann Banaszak. 1991. "Support for Feminism in Nine Western Democracies: The Impact of National and Subnational Contexts." Unpublished paper presented at the Annual Meeting of the American Political Science Association, August 28-September 1.

Portes, Alejandro. 1994. "The Informal Economy and Its Paradoxes." In *Handbook of Economic Sociology,* eds. Neil Smelser and Richard Swedberg, pp. 426-449. Princeton, NJ: Princeton University Press.

Portes, Alejandro, Manuel Castells, and Lauren Benton (eds.). 1989. *The Informal Economy: Studies in Advanced and Less Developed Countries.* Baltimore: Johns Hopkins University Press.

Poster, Mark. 1990. *The Mode of Information: Poststructuralism and Social Context.* Chicago, IL: University of Chicago Press.

Przeworski, A., and J. Sprague. 1986. *Paper Stones: A History of Electoral Socialism.* Chicago, IL: University of Chicago Press.

Raftery, E. Adrian. 1986. "Choosing Models for Cross-Classifications (Comment on Grusky and Hauser)." *American Sociological Review* 51: 145-146.

Raftery, E. Adrian. 1996. "Bayesian Model Selection in Sociology." *Sociological Methodology* 25: in press.

Ragin, Charles. 1987. *The Comparative Method*. Berkeley: University of California Press.

Rakove, Milton L. 1975. *Don't Make No Waves, Don't Back No Losers*. Bloomington: Indiana University Press.

Randall, Vicki. 1982. *Women and Politics: An International Perspective*. London: Macmillan.

Reich. Robert. 1991. *Work of Nations*. New York: Knopf.

Rempel, Michael. 1995. "Contemporary Ideological Cleavages in the United States." Master's paper written for the Department of Sociology, University of Chicago.

Rempel, Michael. 1996. "Expanding the Class Politics Debate: The Social Origins of Urban Political Cleavages in the United States." Paper presented at the American Sociological Association's Annual Meeting, New York.

Riddel, Peter. 1989. *The Thatcher Decade*. London: Basil Blackwell.

Roberti, P. 1978. "Income Inequality in Some Western Countries: Patterns and Trends." *International Journal of Social Economics* 5:1: 23-41.

Robinson, Robert V. 1983. "Explaining Perceptions of Class and Racial Inequality in England and the United States of America." *British Journal of Sociology* 55: 344-366.

Rojo, Teresa. 1990. "Austerity and Urban Innovation in Spain." Paper presented to RC 03 Sessions of World Congress, International Sociological Association, Madrid; published in Spanish.

Roper Organization. 1980. *The 1980 Virginia Slims American Women's Opinion Poll: A Survey of Contemporary Attitudes*.

Rose, Lawrence E., and Ragnar Waldahl. 1982. "The Distribution of Political Participation in Norway: Alternative Perspectives on a Problem of Democratic Theory." *Scandinavian Political Studies* 5: 285-314.

Rose, Richard, and Ian McAllister. 1986. *Voters Begin to Choose: From Closed Class to Open Elections in Britain*. Newbury Park, CA: Sage.

Rothblatt, Sheldon. 1968. *The Revolution of the Dons*. London: Faber.

Sabato, Larry J. 1981. *The Rise of Political Consultants*. New York: Basic Books.

Sarlvik, Bo, and Ivor Crewe. 1983. *Decade of Dealignment*. New York: Cambridge University Press.

Schlesinger, Arthur M., Jr. 1986. *The Cycles of American History*. Boston, MA: Houghton Mifflin.

Shakai Keizai Kokumin Kaigi, eds. 1988. *Sengo Sedai no Kachihenka to Kodoyoshiki no Henyo*. Tokyo: Shakai Keizai Kokumin Kaigi.

Shils, Edward A. 1958. "The Intellectuals and the Powers." *Comparative Studies in Society and History* 1: 5-73.

Singer, Daniel. 1993. "The Ghosts of May." *Nation* (May 31): 729-732.

Skocpol, Theda. 1979. *State and Social Revolution*. Cambridge: Cambridge University Press.

Skocpol, Theda. 1991. "Targeting Within Universalism: Politically Viable Policies to Combat Poverty in the United States." In *The Urban Underclass*, eds. Christopher Jencks and Paul E. Peterson. Washington, DC: The Brookings Institution.

Smith, Tom. 1982. "General Liberalism and Social Change in Post World War II America: A Summary of Trends." *Social Indicators Research* 10: 1-28.

Smith, Tom. 1985. "The Polls: America's Most Important Problems." *Public Opinion Quarterly* 59: 264-274.

Smith, Tom W. 1985a. "Atop a Liberal Plateau? A Summary of Trends Since World War II." In *Research in Urban Policy Vol. 2A*, ed. Terry Nichols Clark. Greenwich, CT: JAI Press.

Smith, Tom W. 1985b. "Working Wives and Women's Rights: The Connection Between the Employment Status of Wives and the Feminist Attitudes of Husbands." *Sex Roles* 12: 501-508.

Sniderman, P., R. A. Brody, and P. Tetlock. 1991. *Reasoning and Choice: Explorations in Political Psychology*. New York: Cambridge University Press.

Spotts, Frederic, and Theodore Weiser. 1986. *Italy: A Difficult Democracy*. Cambridge, England: Cambridge University Press.

Steinmetz, George, and Erik O. Wright. 1989. "The Fall and Rise of the Petty Bourgeoisie." *American Journal of Sociology* 94: 973-1018.

Stouffer, Samuel. 1955. *Communism, Conformity, and Civil Liberties: A Cross-Section of the Nation Speaks Its Mind*. New York: Doubleday.

Summers, R., and A. Heston. 1988. "A New Set of International Comparisons of Real Product and Price Levels Estimates for 130 Countries, 1950-1985." *Review of Income and Wealth* 34: 1-25.

Surazaska, Wisla. 1995. "Local Revolutions in Central Europe: 1990-1994." Paper presented to Conference on Political Culture, Chicago, September.

Swianiewicz, Pawel, and Terry Nichols Clark." Mayors, Parties, and Political Culture in Central Europe." Forthcoming in *Eastern Europe Book*, eds. Harold Badersheim and Larry Rose. Boulder, CO: Westview.

Szelenyi, Ivan, and Bill Martin. 1988. "The Three Waves of New Class Theories." *Theory and Society* 17: 645-667.

Tawney, R. H. 1948. *The Acquisitive Society*. New York: Harcourt, Brace, and World.

Teixeira, Ruy. 1987. *Why Americans Don't Vote: Turnout Decline in the United States, 1960-1984*. New York: Greenwood Press.

Terry, J. 1984. "The Gender Gap: Women's Political Power." *Ottawa: Current Issues Review*.

Thomassen, Jacques A., and Jan van Deth. 1989. "How New Is Dutch Politics?" *West European Politics* 12: 61-78.

Tokei Suri Kenkyujo Kokuminsei Chosa Iinkai, eds. 1961. *Nihonjin no Kokuminsei*. Tokyo: Shiseido.

Tokei Suri Kenkyujo Kokuminsei Chosa Iinkai. 1970. *Daini Nihonjin no Kokuminsei*. Tokyo: Shiseido.

Tokei Suri Kenkyujo Kokuminsei Chosa Iinkai. 1992. *Daigo Nihonjin no Kokuminsei*. Tokyo: Idemitsu Shoten.

Tokyo Kogyo Daigaku Joho Kenkyukai, eds. 1988. *Kodo Joho Shakai*. Tokyo: Japan Times.

Trump, Thomas M. 1991. "Value Formation and Postmaterialism: Inglehart's Theory of Value Change Reconsidered." *Comparative Political Studies* 24: 365-390.

Turner, Bryan. 1988. *Status*. Minneapolis, MN: University of Minnesota Press.

Tyack, David. 1974. *The One Best System*. Cambridge, MA: Harvard University Press.

UNESCO Statistical Yearbook, 1963-1993.

Verba, Sidney, Norman H. Nie, and Jae-on Kim. 1978. *Participation and Political Equality: A Seven Nation Comparison*. Chicago: University of Chicago Press.

Verba, Sidney, et al. 1987. *Elites and the Idea of Equality: A Comparison of Japan, Sweden and the United States.* Cambridge, MA: Harvard University Press.

Verba, Sidney, Kay Lehman Schlozman, Henry Brady, and Norman H. Nie. 1993. "Citizen Activity: Who Participates? What Do They Say?" *American Political Science Review* 87:2 (June): 303-318.

Walker, Daniel. 1976. "Executive Report: Summary of Governor's 'State of the State' Message." *Illinois Issues.* Vol. II, No. 3, pp. 25.

Walker, Daniel. 1984. *Dan Walker Memoir.* Springfield, IL: Sangamon State University.

Ward, Robert E. 1965. "Japan: The Continuity of Modernization." In *Political Culture and Political Development.* Princeton, NJ: Princeton University Press.

Wattenberg, Martin. 1994. *The Decline of American Political Parties, 1952-1992.* Cambridge, MA: Harvard University Press.

Weakliem, David. 1991. "The Two Lefts? Occupation and Party Choice in France, Italy, and the Netherlands." *American Journal of Sociology* 96: 1327-1361.

Weber, Max. 1958. *The Protestant Ethic and the Spirit of Capitalism.* Tr. Talcott Parsons. New York: Charles Scribner's Sons.

Weil, Frederick. 1985. "The Variable Effects of Education on Liberal Attitudes." *American Sociological Review* 50: 458-474.

Welch, Susan. 1977. "Women as Political Animals? A Test of Some Explanations of Male-Female Political Participation Differences." *American Journal of Political Science* 21: 711-730.

Western, Bruce. 1995. "A Comparative Study of Working-Class Disorganization: Union Decline in Eighteen Advanced Capitalist Countries." *American Sociological Review* 60:2 (April): 179-201.

Wheeler, Charles N. III. 1990. "Governor's Race: Messages and Miscalculations." *Illinois Issues.* Vol. XVII, No. 10, pp. 6-7.

Wilcox, Clyde. 1991. "The Causes and Consequences of Feminist Consciousness Among Western European Women." *Comparative Political Studies* 23: 519-545.

Wilensky, Harold L. 1981. "Leftism, Catholicism, and Democratic Corporatism: The Role of Political Parties in Recent Welfare State Development." In *The Development of Welfare States in Europe and America,* eds. Peter Flora and Arnold J. Heidenheimer. New Brunswick, NJ: Transaction Books.

Williams, Raymond. 1958. *Culture and Society, 1780-1950.* New York: Columbia University Press.

Wilson, William Julius. 1987. *The Truly Disadvantaged.* Chicago, IL: University of Chicago Press.

Wolfinger, Raymond E., and Steven Rosenstone. 1980. *Who Votes?* New Haven, CT: Yale University Press.

World Bank. 1995. *World Bank Atlas.* Washington, DC: International Bank for Reconstruction and Development.

World Values Survey. 1981-1982. Fieldwork in spring-summer 1981 for all countries except the United States, South Africa, and Hungary, where fieldwork was carried out in 1982. Fieldwork was carried out by the following organizations: Belgium, Dimarso; Britain and United States, Gallup Poll; Denmark, Observa; France, Faits et Opinions; Hungary, Institute of Sociology-Hungarian Academy of Sciences; Ireland and North Ireland, Irish Marketing Surveys; Italy, DOXA; Japan, Nippon Research Center; Mexico, IMOP; Netherlands, NIPO; South Africa, Markinor; Spain, DATA;

West Germany, Institut fur Demoskopie. Data were kindly made available via Ronald Inglehart and Terry Clark.

Wright, Erik Olin. 1985. *Classes*. New York: Verso.

Wright, Erik O. 1986. "What Is Middle About the Middle Classes?" In *Analytical Marxism*, ed. John Roemer, pp. 114-140. New York: Cambridge University Press.

Wuthnow, Robert, and Wesley Shrum. 1983. "Knowledge Workers as a New Class: Structural and Ideological Convergence among Professional-Technical Workers and Managers." *Work and Occupations* 10: 471-483.

Yamazaki, Masakazu. 1984. *Yawarakai Kojinshigi no Tanjo*. Tokyo: Chuo Koron Sha.

Yankelovich, Daniel. 1981. *New Rules*. New York: Random House.

Yano Tsuneta Kinenkai, eds. 1995. *Nihon Kokusei Zue*. Tokyo: Kokuseisha.

Yuzawa, Yasuhiko. 1987. *Zusetsu Gendai Nihon no Kazoku Mondai*. Tokyo: Nihon Hoso Syuppan Kyokai.

About the Book

The past several decades have seen profound changes in the political landscapes of advanced industrial societies. This volume assesses key political developments and links them to underlying socioeconomic and cultural forces. These forces include the growth of a well-educated middle class, the moderating of bipolar class divisions between wealthy capitalists and struggling workers, and the accelerated rise of new media technologies (especially television) as potent tools shaping the terms of public discussion. Related political transformations include the spread of new social movements on feminist, environmental, and civil liberties issues; economic concerns focusing more on growth, taxes, and middle class programs than on redistribution; the fracturing of core left and right political ideologies; and the growing centrality of electronic media as carriers of political opinions and rhetoric.

In their introduction, Michael Rempel and Terry Clark pull together many seemingly disparate political changes to construct a clear, synthetic framework, identifying eight core components of postindustrial politics. Part Two examines shifts in underlying cultural values. It features a lively exchange between different contributors over whether apolitical, materialistic values have risen or declined since the 1960s. Part Three offers an in-depth look at the political views and party allegiances of the growing middle classes and Part Four examines some of today's most divisive issues.

Although primarily adopting a cross-national perspective, *Citizen Politics in Post-Industrial Societies* includes several case studies of politics in the United States and one in Japan. Unique in its synthetic vision, this volume will stimulate and challenge readers from across the political and theoretical spectrum.